Mott's Illustrated Catalog of

Victorian Plumbing Fixtures

for

Bathrooms and Kitchens

Mott's Illustrated Catalog of

Victorian Plumbing Fixtures

for

Bathrooms and Kitchens

by the

J. L. MOTT IRON WORKS

DOVER PUBLICATIONS, INC.
NEW YORK

Published in Canada by General Publishing Company, Ltd.,
30 Lesmill Road, Don Mills, Toronto, Ontario.
Published in the United Kingdom by Constable and Company, Ltd.

This Dover edition, first published in 1987, is an unabridged
republication of the work originally published by
the J. L. Mott Iron Works, New York, in 1888 under the title
Catalog "G" Illustrating the Plumbing and Sanitary Department.
The color plates of the original edition have been
reproduced here in black and white, and eight of them in color as well.
See also the "Note to the Dover Edition," page 2.

Manufactured in the United States of America
Dover Publications, Inc., 31 East 2nd Street, Mineola, N.Y. 11501

Library of Congress Cataloging-in-Publication Data

J. L. Mott Iron Works.
[Illustrated catalog of Victorian plumbing fixtures
for bathrooms and kitchens]
Mott's illustrated catalog of Victorian plumbing fixtures for
bathrooms and kitchens / by the J. L. Mott Iron Works.
p.   cm.
Reprint. Originally published: Catalog "G" illustrating the
Plumbing and Sanitary Department. New York : J. L. Mott Iron Works,
1888.
Includes index.
ISBN 0-486-25526-3 (pbk.)
1. Plumbing fixtures—United States—Catalogs.
2. Plumbing fixtures—United States—History—19th century.
3. Decoration and ornament—Victorian style.
I. Title.   II. Title: Illustrated catalog of Victorian
plumbing fixtures for bathrooms and kitchens.
III. Title: Victorian plumbing fixtures for bathrooms and kitchens.
TH6255.J2   1987
621'.88—dc19   87-16622
CIP

1888

Catalogue "G"

ILLUSTRATING

The ❊ Plumbing ❊ and ❊ Sanitary ❊ Department

OF

The J. L. Mott Iron Works.

Offices and Show Rooms:

86, 88 and 90 Beekman Street, New York.

AND

311 and 313 Wabash Avenue, Chicago, Ill.

E. D. Slater, Printer, 153 and 155 Fulton Street, New York.

(Original Title Page)

NOTE TO THE DOVER EDITION

This Dover edition faithfully reproduces the unorthodox pagination of the original in which the left-hand pages become odd-numbered beginning with page 229.

A section of color illustrations is included following page 26. These illustrations also appear in black–and–white with full captioning in their original places in the book. Pages originally in color that now appear in black–and–white only are: 56, 59, 72, 229.

PREFACE.

IN presenting this work to Architects, Plumbers, and all interested in the Sanitary features of modern building, would say that in preparing this Catalogue we have endeavored to comprise all our various manufactures heretofore illustrated in our many Catalogues, Supplements and Sheets appertaining to this Department of our business.

The Illustrations will show great improvement in many of our already well known specialties, the result of long and watchful experience.

There will also be found illustrated many new, novel and desirable Sanitary and Plumbing Fixtures and Appliances, the outcome of our research and effort to meet the growing demand for really high class goods, goods not only desirable from a sanitary point of view, but really artistic and beautiful to look upon, and fully up to the present high standard of the inside fittings and interior decorations of our modern houses and public buildings.

Architects writing specifications should be careful to designate each article specified as Plate ---, Mott's Catalogue "G." Also, parties ordering should give Number of Plate in this Catalogue.

Respectfully,

THE J. L. MOTT IRON WORKS.

PLATE 1-G.

BATH ROOM INTERIORS.

IN presenting designs for Bath Room Interiors, our intention is more to give suggestions than to lay down any rigid rule as to the nature or arrangement of fixtures, size of room or style of decoration, all of which, we apprehend, will depend somewhat on the taste of parties building, the space which may be available, and the amount of money to be expended; in all cases, however, we have been careful to present only such goods as we can fully recommend and unhesitatingly warrant from a sanitary point of view.

We are prepared to give estimates on Cabinet Work, in whole or in part, as shown in any of the illustrations. or we will be pleased to estimate on any designs which may be sent us.

BATH ROOM INTERIOR BY THE J. L. MOTT IRON WORKS.

PLATE 1-G.

This very complete Bath Room is designed to show how the various Fixtures illustrated in the following pages, may be fitted up. The Fixtures shown are our "Imperial" Porcelain Bath and Seat Bath, both with Supply Fittings and "Unique" Waste, our "Hygeia" or "Inodoro" Cistern Water Closet, Bidet, and Wash Stand fitted with Oval Wash Basin and "Unique" Waste. The Wood Work is Mahogany, the design Elizabethan. The size of room represented is about 13 feet x 10½ feet; of course the size can be modified should any of the fixtures be dispensed with.

BATH ROOM INTERIOR BY THE J. L. MOTT IRON WORKS.

PLATE 2 - G.

THE above illustration shows not only a most complete but a very artistically designed Bath Room. The fixtures represented are our "Imperial" Porcelain, Porcelain-lined Iron, or Planished Copper Bath Tub, fitted with Copper-lined Combination Shower and Needle Bath (patented), which makes this the most desirable and complete bathing arrangement that can possibly be had in a private bath room; also our "Imperial" Porcelain Seat and Foot Bath, Wash Stand fitted with "Nonpareil" Wash Basin, the "Dolphin" Front-outlet Water Closet, very handsomely made in one piece of earthenware, and furnished in plain ivory or decorated with gold, turquoise or pink lines.

The Combination Needle and Shower Bath is unquestionably the simplest and most effective of any yet devised; by it the desired result is attained without a complicated system of pipes and cocks, and without a possibility of the party using the bath being scalded by accidentally turning on the hot water cock. The combination consists of a wooden casing lined with heavy planished copper, in the interior of which are three vertical Needle Sprays and the Shower; the five Valves shown are lettered Hot, Cold, Supply to Bath, Needle Spray and Shower. The two Valves lettered Hot and Cold are first opened and permit the water to enter a Mixing Column, attached to which is the Thermometer, which registers the degree of temperature of the water; from the Mixing Column the water passes to the Bath Tub, Needle or Shower by opening the respective valves. Assuming the hot water supply to be at boiling point, the water passing through the Mixing Column can never be of a higher temperature than 98°; any desired temperature (lower than 98°) can be obtained by a further opening or closing of the hot or cold water valve, as the case may be. To fill the Bath Tub the valve lettered "Supply to Bath" is opened, the water entering at the foot of the tub without noise or steam. The Needle and Shower may be used together or separately. The Waste employed, but which cannot be shown by the illustration, is the Demarest Patent Standing Waste and Overflow, which is illustrated and described on the following pages.

BATH ROOM INTERIOR BY THE J. L. MOTT IRON WORKS.

PLATE 3 - G.

WE present this Interior as a suggestion to those who prefer to have all plumbing fixtures set up open, dispensing as far as possible with cabinet work, so that they may be readily accessible on all sides. Obviously, this renders it imperative that the various fixtures, such as Bath Tub, Water Closet, etc., be not only perfect from a practical and sanitary standpoint, but that they be handsome and artistic in appearance, and made and finished in a first-class manner; that we have fully appreciated this will be conceded by a reference to the above Interior and by an examination of the goods themselves.

The Interior comprises Mott's Porcelain-lined Roman Bath, with Supply and Waste Fittings and Hardwood Rim (the Legs can be made of cast brass or bronze to order); the "Inodoro" Embossed All-Porcelain Water Closet, with Cabinet-finish Cistern and Open Seat and Back; Mott's Open Lavatory, with "Nonpareil" Basin or with Oval Basin and "Unique" Waste; Porcelain-lined Seat Bath, with Supply and Waste Fittings and Hardwood Rim (the Legs can be made of cast brass or bronze to order) A detailed illustration and description of these appliances will be found on the following pages of this Catalogue.

BATH ROOM INTERIOR BY THE J. L. MOTT IRON WORKS.

PLATE 4 - G.

THE above illustration gives our idea of a Nursery Bath Room ; the fixtures consisting of a Children's Bath Tub, with Supply Fittings and Patent "Unique" Waste, no part of Fittings projecting into the Bath, the handles on top are all rounded and finished without any sharp corners, so there can be no chance of children getting bruised or hurt from slipping or falling while in the Bath Tub. The Wash Stand can be fitted with our regular Oval Basin with Patent "Unique" Waste, or with our Patent "Nonpareil" Basin. The height of Wash Stand should be from 24 to 27 inches. The Water Closet shown is the " Inodoro," with No. 4½ Syphon Cistern, arranged with Seat Pull, the seat being made with a step for children's use. The Slop Sink is our " Imperial" Porcelain, with hardwood rim and bronzed legs, which seems to us a very necessary fixture in a Bath Room exclusively for Nursery use, as it can be used by the nurse not only as a slop receiver, but to wash out and cleanse vessels of all kinds, also to rinse out cloths, etc. The Chiffonier, of course, is intended to hold the children's underclothes, etc., while the top part can be used for soaps and other toilet articles. The upholstered Bench is to stand or seat the children on while dressing ; the cover is hinged so the box can be used to hold both towels and wrappers.

BATH ROOM INTERIOR BY THE J. L. MOTT IRON WORKS.

PLATE 5 - G.

BATH ROOM INTERIOR, "EASTLAKE" DESIGN.

THE Fixtures encased are our "Imperial" Porcelain or Porcelain-lined Iron Bath Tub, with Supply and Waste Fittings; the "Hygeia," "Inodoro," "Triplex" or "Undine" Water Closet; the "Imperial" Porcelain Foot or Children's Bath, and Wash Stand with "Nonpareil" Basin or Oval Basin with "Unique" Waste. The cabinet work may be of mahogany, cherry or ash: the tiles are hand painted. Dimensions of Bath Room about 12 ft. by from 6 to 7 ft. For detailed illustrations and descriptions of the above, please refer to the following pages of this Catalogue.

BATH ROOM INTERIOR BY THE J. L. MOTT IRON WORKS.

PLATE 6 - G.

BATH ROOM INTERIOR, "EASTLAKE" DESIGN.

THE Fixtures encased are the same as those described by Plate 5 - G, except that the "Demarest" Valve Water Closet (to be supplied direct from main, or large tank) is substituted for a Cistern Water Closet. For detailed illustrations and descriptions of the above, please refer to the following pages of this Catalogue.

BATH ROOM INTERIOR BY THE J. L. MOTT IRON WORKS.

PLATE 7-G.

BATH ROOM INTERIOR, "EASTLAKE" DESIGN.

THE Fixtures encased are our "Imperial" Porcelain, Porcelain-lined Iron, or Planished Copper Bath Tub, with Supply and Waste Fittings, the "Hygeia," "Inodoro," "Triplex" or "Undine" Water Closet, Wash Stand with Oval Basin and "Unique" Waste, and Porcelain Oval Foot Bath with Supply and Waste Fittings. The cabinet work may be of cherry, black walnut or ash. Dimensions of Bath Room about 10½ feet by 6 feet.

For detailed illustrations and descriptions of the above, please refer to the following pages of this Catalogue.

BATH ROOM INTERIOR BY THE J. L. MOTT IRON WORKS.

PLATE 8 - G.

BATH ROOM INTERIOR, "EASTLAKE" DESIGN.

THE Fixtures encased are the same as those described by Plate 7-G, except that the "Demarest" or "Premier" Valve Water Closet (to be supplied direct from main, or large tank) is substituted for a Cistern Water Closet. For detailed illustrations and descriptions of the above, please refer to the following pages of this Catalogue.

MOTT'S PATENT BATH AND SHOWER COMBINATION.

PLATE 9 - G.

BATH AND SHOWER COMBINATION.

COMPRISING

The "Imperial" Porcelain, Porcelain-lined Iron or Planished Copper Bath, with Supply and Waste Fittings and Patent Shower and Curtain.

THE Patent Shower and Curtain may be used in conjunction with our "Imperial" Porcelain, Porcelain-lined Iron or Planished Copper Baths when they are encased as illustrated above or when they are set up open; in the latter case the Polished or Nickel-plated Brass Pipes run up and are attached to the tile or wood wainscoted wall.   When the Shower is to be used the Curtain is removed from the hook and envelops the bather, who can have a perfect shower bath without splashing the cabinet work, wall or floor.

When the two lower valves, lettered "Hot" and "Cold," are opened, the water passes into the mixing column, attached to which is a thermometer; the latter registers the degree of temperature of the water.   From the mixing column the water passes to the shower by opening the upper valve.

THE "IMPERIAL" PORCELAIN BATHS.

THE "Imperial" Porcelain Bath is moulded and glazed in one piece, and is without doubt the finest piece of ware that has yet been produced of so large a size by any potter. It is perfectly modeled, is delicate and uniform in color, with a glaze finish which is simply wonderful on so large a vessel as a Bath Tub. We would call special attention to the weights of these Baths, as being very much less than anything of the kind made hitherto; in fact, this has been the great desideratum in the manufacture of large vessels from clay in its various forms, they having invariably been so heavy and clumsy as to debar them from use in many places, and at the same time adding very much to the expense of and danger in freighting and handling. From a sanitary point of view, of course, there can be but one opinion as to their superiority: they are absolutely non-absorbent, requiring only to be wiped out with a sponge to be made perfectly clean, and even on the score of economy recommend themselves, as they will never wear out and entail no labor scouring or burnishing.

As will be observed by the following illustrations, we are prepared to furnish these Baths in various tints, handsomely decorated and inlaid with English tile. The Baths with Rolled Edge are very handsome and specially adapted to be set up open, as indicated by Plates 14 and 15 - G, no cabinet work whatever being required.

In the manufacture of large pieces of porcelain, such as Baths, a greater or less number when taken out of the kiln are found to have slight defects, which in no way detract from the practical value or fine appearance of the article; in fact, our "Seconds," as we term them, are equal to the best ware of any other make we have yet seen and are only classed as such in view of the very high standard we have established for our "Firsts." These "Seconds" are well adapted for use not only in private residences, but especially in hospitals, asylums, apartment houses, public buildings and baths, where cost is a consideration.

"IMPERIAL" PORCELAIN BATHS.

Plate 10-G.

"Imperial" Porcelain Roman Bath, with Marble Rim and Legs, Supply Fittings, and "Unique" Waste.
Dimensions of bath: length outside, 5 feet 4 inches; width outside, 2 feet 5 inches; depth inside, 1 foot 7 inches.

Reproduced in color on Plate A following page 26.

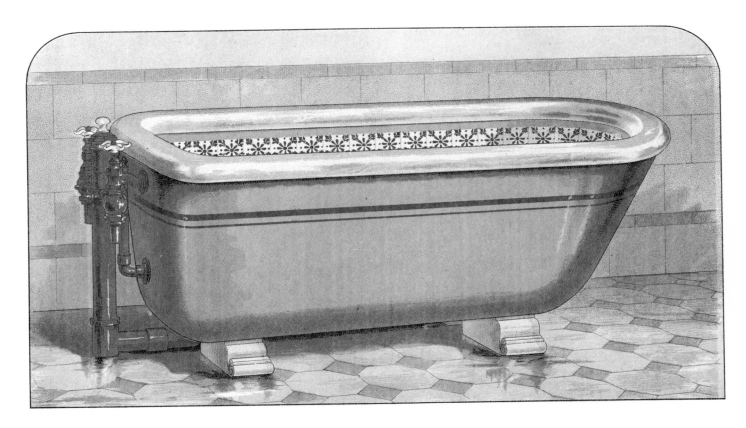

Plate 11-G.

"Imperial" Porcelain Bath, light pink tint, inlaid with white and gold English tiles, with Marble Rim and Legs, all polished or all nickel-plated
Supply Fittings, and "Unique" Waste.   For dimensions of baths, see page 22.

Major, Knapp & Co. 56 & 58 Park Place, N.Y.

"IMPERIAL" PORCELAIN BATHS.

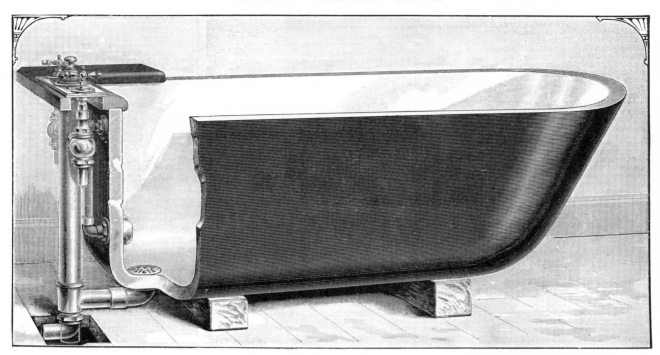

PLATE 12-G.

"Imperial" Porcelain Bath with Supply Fittings and "Unique" Waste and Overflow. Two Sizes, A and B.

THE above method of supply and waste is in our opinion the best, and is the one most generally used in private bath rooms with cabinet finish. The Supply Valves are of the best known form of compression, durable and easy in movement. The "Unique" Combined Waste and Overflow is absolutely the simplest, most effective and durable that has yet been devised. The illustration shows the Stand Pipe of the Waste seated as when the tub is being filled ; to empty the latter the Stand Pipe is raised and turned slightly to the right or left ; a still further turn will permit the Stand Pipe to be taken out, when it and the interior of tube may be cleaned. The sectional cut on page 22 will more fully explain the operation of this Waste.

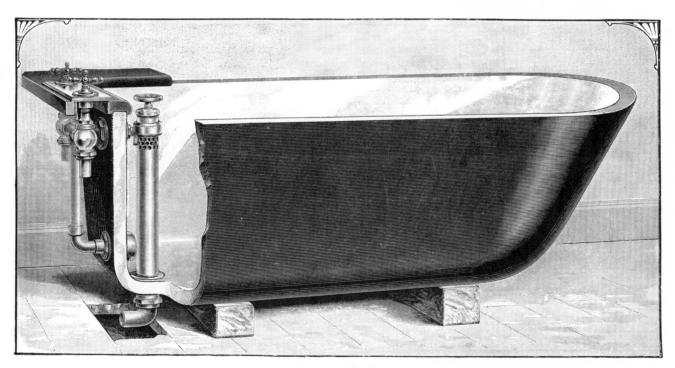

PLATE 13-G.

"Imperial" Porcelain Bath, with Supply Fittings and "Demarest" Patent Standing Waste and Overflow. Two sizes, A and B.

TO those who prefer to have the Waste and Overflow inside the Bath Tub, we can recommend the "Demarest" Patent Standing Waste and Overflow as being superior to anything of the kind in the market. The Stand Pipe is shown in the illustration seated ; to empty the Bath the Stand Pipe is raised and given a slight turn to the right or left ; a still further turn will allow of it being removed for cleaning.

For dimensions of Baths, see page 22.

IMPERIAL PORCELAIN BATHS.

PLATE 14 - G.

"Imperial" Porcelain Rolled-edge Bath, with all exposed parts of Brass Fittings Polished, Nickel or Silver-plated, Unique Waste and Overflow, Bronzed Iron, Nickel-plated or Polished Cast Brass Legs. Two sizes, A and B.

A S indicated by the illustration, the "Imperial" Porcelain Rolled-Edge Bath is intended to be set up without cabinet work, and where tile or marble enters more or less into the finish and decoration of the room. This bath is made of one piece of porcelain, the rolled edge being glazed as well as the interior of the bath ; the outside of the bath, below the rolled edge, is intended to be rubbed down and finished to match the surroundings, and when so treated makes, in conjunction with the nickel or silver-plated brass fittings and legs, a really handsome and artistic bathing tub.

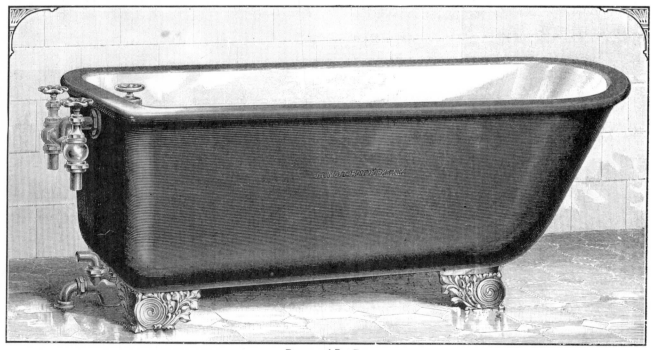

PLATE 15 - G.

"Imperial" Porcelain Rolled-edge Bath, with all exposed parts of Brass Fittings Polished, Nickel or Silver-plated, Demarest Patent Standing Waste and Overflow, Cast Brass Trap, and Bronzed Iron, Nickel-plated or Polished Cast Brass Legs. Two sizes, A and B.

For dimensions, see page 22.

"IMPERIAL" PORCELAIN BATHS.

PLATE 16-G.

"Imperial" Porcelain Bath with Supply Fittings, "Unique" Waste and Overflow, Hardwood Rim and Bronzed Iron or Cast Brass Legs; all exposed parts of Brass Work being Polished, Nickel, or Silver-plated. Two sizes, A and B.

PLATE 17-G.

"Imperial" Porcelain Bath with Improved Ebony Handle Double Bath Cock and "Unique" Waste and Overflow. Two sizes, A and B. The Double Bath Cock is furnished with Rubber Tube and Sprinkler for Shower.

For dimensions, see page 22.

"IMPERIAL" PORCELAIN BATHS.

PLATE 18-G.

"Imperial" Porcelain Bath with Improved Ebony Handle Double Bath Cock, Nickel or Silver-plated Brass Waste Plug, Rubber Stopper, Chain and Common Overflow.   Two sizes, A and B.

The Double Bath Cock is furnished with Rubber Tube and Sprinkler for Shower.

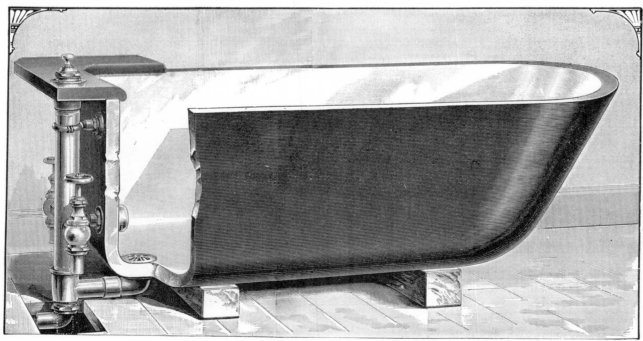

PLATE 19-G.

"Imperial" Porcelain Bath with Supply Valves and "Unique" Waste and Overflow.   Two sizes, A and B.

THE above is adapted for use in Asylums and Hospitals where it is desirable to have the Supply Fittings out of the reach of patient; Detachable Key Handles instead of the Wheels will be furnished when so ordered. Plug and Chain, as shown by Plate 18-G, may be used instead of the "Unique" Waste. If desired, this Bath can be furnished with Hardwood Rim, as shown by Plate 16-G.

For dimensions, see page 22.

"Imperial" Porcelain Baths.

PLATE 20-G.

"Imperial" Porcelain Bath with Supply Fittings and the "Simplex" Patent Standing Waste and Overflow; the Cocks are of the Improved Pattern and with Ebony Handles.   Two Sizes, A and B.

AS a Standing Overflow in its simplest form the above is unquestionably superior to any yet made.   By reference to the illustration it will be seen that the movement of the Stand Pipe is controlled by the inner tube, which also serves to retain the Stand Pipe in a perpendicular position, thus insuring a permanently tight seat.   The Tub is emptied by raising the Stand Pipe and giving it a slight turn to right or left; by a further turn it can be taken out and cleaned, and should it be accidentally dropped the rubber cushion at each end will preclude the possibility of its being dented or bruised or in any way injuring the inside of the Bath.

PLATE 21-G.

"Imperial" Porcelain Bath with Brass Plug, Rubber Stopper, Chain and Common Overflow.   Two sizes, A and B.

For dimensions, see page 22.

DIAGRAMS SHOWING SPACE REQUIRED TO SET "IMPERIAL" BATHS.

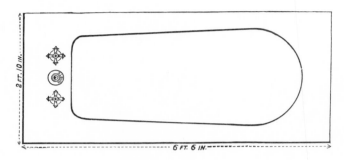

PLATE 22 - G.

PLAN OF TOP OF WOOD CASING FOR SIZE A.

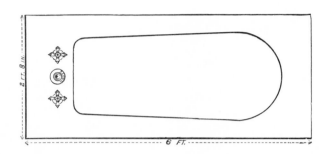

PLATE 23 - G.

PLAN OF TOP OF WOOD CASING FOR SIZE B.

These plans give the exact proportions of the openings of the two sizes of Baths, also the dimensions of top wood work. If space is limited, however, the length can be reduced as much as six inches.

DIMENSIONS AND WEIGHTS.

	AVERAGE WEIGHT.	WEIGHT IN SHIPPING ORDER.
SIZE A.—Outside dimensions : length 66 inches, width at head 30 inches, width at foot 24 inches, depth 22½ inches,	520 lbs.	600 lbs.
" B.— " " " 60 " " " 30 " " " 24 " " 22½ "	430 "	500 "

Thickness of Baths, 1¾ inches.

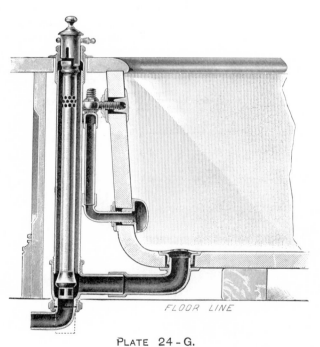

PLATE 24 - G.

Section of Plate 12-G, showing the "Unique" Waste and Overflow.

PLATE 25 - G.

PLATE 26 - G.

PLATE 27 - G.

PLATE 28 - G.

The above four illustrations show the various styles of handles we furnish with our Bath Tubs.

AS indicated by illustration, Plate 24-G, the "Unique" Waste consists of a Stand Pipe, with perforations near the top for overflow, moving within a Tube, the movement of Stand Pipe for regulating the retention and egress of water in the tub being controlled by a bayonet lock. To bring the Stand Pipe in the position shown by above illustration, it is raised from its seat and given a slight turn to the right or left; a still further turn will allow the Stand Pipe to be removed for cleaning without the use of any tool whatever.

MOTT'S PORCELAIN=LINED FRENCH AND ROMAN BATHS.

THESE celebrated Baths are so well known and their high quality so well understood by architects and the trade generally, that it seems almost unneccessary to make any special reference to them at this time, their very general use for the last ten years throughout the country, not only in fine private work but in the largest and best equipped of our hospitals and asylums, having, we think, fully established their superiority to all others.

The following illustrations show the Baths with an almost endless variety of fittings ; these are not only finished and fitted in the most thorough manner, but are in all cases improvements upon the old methods.

The "Roman" Bath is the outcome of the growing desire to have plumbing fixtures set up without any, or at least with very little cabinet work, and for this purpose we imagine this Bath will become a favorite, as it does away with the exposure of the pipes and fittings, and is very artistic and symmetrical. The fittings, being at back of the tub, can be easily reached by the bather while in the bath.

MOTT'S PORCELAIN-LINED ROMAN BATH.

PATENT APPLIED FOR.

PLATE 29-G.

Porcelain-lined Roman Bath with Supply Fittings and "Unique" Waste and Overflow, Bronzed Iron, Polished or Nickel-plated Cast Brass Legs and Hardwood Rim.

THE illustration represents the Roman Bath with the Hardwood Rim finishing close up to the wall at back; if desired, however, the Rim can be furnished to cover the top of Bath only, the handles being back of the Rim and not passing through it. A reference to Plate 14-G will explain the latter arrangement, which would render accessible for cleaning all parts of the wall, fittings and Bath.

THREE SIZES:

A—4 feet 6 inches long, 2 feet 3 inches wide outside, inside depth at outlet 18½ inches, height on legs, 24½ inches.
B—5 " 0 " " 2 " 3 " " " " " " 18½ " " " 24½ "
C—5 " 6 " " 2 " 3 " " " " " " 18½ " " " 24½ "

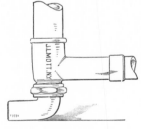

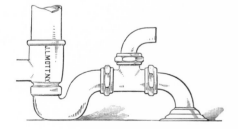

PLATE 30-G.   PLATE 31-G.   PLATE 32-G.

When ordering the Roman Bath, please state if it is desired with Straight or Bent Coupling, as shown by Plates 30 and 31-G, or with Cast Brass Trap, as shown by Plate 32-G.

MOTT'S PORCELAIN-LINED FRENCH BATHS.

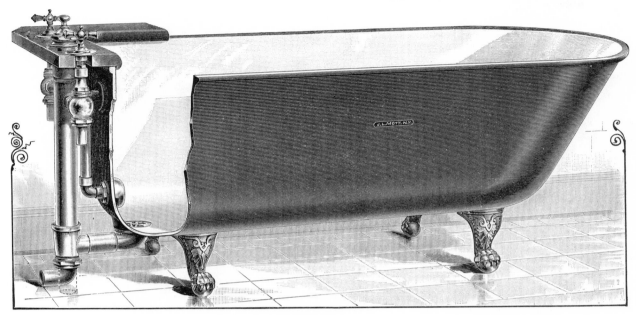

PLATE 33 - G.

Porcelain-lined French Bath with Supply Fittings and "Unique" Waste and Overflow.

THE above method of supply and waste is in our opinion the best and the one most generally used in private bath rooms with cabinet finish. The Supply Valves are of the best known form of compression, durable and easy in movement. The 'Unique' Combined Waste and Overflow is absolutely the simplest, most effective and durable that has yet been devised. The illustration shows the Stand Pipe of the Waste seated as when the tub is being filled; to empty the latter the Stand Pipe is raised and turned slightly to the right or left; a still further turn will permit the Stand Pipe to be taken out, when it and the interior of tube may be cleaned. The sectional cut on page 22 will more fully explain the operation of this Waste.

PLATE 34 - G.

Porcelain-lined French Bath with Supply Fittings and "Unique" Waste and Overflow; the Cocks are of the Improved Pattern and with Ebony Handles.

Sizes: 3, 3½, 4, 4½, 5, 5½ and 6 feet long by 24 inches wide outside, and 19 inches deep inside; height on legs, 25 inches.

MOTT'S PORCELAIN-LINED BATHS.

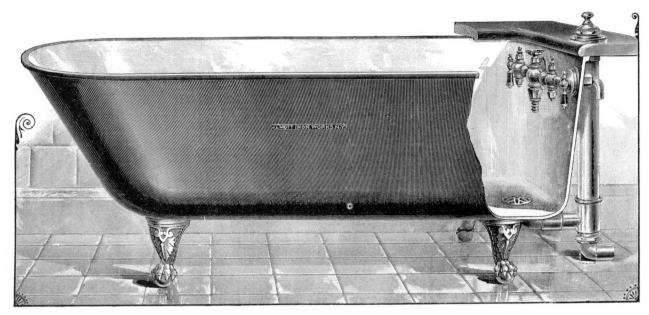

PLATE 35 - G.

Porcelain-lined French Bath with Improved Ebony Handle Double Bath Cock and "Unique" Waste and Overflow. The Double Bath Cock
is furnished with Rubber Tube and Sprinkler for Shower.

PLATE 36 - G.

Porcelain-lined French Bath with Improved Ebony Handle Double Bath Cock, "Unique" Waste and Overflow, Hardwood Rim, Brass Trap,
Supply Pipes and Air Chambers, and Bronzed Iron or Cast Brass Legs; all exposed parts of Brass Fittings
being Polished, Nickel or Silver-Plated.

THE Porcelain-lined Bath as represented by the illustration, forms a most complete and handsome fixture, especially designed for use in
private and public bath rooms where cabinet work is dispensed with. The exterior of the Bath may be painted or decorated to harmonize
with the prevailing colors in the room in which it is placed. The Hardwood Rim may be of mahogany, cherry, black walnut or ash.

For sizes, see page 25.

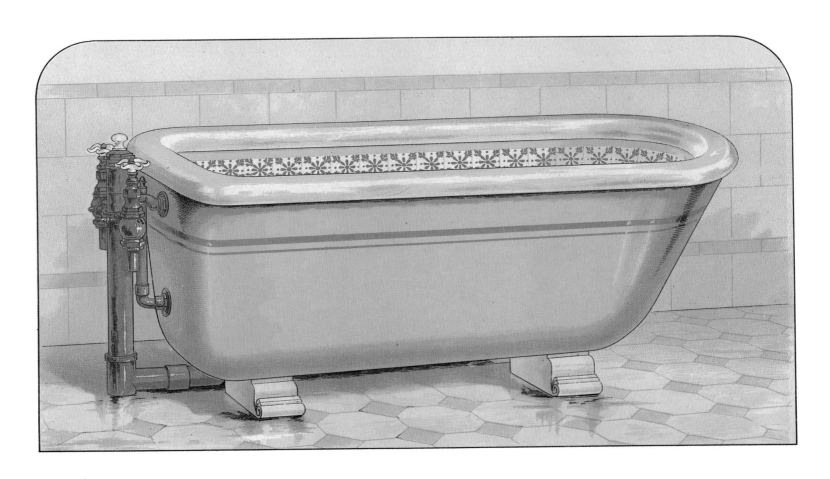

PLATE A

See page 15 for identifications.

PLATE B

See page 163 for identifications.

Plate C

See page 164 for identifications.

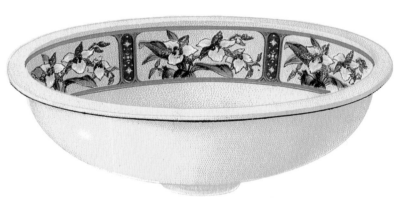

PLATE D

See page 165 for identifications.

PLATE E

See page 166 for identifications.

PLATE F

See page 167 for identifications.

PLATE G

See page 168 for identifications.

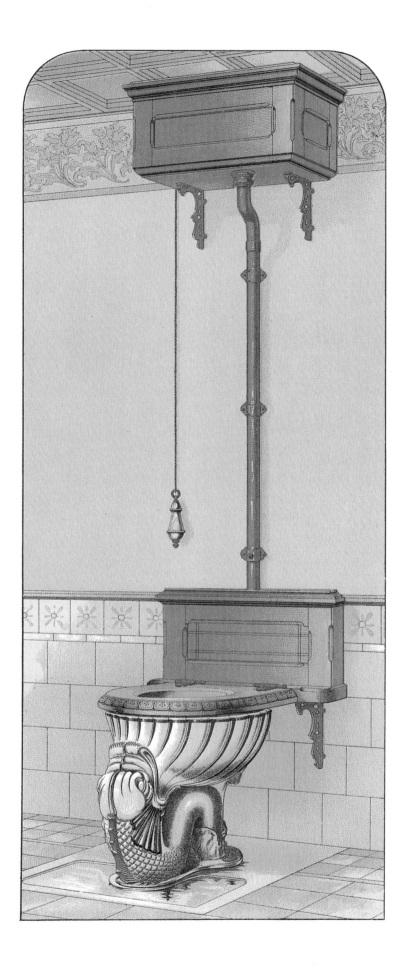 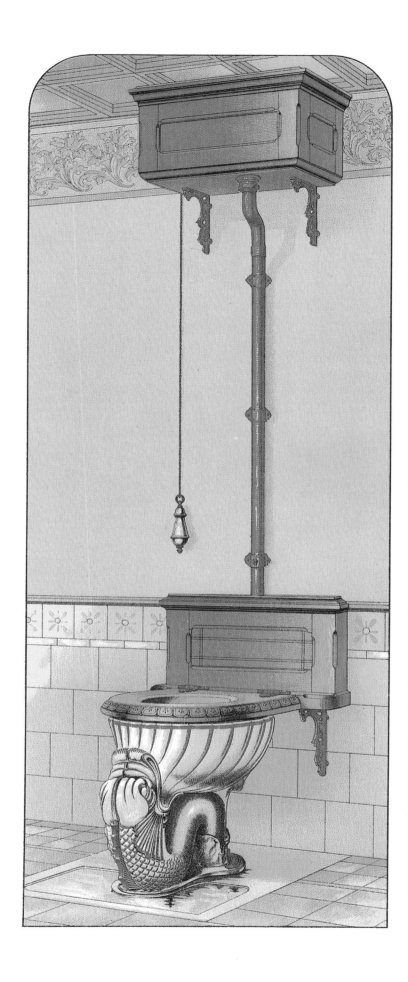

Plate H

See page 75 for identifications.

Mott's Porcelain-Lined French Baths.

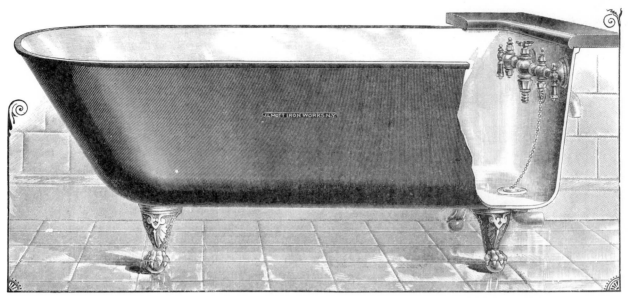

Plate 37 - G.

Porcelain-lined French Bath with Improved Ebony Handle Double Bath Cock, Plug. Rubber Stopper, Chain and Common Overflow. The Double Bath Cock is furnished with Attachable Rubber Tube and Sprinkler for Shower.

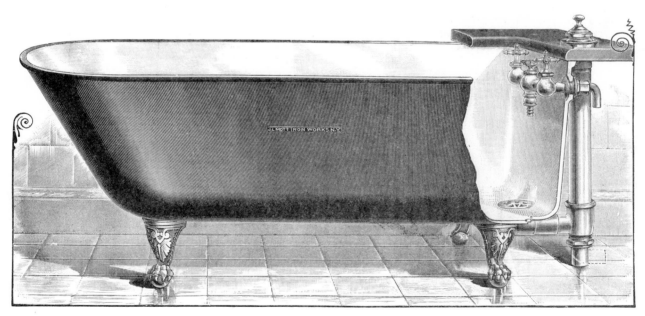

Plate 38 - G.

Porcelain-lined French Bath with Compression Double Bath Cock and "Unique" Waste and Overflow. The Double Bath Cock is furnished with Attachable Rubber Tube and Sprinkler for Shower.

For dimensions of Baths, see page 25.

MOTT'S PORCELAIN-LINED FRENCH BATHS.

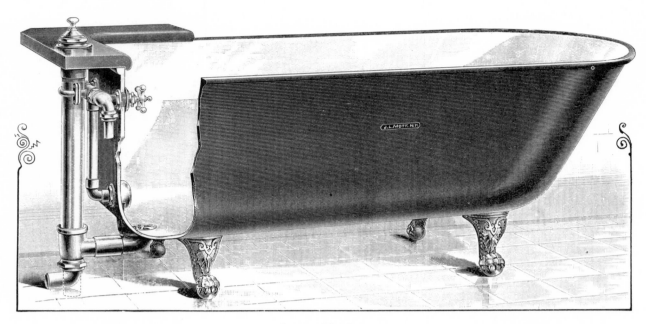

PLATE 39-G.

Porcelain-lined French Bath with Bottom Supply Fittings and "Unique" Waste and Overflow; Handles inside the Bath.

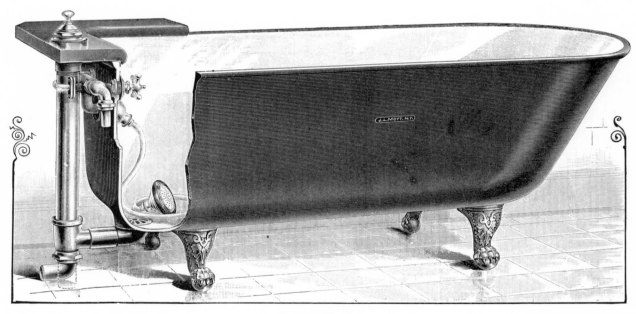

PLATE 40-G.

Porcelain-lined French Bath with Top Supply Fittings, "Unique" Waste and Overflow, and Attachable Rubber Tube and Sprinkler for Shower; Handles inside the Bath.

THE illustration shows the Rubber Tube and Sprinkler attached to the Supply Bell as when Shower is to be used.

For dimensions of Baths, see page 25.

MOTT'S PORCELAIN-LINED FRENCH BATHS.

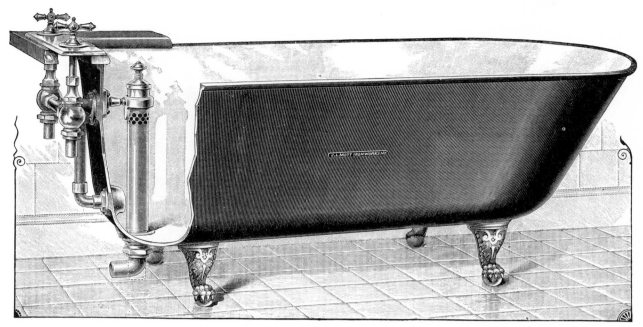

PLATE 41-G.

Porcelain-lined French Bath with Demarest's Patent Standing Waste and Overflow and Bottom Supply Fittings.

THE illustration shows the Stand Pipe seated—that is, the Tub is ready to be filled with water. To empty the Tub, the Stand Pipe is raised and given a slight turn to the right or left, the movement being controlled by the Ring near the top of Stand Pipe; a still further turn will permit the Stand Pipe to be taken out to be cleaned. On the bottom of Overflow Tube there is a Strainer which prevents extraneous matter from getting into the Pipes, and which is also the guide. The Demarest Standing Overflow is unquestionably the best of that form in the market.

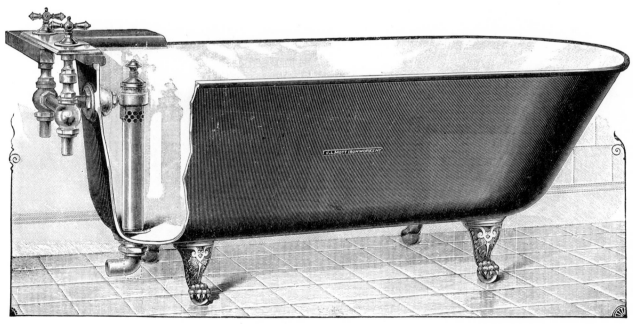

PLATE 42-G.

Porcelain-lined French Bath with Demarest's Patent Standing Waste and Overflow and Top Supply Fittings.

For dimensions of Baths, see page 25.

MOTT'S PORCELAIN-LINED FRENCH BATHS.

PLATE 43 - G.

Porcelain-lined French Bath with Top-Supply Fittings and Patent "Simplex" Standing Waste and Overflow.

PLATE 44 - G.

Porcelain-lined, Galvanized or Painted French Bath with Compression Faucets and Patent "Simplex" Standing Waste and Overflow.

A S a Standing Overflow in its simplest form the above is unquestionably superior to any yet made. By reference to the illustration it will be seen that the movement of the Stand Pipe is controlled by the inner tube, which also serves to retain the Stand Pipe in a perpendicular position, thus insuring a permanently tight seat. The Tub is emptied by raising the Stand Pipe and giving it a slight turn to right or left; by a further turn it can be taken out and cleaned, and should it be accidentally dropped the rubber cushion at each end will preclude the possibility of its being dented or bruised or in any way injuring the inside of the Bath.

For dimensions of Baths, see page 25.

MOTT'S PORCELAIN-LINED FRENCH BATHS.

PLATE 45-G.

Porcelain-lined French Bath with Bottom-Supply Fittings, Connected Overflow and Waste, Rubber Stopper and Chain.

PLATE 46-G.

Porcelain-lined French Bath with Compression Double Bath Cock, Connected Overflow and Waste, Rubber Stopper and Chain. The Double Bath Cock is furnished with Attachable Rubber Tube and Sprinkler for Shower.

THE Brass Cap at Top of Connected Overflow and Waste may be unscrewed when it is desired to cleanse the interior of Overflow Tube; or it may be taken off permanently and a Vent Pipe attached for ventilating the Overflow and Waste.

For dimensions of Baths, see page 25.

MOTT'S FRENCH BATHS.

PLATE 47 - G.

Porcelain-lined, Galvanized or Painted French Bath with Compression Double Bath Cock, Common Overflow, Brass Plug, Rubber Stopper and Chain.
The Double Bath Cock is furnished with Attachable Rubber Tube and Sprinkler for Shower.

PLATE 48 - G.

Porcelain-lined, Galvanized or Painted French Bath with Common Overflow, Brass Plug, Rubber Stopper and Chain.

For dimensions of Baths, see page 25.

MOTT'S FRENCH BATHS FOR HOSPITALS AND PRISONS.

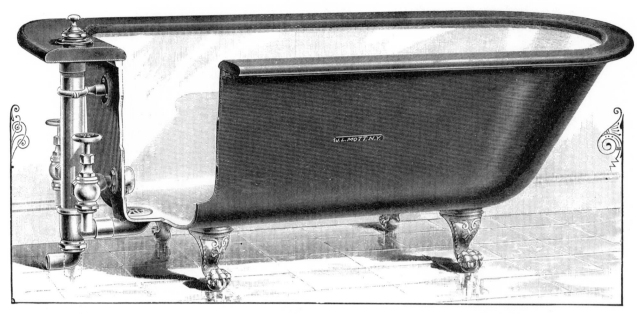

PLATE 49 - G.

Porcelain-lined, Galvanized or Painted French Bath with Supply Fittings, "Unique" Waste and Overflow and Hardwood Rim. The Supply Valves can be furnished with Detachable Key Handles when so ordered.

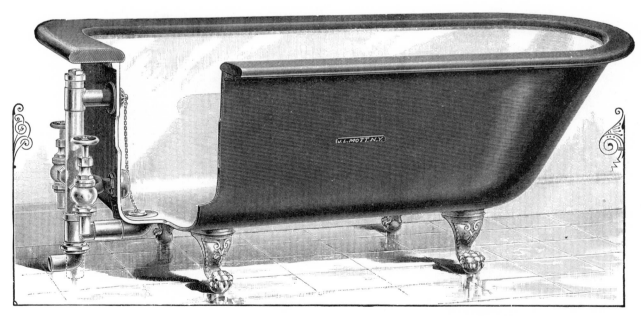

PLATE 50 - G.

Porcelain-lined, Galvanized or Painted French Bath with Supply Fittings, Connected Overflow and Waste, Brass Plug, Rubber Stopper and Chain, and Hardwood Rim. The Supply Valves can be furnished with Detachable Key Handles when so ordered.

For dimensions of Baths, see page 25.

MOTT'S FRENCH BATHS.

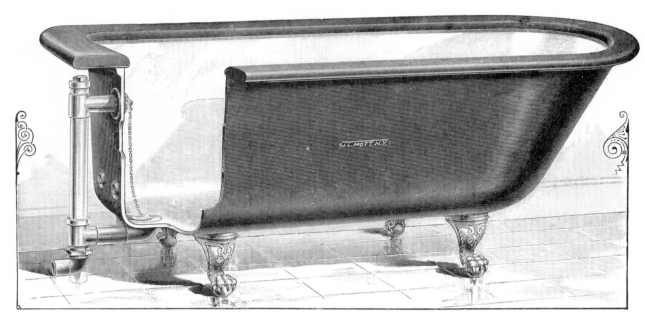

PLATE 51-G.

Porcelain-lined, Galvanized or Painted French Bath with Connected Waste and Overflow, Rubber Stopper, Chain and Hardwood Rim; Inlets tapped for Iron Pipe Supply.

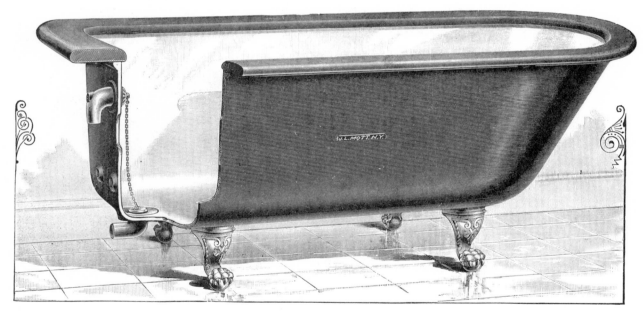

PLATE 52-G.

Porcelain-lined, Galvanized or Painted French Bath with Common Overflow, Plug, Rubber Stopper, Chain and Hardwood Rim; Inlets tapped for Iron Pipe Supply.

For dimensions of Baths, see page 25.

MOTT'S PAINTED IRON BATH TUBS.
WITH PATENT OVERFLOW.

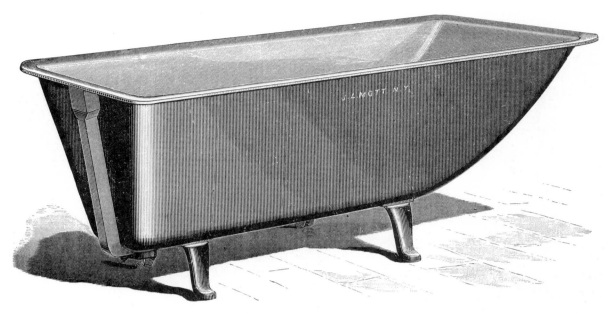

PLATE 53-G.

MOTT'S BATH WITH PATENT OVERFLOW.

For Sizes see below.

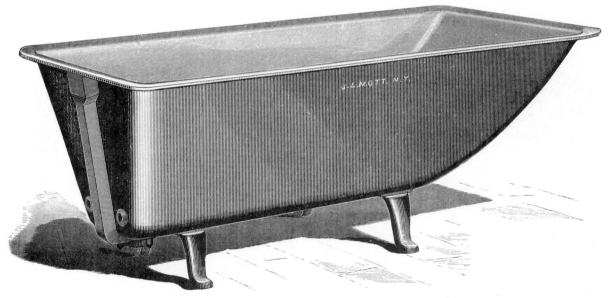

PLATE 54-G.

MOTT'S BATH WITH PATENT OVERFLOW.

Inlets Tapped for ¾ inch Iron Pipe Supply.

For Asylum and Hospital use.

Length.	Width.	Depth.	Height on Legs.
No. 1, 66 inches.	25½ inches.	19 inches.	23 inches.
No. 2, 72 inches.	25½ inches.	19 inches.	23 inches.

COPPER BATH TUBS WITH PATENT SUPPLY AND WASTE FITTINGS.

To meet a demand for Copper Bath Tubs having a better and more complete form of Supply and Waste Fittings than has heretofore been obtainable, we offer those illustrated and described on this and the following pages. The Supply and Waste Fittings are essentially the same as those which have been illustrated and described in connection with our Porcelain-lined Iron and "Imperial" Porcelain Baths on previous pages of this Catalogue; they are made and finished in the best possible manner and warranted effective and durable.

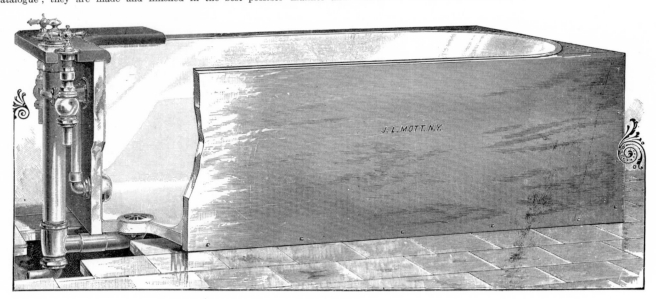

PLATE 55-G.

COPPER BATH,

With Supply Fittings and "Unique" Waste and Overflow.

French Shape Tub, 4½, 5, 5½ and 6 feet long; 26 inches wide and 22 inches deep.

Regular Shape Tub, 5, 5½ and 6 feet long; 24 inches wide and 20 inches deep.

Weight, 14, 16, 18 and 20 ounces to the square foot.

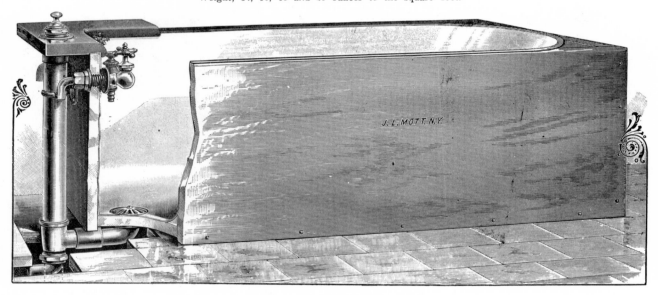

PLATE 56-G.

COPPER BATH,

With "Unique" Waste and Overflow and Compression Double Bath Cock; the latter is furnished with Attachable Rubber Tube and **Sprinkler**.

For Sizes and Weights, see Plate 55-G.

Plates 55-G and 56-G are furnished with the Fittings all attached and ready for use, so that the Plumber has only the Supply and Waste Connections to make.

NOTE:—When ordering it is necessary to state whether Bath is desired French or Regular Shape.

COPPER BATH TUBS, WITH PATENT SUPPLY AND WASTE FITTINGS.

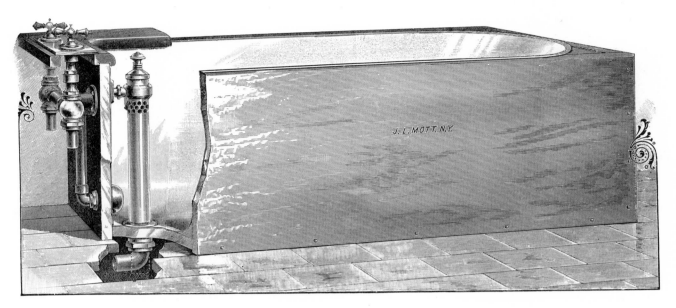

PLATE 57-G.

COPPER BATH,

With Supply Fittings and "Demarest" Patent Standing Waste and Overflow.

Also furnished with Top Supply if so ordered.

For Sizes and Weights, see Plate 55–G.

The illustration shows the Demarest Patent Standing Waste seated—that is, the Tub is ready to be filled with Water. To empty the Tub it is only necessary to slightly raise the Stand Pipe and give it a turn to the right or left; a still further turn will allow the Stand Pipe to be taken out and cleaned. The Strainer on bottom of overflow tube, which prevents extraneous matter from getting into the pipes, is also the guide.

PLATE 58-G.

COPPER BATH,

With Patent "Simplex" Waste and Compression Faucets.

As a Standing Overflow in its simplest form the above is unquestionably superior to any yet made. By reference to the illustration it will be seen that the movement of the Stand Pipe is controlled by the inner tube, which also serves to retain the Stand Pipe in a perpendicular position, thus insuring a perfectly tight seat. The Tub is emptied by raising the Stand Pipe and giving it a slight turn to right or left; the latter can readily be taken out and cleaned, and should it accidentally be dropped into the Tub the Rubber Cushion at each end will prevent the Copper from being dented or otherwise injured.

For Sizes and Weights, see Plate 55–G.

Plates 57–G and 58–G are furnished with the Fittings all attached and ready for use so that the Plumber has only the Supply and Waste Connections to make.

COPPER BATHS, WITH PATENT SUPPLY AND WASTE FITTINGS.

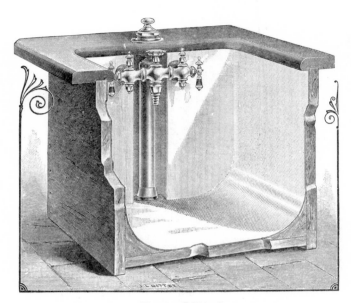

PLATE 58½-G.

THE "NONPAREIL" PATENT COPPER BATH,

With Improved Ebony Handle Double Bath Cock with Attachable Rubber Tube and Sprinkler; also furnished with Compression Double Bath Cock.

DIMENSIONS : 4½, 5, 5½ and 6 feet, not including recess which adds 6 inches to length of Tub.   Width, 26 inches.   Depth, 22 inches.

The illustration shows the Stand Pipe seated. To empty the Bath, the Stand Pipe is raised and given a slight turn to the right or left ; a still further turn permits the Stand Pipe to be taken out and cleaned without the use of any tool whatever.

PLATE 59-G.

COPPER BATH,

With Recess, Patent Simplex Waste and Overflow and Compression Faucets.

DIMENSIONS : Four Sizes, 4½, 5, 5½ and 6 feet, not including recess which adds 6 inches to length of Tub.   Width, 26 inches.

Depth, 22 inches.

For description of "Simplex" Waste, see Plate 58-G.

Plate 58½-G and 59-G are furnished with the Fittings attached.

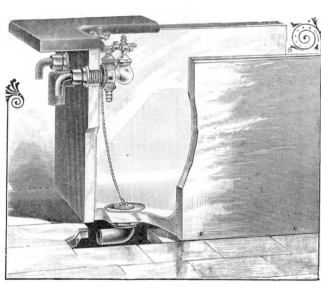

PLATE 59½-G.

COPPER BATH,

With Compression Double Bath Cock, Common Overflow and Plug and Chain.

The Bath Cock is furnished with attachable Rubber Tube and Sprinkler.

French Shape Bath, 4½, 5, 5½ and 6 feet long.   Width, 26 inches.   Depth, 22 inches.

Regular Shape Bath, 5, 5½ and 6 feet long.   Width, 24 inches.   Depth, 20 inches.

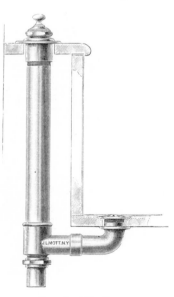

PLATE 60-G.

THE "UNIQUE" PATENT WASTE,

For Copper Bath without Overflow.

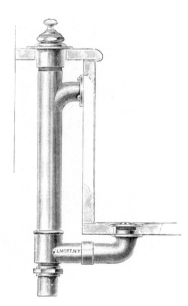

PLATE 60½-G.

THE "UNIQUE" PATENT WASTE,

For Copper Bath with Overflow.

The "Unique" Patent Waste is unquestionably the simplest, most effective and durable that has yet been devised.   For sectional view and description see Plate 24-G.

By reference to Plate 24-G it will be seen that the Overflow is within the Waste. The Waste as shown by Plate 60-G is designed to be used on a Bath without Overflow. For a Bath as regularly made, namely with Overflow Opening, the Waste as shown by Plate 60½-G is furnished.

Mott's Patent Combination Bathing Apparatus.

PLATE 61-G.

MOTT'S PATENT COMBINATION BATHING APPARATUS.

COMPRISING

The "Imperial" Porcelain, or Porcelain-lined Iron, or Planished Copper Bath with Needle Spray and Shower, (and with Liver Spray if so ordered.)

PLATE 61-G represents what is unquestionably the simplest, most effective and complete Bathing Apparatus of its kind yet devised; by it the desired result is attained without a complicated system of Pipes and Valves. The combination consists of an "Imperial" Porcelain, or Porcelain lined Iron, or Copper Bath with the "Unique" Waste and extra heavy Circular Tinned and Planished Copper Hood in the interior of which are the Needle Spray and Shower. The two Valves lettered "Hot" and "Cold" control the Supply and permit the water to enter the Mixing Chamber, attached to which is the Thermometer which registers the temperature of the water; then the Valves lettered, "Needle," "Shower" or "Supply to Bath" can be opened as desired.

The Needle and Shower may be used together or separately. The Needle Spray will be furnished horizontal as shown or vertical as shown by Plate 2-G.

Dimensions: Height from bottom of Bath to top of Hood, 7 feet 2 inches. Inside diameter of Hood, 2 feet 9 inches. This gives abundant room for a free movement of the arms within the Hood and allows a proper diffusion of the Needle Spray.

Mott's Showers and Shampoos.

Plate 62-G.

NICKEL-PLATED BRASS SHAMPOO,

For Rubbing slabs in Turkish and Russian Baths.

The Sprinkler is 3¼ inches in diameter, and is encircled by Rubber Band or Cushion. Plate 62–G as shown is arranged for Supply to run behind wall; it can also be furnished for Supply to run in front of wall.

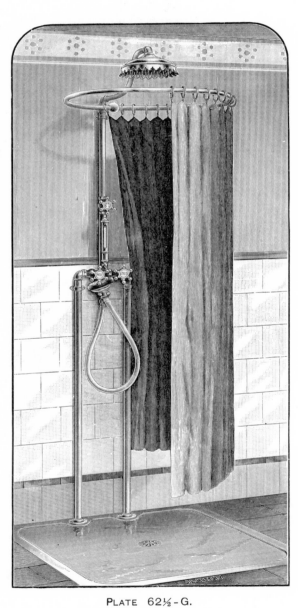

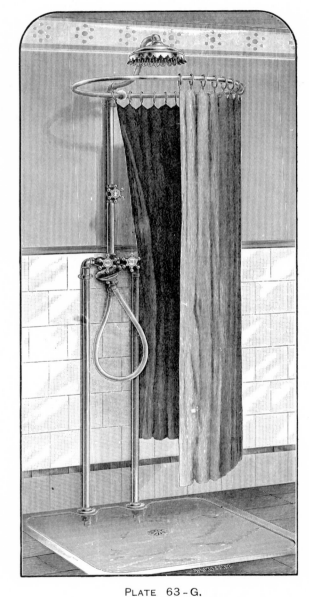

Plate 62½-G.

NICKEL-PLATED BRASS SHOWER,

With Thermometer, Shampoo, Curtain Ring, Curtain and Supply Pipes to Floor.
Also furnished without Curtain Ring and Curtain if so ordered.

The novel and special feature of Plate 62½-G is that by means of the Mixing Chamber and Thermometer, the temperature of the water can be gauged and is registered before opening the Upper Valve which allows water to pass to the Shower.

Plate 63-G.

NICKEL-PLATED BRASS SHOWER,

With Shampoo, Curtain Ring, Curtain and Supply Pipes to Floor.

Diameter of Shower, 8½ inches. Diameter of Curtain Ring, 25 inches.

Plates 62½-G and 63-G are adapted for use in Bathing Establishments and over Baths where it is desired to confine the spray within the Curtain.

Mott's Needle and Shower Baths, &c.

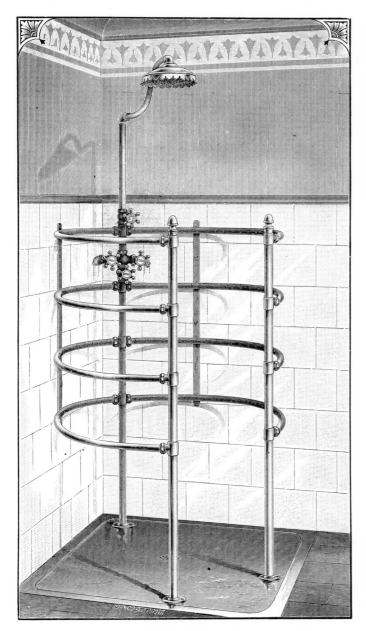

PLATE 63½-G.

PLATE 64-G.

Mott's Combination Needle and Shower Bath,

For Cold and Hot Water.

Nickel-plated Brass Shower,

With Self-closing Upper Valve, Shampoo and Supply Pipes to floor.

Also furnished with Curtain Ring and Curtain as shown by Plate 65-G;
and for Cold water only, if so ordered.

Diameter of Needle Bath, 3 feet 2 inches.   Diameter of Shower, 8½ inches.

Plate 63½-G is intended for use in Bathing Establishments, Athletic Club Rooms and Private Bath Rooms where a less complete and less expensive combination than that shown by Plate 65-G, will answer the requirements.   It can be placed in a Marble or Slate Stall as shown by Plate 66-G, or it can be furnished with Curtain Ring and Curtain as shown by Plate 65-G.

DIMENSIONS : Diameter of Tubular Shower, 8½ inches.
Distance from Floor to centre of Hot and Cold Valves, 4 feet.
Distance from centre of Hot and Cold Valves, to top of Shower, 3 feet.
Lateral distance from Wall to centre of Shower, 19 inches.

This Shower is adapted for use in Bathing Establishments, Athletic Club Rooms, and over Baths where it is not desired to confine the spray by a Curtain as shown by Plate 63-G.   Plate 64-G can however, be furnished with Curtain Ring and Shower as shown by Plate 63-G, if so ordered.   The Upper Valve is self-closing and water will descend from Shower only while the Pull is drawn down.

MOTT'S PATENT NEEDLE AND SHOWER BATHS.

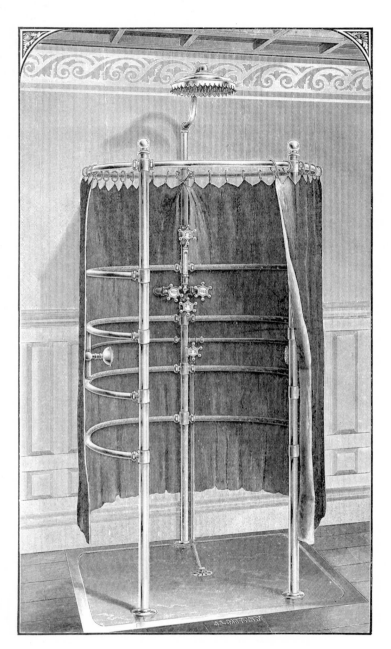

PLATE 64½-G.

NICKEL-PLATED BRASS SHOWER,

With Shampoo and Supply Pipes to Floor.

DIMENSIONS : Diameter of Tubular Shower, 8½ inches.
Distance from Floor to centre of Hot and Cold Valves, 4 feet.
Distance from centre of Hot and Cold Valves to top of Shower, 3 feet 6 inches.
Lateral distance from Wall to centre of Shower, 17 inches.

Plate 64½–G can be furnished of dimensions other than above, to order.

This Shower is adapted for use in Bathing Establishments, Athletic
Club Rooms, and over Baths where it is not desired to confine the spray
by a Curtain as shown by Plate 63–G.

PLATE 65 -G.

MOTT'S PATENT CIRCULAR COMBINATION NEEDLE, SHOWER,
LIVER AND DOUCHE SPRAY BATH,
With Thermometer and Curtain.

DIMENSIONS : Height to top of Shower, 7 feet 6 inches ; Diameter of Needle Bath,
3 feet 5 inches ; Diameter of Shower, 11 inches.   Countersunk
Marble or Slate Base, 3 feet 9 inches × 3 feet 6 inches.

For description of Plate 65–G see Plate 66–G.   In principle of construction and
in operation they are essentially the same, the difference being in the shape and
dimensions.

The two Vertical columns in the foreground of Plate 65–G are perforated as
well as the Horizontal columns, hence the Needle Spray is abundant and thorough.

A feature of the above is that it can be put up without being placed in a Marble
or Slate Stall, the Rubber Curtain effectually confining the spray within the
prescribed limits of the Countersunk Base shown in the illustration.   If preferred,
however, it can be placed in Marble or Slate Stall, same as Plate 66–G.

MOTT'S PATENT COMBINED NEEDLE, SHOWER AND DOUCHE BATH.

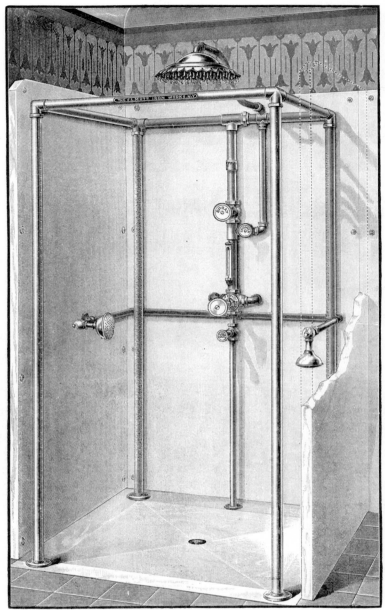

PLATE 66-G.

THE illustration represents a most complete Bath, combining Needle, Spray, Shower, Liver Spray and Douche. Our object has been to produce an apparatus at once simple and efficient, one that would accomplish the desired purpose without the complicated system of pipes and cocks employed in all Combination Baths heretofore made, also to obviate any possibility of the party using the bath to be scalded by accidentally turning on a hot water cock. In this apparatus (assuming the hot-water supply to be at boiling point) the water passing through mixing column can never be of a higher temperature than 98 degrees. Any desired temperature (lower than 98 degrees) can be obtained by turning the wheel governing the mixing column towards cold, tepid or hot, the thermometer attached to the mixing column registering the degree.

The four vertical columns which give the main or Needle Spray are perforated at an angle which throws the spray so that it will entirely cover the body of the bather. A very ingenious feature is that of the Liver Sprays, which can be adjusted to suit the varying heights of the different parties using the bath. The Rose Jet shown in the centre of the bottom slab may be unscrewed, when the Douche or Bidet will be ready for use. In conclusion, we mention the important features and advantages of this Bath as compared with those heretofore made :

FIRST.—Its perfect safety : the hot and cold water supplies being so graduated that it is impossible for the bather to be scalded.

SECOND.—Any desired temperature (below 98 degrees) can be obtained, the degree being registered by the thermometer attached to mixing column, before the sprays are turned on.

THIRD.—The number of stop valves and pipes is so few that the bather is not apt to get confused by their number or uses.

FOURTH.—The four different sprays, Needle, Liver, Shower and Douche, are all combined and may be used together or separately, at the immediate control of the bather.

As regards the workmanship, we have only to say that it is of the very best, being made with the same care and thoroughness which characterizes all our work in this department.

The above occupies a space of 7 ft. × 3 ft. 6 in. × 3 ft. 6 in., but can be made an inch or two less or more, or otherwise modified to suit. The Marble or Slate Stall may be dispensed with where it is not necessary to confine the spray within its limits ; in this case the Needle Bath is arranged to stand alone, provision being made to secure it firmly to the floor.

CABINET WORK FOR BATH TUBS.

PLATE 67 - G.

"Elizabethan" Design.

Furnished in Mahogany and Cherry.

Cabinet Work for Seat, Foot and Child's Baths can be furnished in this design.

CABINET WORK FOR BATH TUBS.

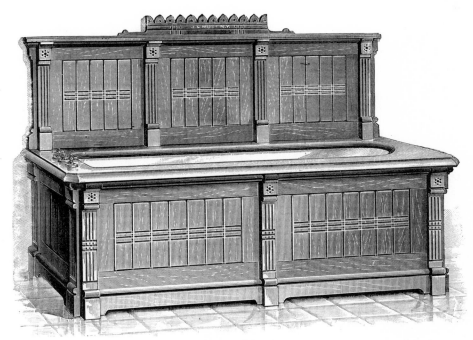

PLATE 68 - G.

"Eastlake" design.

Furnished in Black Walnut, Cherry and Ash.

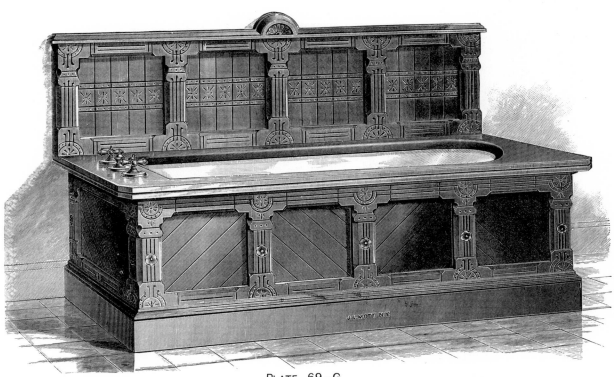

PLATE 69 - G.

"Eastlake" design.

Furnished in Mahogany or Cherry.

Cabinet Work for Seat, Foot and Child's Baths can be furnished in above designs.

CABINET WORK FOR BATH TUBS.

PLATE 70 - G.

Case with Marble Back.

Furnished in Cherry, Black Walnut and Ash

PLATE 71 - G.

Furnished in Cherry, Black Walnut and Ash.

Cabinet Work for Seat, Foot and Child's Baths can be furnished in above designs.

"Imperial" Porcelain Seat Baths.

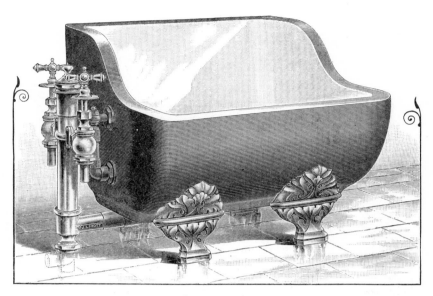

PLATE 72 - G.

"Imperial" Porcelain Seat Bath with Supply Fittings and "Unique" Waste and Overflow. Furnished with or without Cast Iron Legs. The Fittings can be at the left as shown, or at the right if so ordered.

Outside Dimensions : length, 25½ inches ; width, 22½ inches ; height at front on legs, 17 inches ; height at back on legs, 22½ inches ; thickness, 1½ inches.

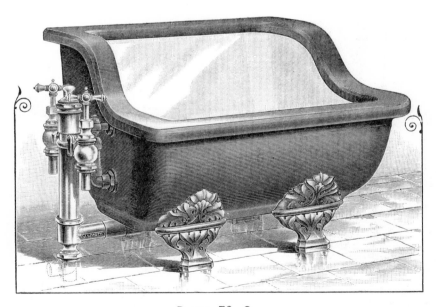

PLATE 73 - G.

"Imperial" Porcelain Seat Bath with Supply Fittings, "Unique" Waste and Overflow, Hardwood Rim and Bronzed Iron, Polished or Nickel-plated Cast Brass Legs ; all exposed parts of Brass Fittings being Polished or Nickel-plated. Can also be furnished with Brass Trap, as shown by Plate 32-G. The Seat Bath is furnished with Fittings at the left as shown, or at the right if so ordered.

A SEAT BATH is a most useful and desirable Fixture in a well appointed bath-room, serving a double purpose, as it is equally well adapted for use as a Foot Bath.

PORCELAIN-LINED IRON SEAT BATHS.

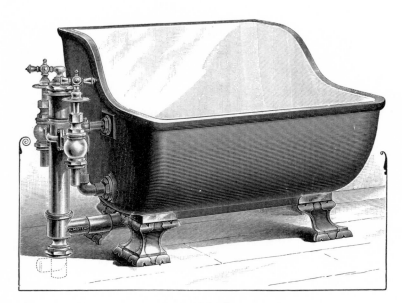

PLATE 74 - G.

Porcelain-lined Seat Bath with Supply Fittings and "Unique" Waste and Overflow.

Furnished with Fittings at the left as shown, or at the right if so ordered.

Dimensions : length, 24 inches ; width, 22½ inches, height at front, 16 inches ; height at rear, 21 inches.

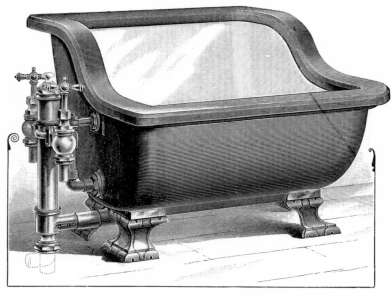

PLATE 75 - G.

Porcelain-lined Seat Bath with Supply Fittings, "Unique" Waste and Overflow, Hardwood Rim and Bronzed Iron, Polished or Nickel-plated Cast
Brass Legs ; all exposed parts of Brass Fittings being Polished or Nickel-plated. The Bath is furnished
with Fittings at the left as shown, or at the right if so ordered.

A SEAT BATH is a most useful and desirable Fixture in a well appointed bath-room, serving a double purpose, as it is equally well adapted
for use as a Foot Bath.

"IMPERIAL" PORCELAIN CHILD'S BATHS.

PLATE 76 - G.

"Imperial" Porcelain Child's Bath with Rolled Edge, Supply Fittings, "Unique" Waste and Overflow, and Bronzed Iron, Polished, or Nickel-plated Cast Brass Legs.

Outside dimensions, including Rolled Edge : length, 29 inches ; width, 22 inches ; inside depth, 13 inches.

PLATE 77 - G.

"Imperial" Porcelain Child's Bath with Supply Fittings, "Unique" Waste and Overflow, Hardwood Rim, and Bronzed Iron, Polished or Nickel-plated Cast Brass Legs.

Outside dimensions, not including Hardwood Rim : length, 27½ inches ; width, 20 inches ; inside depth, 13 inches.

"IMPERIAL" PORCELAIN CHILD'S BATHS.

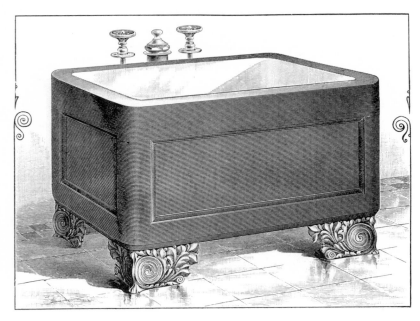

PLATE 78-G.

"Imperial" Porcelain Child's Bath with Bottom Supply Fittings and "Unique" Waste and Overflow. Furnished with or without Cast Iron Legs.

Outside dimensions: length, 27½ inches; width, 20 inches; inside depth, 13 inches; height on legs, 19 inches.

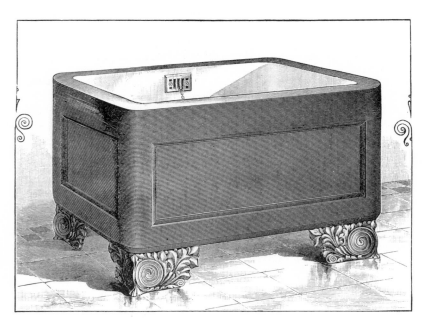

PLATE 79-G.

"Imperial" Porcelain Child's Bath with Common Overflow, Nickel-plated Plug, Rubber Stopper and Chain. Furnished with or without Cast Iron Legs.

For dimensions see Plate 78-G.

PORCELAIN-LINED IRON FOOT BATHS.

PLATE 80 - G.

Porcelain-lined Foot Bath with Supply Fittings and "Unique" Waste and Overflow.

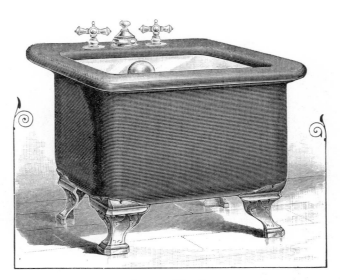

PLATE 81 - G.

Porcelain-lined Foot Bath with Supply Fittings and "Unique" Waste and Overflow, Bronzed Iron, Polished or Nickel-plated Cast Brass Legs
and Hardwood Rim.

Dimensions : length outside, 20¼ inches ; width outside, 17¼ inches ; depth inside, 11 inches ; height on legs, 16 inches.

PORCELAIN-LINED IRON AND OVAL PORCELAIN FOOT BATHS.

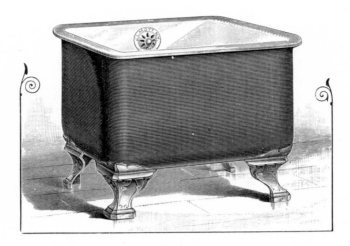

PLATE 82 - G.

Porcelain-lined Iron Foot Bath with Brass Waste Plug, Rubber Stopper, Chain and Common Overflow.

Dimensions: length outside, 20¼ inches; width outside, 17¼ inches; depth inside, 11 inches; height on legs, 16 inches.

PLATE 83 - G.

PLATE 84 - G.

Oval Porcelain Foot Bath with Common Overflow, Brass Waste Plug, Rubber Stopper and Chain.

Oval Porcelain Foot Bath with Top Supply Fittings and "Unique" Waste and Overflow.

Dimensions: 19 × 17 × 10 inches deep.

Copper Seat and Foot Baths.

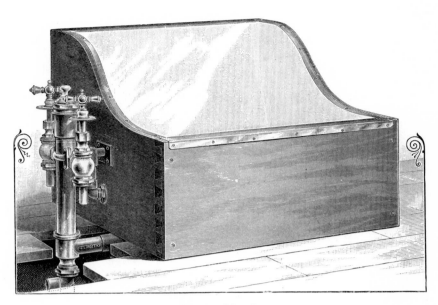

PLATE 85 - G.

Copper Seat Bath with Supply Fittings and "Unique" Waste and Overflow.   Furnished with Fittings at the left as shown, or at the right if so ordered.

Outside Dimensions: length, 24 inches; width, 23 inches; height at front, 12 inches; height at back, 22 inches.

Weight of Copper, 14, 16, 18 and 20 oz. to the square foot.

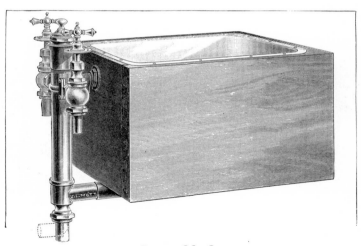

PLATE 86 - G.

Copper Foot Bath with Supply Fittings and "Unique" Waste and Overflow. Furnished with Fittings at the left as shown, or at the right if so ordered.

Dimensions: length outside, 20 inches; width outside, 14 inches; depth inside, 11 inches.

Weight of Copper, 14, 16, 18 and 20 oz. to the square foot.

THE "INODORO" AND "PURITA" BACK-OUTLET WASH-OUT VENTILATING WATER CLOSETS.

PATENTED.

THERE are many points of advantage possessed by a properly constructed Wash-out Water Closet which warrant its being considered equal, if not superior, to any other form yet produced. From a sanitary standpoint it represents absolute perfection; it is simple, rapid and thorough in operation and devoid of all moving or mechanical parts liable to derangement, and there is at all times a sufficient body of water in the Bowl. The foregoing we claim in a high degree for the "Inodoro" as illustrated on the following pages. It is a beautiful piece of porcelain made for us in England and guaranteed not to craze or discolor. The Flushing Rim is designed to give the greatest Wash-out force with the least amount of water, and to insure that all parts of the Bowl are flushed. The "Inodoro" is made with Trap or Sewer Vent, and with Local or Bowl Vent; the latter of course is rarely used unless when it can be connected with a hot flue.

The Embossed "Inodoro," in Plain White and Ivory Tint, also Decorated, is the outcome of the tendency to have all plumbing fixtures set up open, dispensing as far as possible with Cabinet Work, so they may be accessible on all sides. For this purpose we know of no Water Closet better adapted than the Embossed "Inodoro," which combines a really handsome and artistic appearance with all practical and sanitary requisites.

As shown by the following cuts, we also make the "Inodoro" with an Offset; this Closet, however, is only used to take the place of an old closet where the Trap is already under the floor and cannot well be removed.

SECTIONAL VIEWS OF THE "INODORO" AND "PURITA."

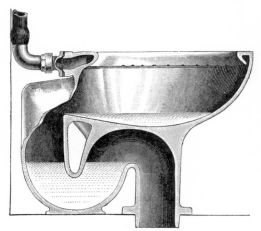

PLATE 87-G.

Section of the "Inodoro."

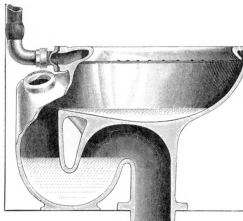

PLATE 88-G.

Section of the "Inodoro" with Local or Bowl Vent.

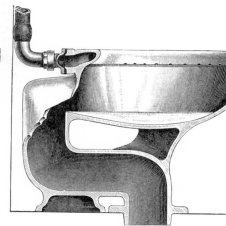

PLATE 89-G.

Section of the "Inodoro" with Offset.

Each "Inodoro" is furnished with our Patent Brass Inlet, Brass Vent Coupling and Brass Lag Bolts and Washers.

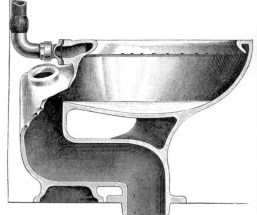

PLATE 90-G.

Section of "Inodoro" with Offset and Local or Bowl Vent.

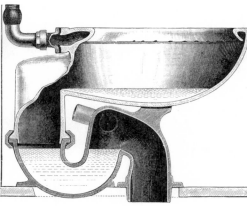

PLATE 91-G.

Section of the "Purita," with Trap having Flange for Lead Waste Pipe Connection.

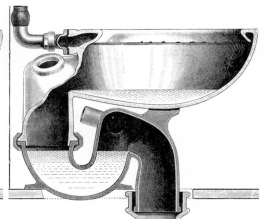

PLATE 92-G.

Section of the "Purita," with Trap having Spigot to caulk into Hub of Soil Pipe and with Local or Bowl Vent.

The "Purita" is in all respects the same as the "Inodoro," only the Trap is Enameled Iron; the Brass Vent is reversible and can be used on either right or left side of the Trap. Each "Purita" is furnished with Patent Brass Inlet and Vent Coupling.

THE "INODORO," EMBOSSED.

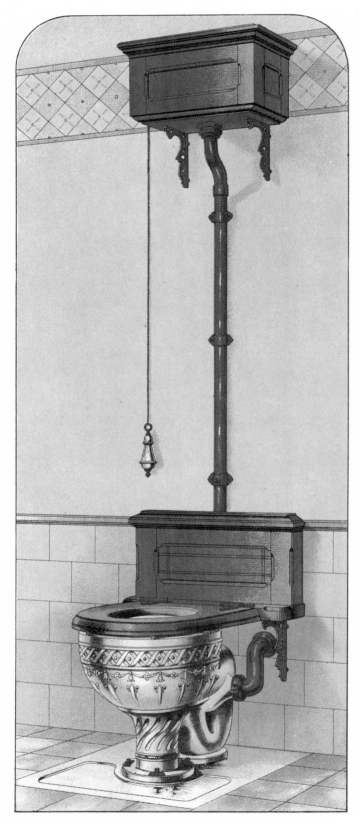

Plate 93-G.

Plate 94-G.

For description, see opposite page.

THE "INODORO" EMBOSSED.

DESIGN PATENTED.

PLATE 93-G.

THE "INODORO," EMBOSSED, IVORY-TINTED PORCELAIN,

With Open Seat and Back, No. 4½ Cabinet-finish Copper-lined
Cistern (Design B), Nickel-plated or Polished Brass Flush Pipe,
Nickel-plated or Polished Brass Curved Trap Vent,
Nickel-plated or Polished Brass Brackets for Seat
and Cistern, Pull and Chain.

PLATE 94-G.

THE "INODORO," EMBOSSED, WHITE PORCELAIN,

With Open Seat and Back, No. 4½ Cabinet-finish
Copper-lined Cistern, (Design B), Nickel–plated or Polished
Brass Flush Pipe, Nickel-plated or Polished Brass Straight
Trap Vent, Nickel-plated or Polished Brass Brackets
for Seat and Cistern, Pull and Chain.

THE Seat and Cistern may be of Cherry, Ash, Black Walnut or Mahogany; when ordering it will be necessary to state which is desired. The Brass Flush Pipe (patent applied for) is an important feature and adds greatly to the appearance of the apparatus, while its cost does not exceed that of lead pipe, taking into consideration the expense of bending, fitting and encasing the latter. With each Brass Flush Pipe is furnished the Offset as shown and an Adjustable Bottom Bend and Coupling, which enables the plumber to make the connection quickly and easily.

With the No. 4½ Cistern the Syphon is started by drawing down the Pull and releasing it at once, when the contents (about three gallons) descend rapidly and with force to the Closet. Where the water supply is constant this Cistern we think superior to all others, as it is not only neat and sightly but is simple and reliable in every way. Dimensions 18 × 9 × 10 inches deep.

The Polished or Nickel-plated Brass Vent for Trap is furnished curved as shown by Plate 93-G, or straight as shown by Plate 94-G. It is intended to be caulked into the Hub of the Iron Vent Pipe which comes flush with the wall, the Polished or Nickel-plated Brass Escutcheon making a finish.

The illustrations show the "Inodoro" placed upon a Counter-sunk Marble Floor Slab which is, in our opinion, superior to all other methods of setting, and also heightens the general neat and attractive appearance of the apparatus.

For sectional view and description of the "Inodoro" see page 54.

THE "INODORO" EMBOSSED.

DESIGN PATENTED.

PLATE 95-G.

THE "INODORO," EMBOSSED, IVORY-TINTED PORCELAIN AND TURQUOISE,

With Open Seat and Back, No. 21½ Cabinet-finish Copper-lined
Cistern (Design B), Nickel-plated or Polished Brass Flush Pipe,
Nickel-plated or Polished Brass Curved Trap Vent,
Nickel-plated or Polished Brass Brackets for Seat
and Cistern, Pull and Chain.

PLATE 96-G.

THE "INODORO," EMBOSSED, IVORY-TINTED PORCELAIN AND GOLD,

With Carved Open Seat and Back, No. 21½ Cabinet-finish
Copper-lined Cistern, (Design B), Nickel-plated or Polished
Brass Flush Pipe, Nickel-plated or Polished Brass Curved
Trap Vent, Nickel-plated or Polished Brass Brackets
for Seat and Cistern, Pull and Chain.

The "Inodoro" Embossed, Plates 95 and 96-G, will be furnished White instead of Ivory-tinted, if so ordered.

THE Seat and Cistern may be of Cherry, Ash, Black Walnut or Mahogany; when ordering it will be necessary to state which is desired. The Brass Flush Pipe (patent applied for) is an important feature and adds greatly to the appearance of the apparatus, while its cost does not exceed that of lead, taking into consideration the expense of bending, fitting and encasing the latter. With each Flush Pipe is furnished the Offset as shown and an Adjustable Bottom Bend and Coupling, which enables the plumber to make the connection quickly and easily.

The Polished or Nickel-plated Brass Vent for Trap is furnished curved as shown by Plates 95 and 96-G, or straight as shown by Plate 94-G. It is intended to be caulked into the Hub of the Iron Vent Pipe which comes flush with the wall, the Polished or Nickel-plated Brass Escutcheon making a finish.

The illustrations represent the "Inodoro" placed upon a Counter-sunk Marble Floor Slab, which is well adapted for the purpose and heightens the general neat and attractive appearance of the apparatus.

With the No. 21½ Cistern a momentary retention of Pull will insure a thorough and forcible flush of the Closet and Trap. The dimensions are 24 × 14 × 10 inches deep, and the capacity (8 gallons) sufficient for two or three successive flushes.

For sectional view and description of "Inodoro" see page 54.

THE "INODORO," EMBOSSED.

Plate 95-G.

Plate 96-G.

For description, see opposite page.

THE "INODORO" EMBOSSED.

PLATE 97 - G.

THE "INODORO," EMBOSSED, IVORY-TINTED OR WHITE PORCELAIN,

With Open Seat and Back, No. 4½ or 21½ Stained Copper-lined Cistern,
Polished or Nickel-plated Brass Flush Pipe, Japanned Brackets,
Nickel-plated Chain and Pull. Also furnished with
Iron or Plain Wood Cistern.

For description of No. 4½ and No. 21½ Cistern see page 62.

PLATE 98 - G.

THE "INODORO," EMBOSSED, IVORY-TINTED OR WHITE PORCELAIN,

With Stained Copper-lined No. 11 Afterwash Cistern, Automatic Open
Seat and Back with Bronzed or Brass plated Brackets, Japanned
Cistern Brackets, Polished or Nickel-plated Brass Flush
Pipe, and Chain. Also furnished with Iron or
Plain Wood Cistern.

PLATE 98-G is automatic in action ; when the seat is relieved about two and a half gallons of water descend and thoroughly flush the Closet. A novel feature of this apparatus is the combination of Bracket and Lever and Friction Roller on the end of the Lever : the Seat rests on the Roller and when depressed operates the Lever without loss of power and without friction.

The Brass Flush Pipe is an important feature and adds greatly to the appearance of the apparatus, while its cost does not exceed that of lead, taking into consideration the expense of bending, fitting and encasing the latter. With each Flush Pipe is furnished the Offset as shown, and an Adjustable Bottom Bend and Coupling which enables the plumber to make the connection quickly and easily.

Our Stained Cisterns are made of seasoned White-wood, stained to represent Cherry or Black Walnut, and unless examined closely it is difficult to discover that they are not the real wood. Being neat in appearance and costing but a trifle more than a plain wood cistern, they are adapted for use in Hotels, Government and Public Buildings, where water closets are frequently put up under such conditions that the Stained Cisterns will answer as well as Cabinet-finished.

THE "INODORO."

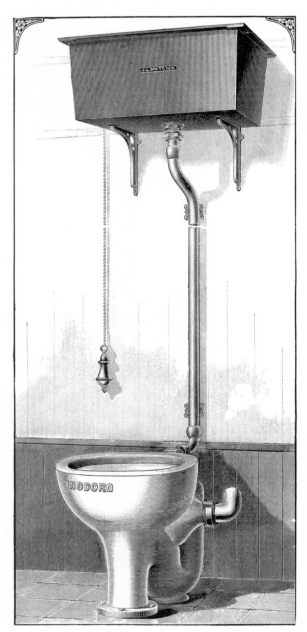

PLATE 99-G.

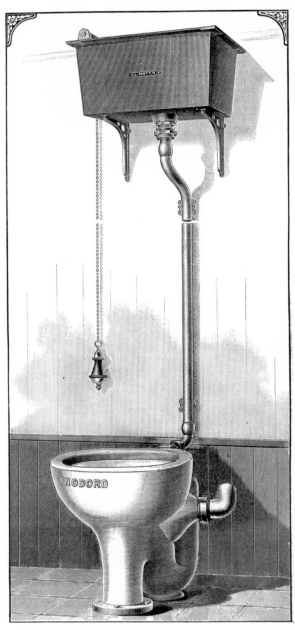

PLATE 100-G.

THE "INODORO," IVORY-TINTED OR WHITE PORCELAIN,

With No. 21½ Cistern, Brackets, Nickel-plated Chain and Ebony Pull.

With the No. 21½ Cistern a momentary retention of Pull will insure a thorough and forcible flush of the Closet and Trap. The dimensions are 24 × 14 × 10 inches deep, and the capacity (8 gallons).

THE "INODORO," IVORY-TINTED OR WHITE PORCELAIN,

With No. 4½ Syphon Cistern, Brackets, Nickel-plated Chain and Ebony Pull.

With the No. 4½ Cistern the Syphon is started by drawing down the Pull and releasing it at once, when the contents of the Cistern (about three gallons) descend rapidly and with force to the Closet. The dimensions are 18 × 9 × 10 inches deep.

The "Inodoro" will be furnished with Offset as shown by Plate 89-G, when it is to be put up with Trap below the floor.

For sectional view and description of "Inodoro" see page 54.

THE "INODORO."

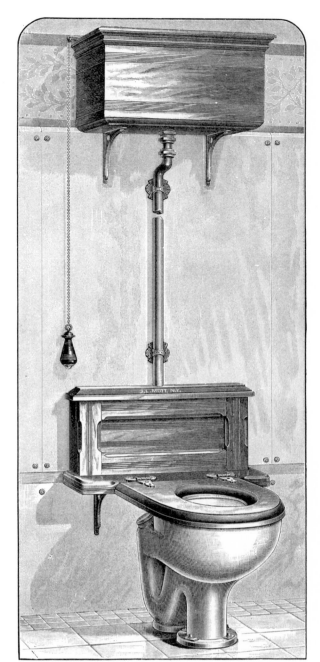

PLATE 101-G.

THE "INODORO," IVORY-TINTED OR WHITE PORCELAIN,

With Open Seat and Back, No. 4½ or 21½ Cabinet-finish Copper-
lined Cistern (Design A), Japanned Brackets, Nickel-
plated Chain and Pull, Nickel-plated or
Polished Brass Flush Pipe.

For description of No. 4½ and No. 21½ Cisterns see page 62.

The Seat and Cistern may be of cherry, black walnut, ash or mahogany; when ordering it will be necessary to state which is desired.

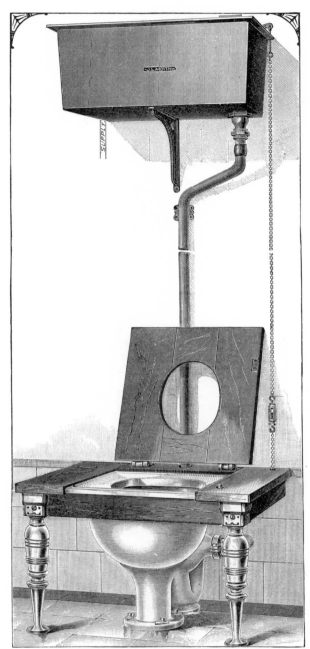

PLATE 102-G.

THE "INODORO," IVORY-TINTED OR WHITE PORCELAIN,

With No. 11 After-wash Waste-preventing Cistern, Porcelain Slop
Safe, Cherry, Black Walnut or Ash Seat, with Bronzed
Iron Legs, Bracket and Chain.

This Water Closet apparatus is automatic in action; when the
seat is relieved about 2½ gallons of water descend and thoroughly
flush the closet.

THE Brass Flush Pipe is an important feature, and adds greatly to the appearance of the apparatus, while its cost does not exceed that of
lead, taking into consideration the expense of bending, fitting and encasing the latter. With each Flush Pipe is furnished the Offset as
shown, and an Adjustable Bottom Bend and Coupling which enables the plumber to make the connection quickly and easily.

For sectional view and description of "Inodoro" see page 54.

THE "INODORO."

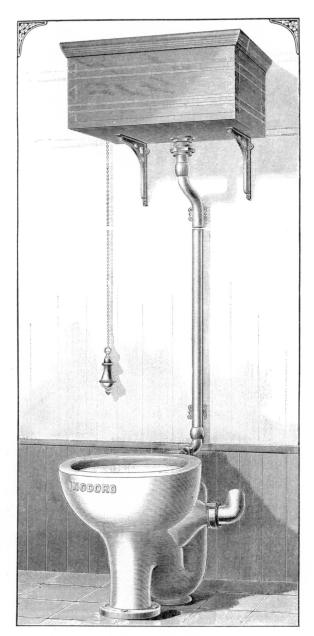

PLATE 103-G.

THE "INODORO," IVORY-TINTED OR WHITE PORCELAIN,

With No. 21½ Copper-lined Stained Wood Cistern, Brackets, Nickel-plated Chain, and Pull.

With the No. 21½ Cistern a momentary retention of Pull will insure a thorough and forcible flush of the Closet. The dimensions are 24 × 14 × 10 inches deep, and the capacity 8 gallons.

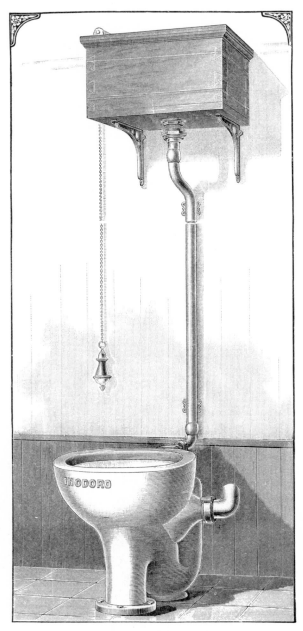

PLATE 104-G.

THE "INODORO," IVORY-TINTED OR WHITE PORCELAIN,

With No. 4½ Copper-lined Stained Wood Cistern, Brackets, Nickel-plated Chain, and Pull.

With the No. 4½ Cistern the Syphon is started by drawing down the Pull and releasing it at once, when the contents of the Cistern (about 3 gallons) descend rapidly and forcibly to the Closet. The dimensions are 18 × 9 × 10 inches deep.

OUR Stained Cisterns are made of seasoned White-wood, stained to represent Cherry or Black Walnut, and unless examined critically it is difficult to discover that they are not the real wood ; being neat in appearance and costing but a trifle more than a plain Wood Cistern, they are especially suitable for use in Hotels, Government and Public Buildings, etc., where the Water Closets are frequently put up under such conditions that the Stained Cisterns would answer as well as Cabinet-finish.

For sectional view and description of the "Inodoro" see page 54.

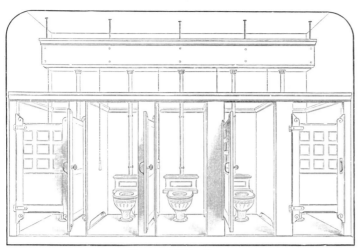

PLATE 105-G.

SECTIONS OF PLATE 107-G.

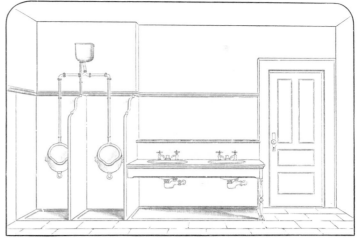

PLATE 106-G.

PLATE 107-G.

THE Interior as above represented is practically an illustration of a series of Lavatory and Water Closet rooms in one of the largest and best equipped office buildings in New York City. While the work is most elaborate and complete, yet the selection of the plumbing appliances proper was made with a special view as to their simplicity, non-liability to get out of order, high quality and fine appearance. The entire apartment is of Italian Marble, including Floor, Walls, Ceiling, Partitions and Casings for Water Closet Cisterns, the only Cabinet Work being the Open Seat for Water Closets and the Doors for Water Closet Compartments. The Water Closets are the "Inodoro," Embossed, Ivory-tinted Porcelain, Plate 93-G, with Copper-lined Wood Cistern, Polished Brass Curved Trap Vent caulked into Hub of Iron Vent Pipe, and Polished Brass Local or Bowl Vent connected with Hot Flue by a Copper Pipe. The Flush Pipe for Water Closets is of Polished Brass, as shown by Plate 108-G. The Flush Tank for Urinals is our Patent Automatic, made of Polished Cast Brass, but which of course we can furnish in Copper-lined Wood or Cast Iron. The Wash Basin is Oval, size 19 × 15, with the "Unique" Waste and Polished Cast Brass Trap. The Leg supporting Marble Slab is also of Polished Cast Brass.

We present this Interior as a suggestion to Plumbers and Architects and others who may be interested in the construction of large buildings.

NICKEL-PLATED AND POLISHED BRASS FLUSH PIPE FOR WATER CLOSETS.

PATENT APPLIED FOR.

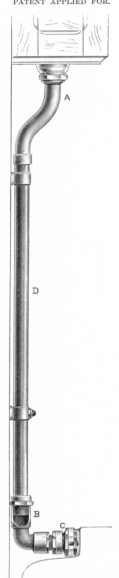

PLATE 108-G.

Nickel-plated or Polished Brass Flush Pipe.

With each Brass Flush Pipe is furnished the Offset A and the Adjustable Bottom Bend and Coupling B C, also, plain strap, and strap with rubber bumper. The Offset A is made of three different sizes to suit our various cisterns, viz :

For Nos. 4½ and 21½ Cisterns the Offset is 4 inches.
" Nos. 10   " 2   "   "   " 5¾ "
" Nos. 11   " 11½ "   "   " 9½ "

The Pipe D is screwed into Socket on bottom of Offset A. The connection between Pipe D and Lower Bend B is made by a slip joint having a play of two inches.

The Adjustable Coupling C may be regulated to suit the distance from wall to face of coupling on Closet.

The Pipe D is furnished six feet long, which gives a distance of about seven feet from bottom of cistern to top of Closet ; if the distance be less the plumber can saw off as much as may be necessary from bottom of pipe ; if the distance be greater than seven feet we can furnish the Pipe D correspondingly longer.

The superiority of Brass Flush Pipe for Water Closets will readily be conceded, and that it has not been more extensively used heretofore was due to its comparative greater cost, not so much of the material but of the labor in bending and fitting, which could only be done by an experienced plumber. By means of our Adjustable Bottom Bend and Coupling any plumber can make the connections quickly and easily, so that the cost of our Brass Flush Pipe will not exceed that of lead, taking into consideration the expense of bending, fitting and encasing the latter.

FLOOR CONNECTIONS FOR ALL-PORCELAIN WATER CLOSETS.

PLATE 109-G.

Brass Floor Flange for Lead Pipe Connection.

The Lead Pipe or Bend is soldered to the Brass Flange, the marble, tile or wood floor being countersunk to receive the latter.

PATENT FLOOR CONNECTIONS,

With Adjustable Screwed Brass Flange, Brass Bolts and Nuts.

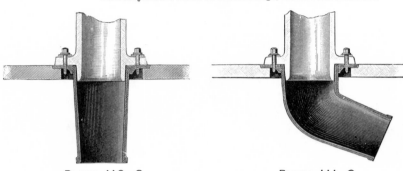

PLATE 110-G.   PLATE 111-G.
Straightway.   Sixth Bend.

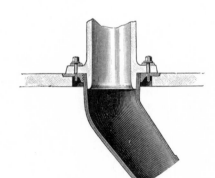   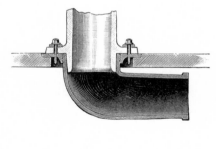

PLATE 112-G.   PLATE 113-G.
Eighth Bend.   Short Quarter Bend.

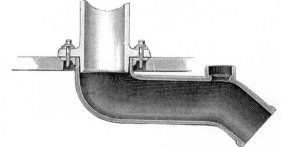

PLATE 114-G.

Long Quarter Bend to connect into Y Branch, with two-inch inlet for waste from bath, basin or urinal.

These connections are of cast iron with screwed brass flange, which enables the plumber to turn the fitting to any angle required. The bolts and nuts are of finished brass.

THE "PURITA."

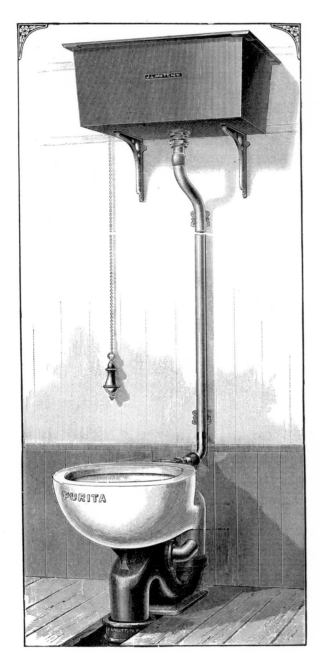

PLATE 115-G.

THE "PURITA,"

With No. 21½ Cistern, Brackets, Nickel-plated Chain, and Pull.

With the No. 21½ Cistern a momentary retention of Pull will insure a thorough and forcible flush of the Closet and Trap. The dimensions are 24 × 14 × 10 inches deep, and the capacity eight gallons.

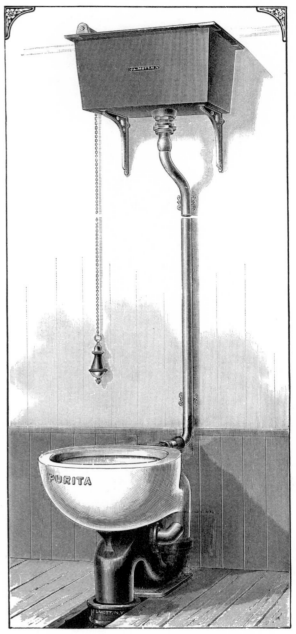

PLATE 116-G.

THE "PURITA,"

With No. 4½ Syphon Cistern, Brackets, Nickel-plated Chain, and Pull.

With the No. 4½ Cistern the Syphon is started by drawing down the Pull and releasing it at once, when the contents of the Cistern (about three gallons) descend rapidly and with force to the Closet. The dimensions are 18 × 9 × 10 inches deep.

THE "Purita" is shown with Trap to caulk into Hub of Soil Pipe, but can be furnished with Flange for Lead Pipe Connection as shown by Plate 91-G, if so ordered.

THE "PURITA."

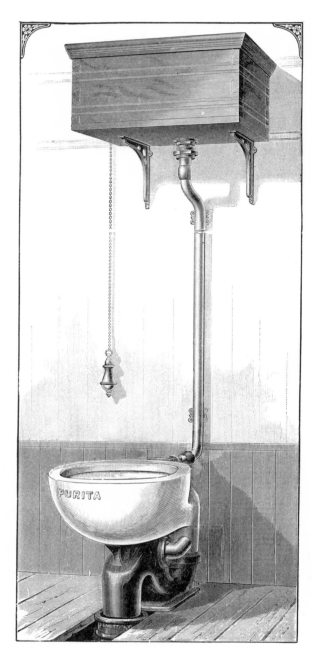

PLATE 117-G.

THE "PURITA,"

With No. 4½ or No. 21½ Copper-lined Stained Wood Cistern,
Brackets, Chain and Pull.

For description of No. 4½ and No. 21½ Cistern see page 67;
for remarks relative to our Stained Wood Cisterns see page 64.

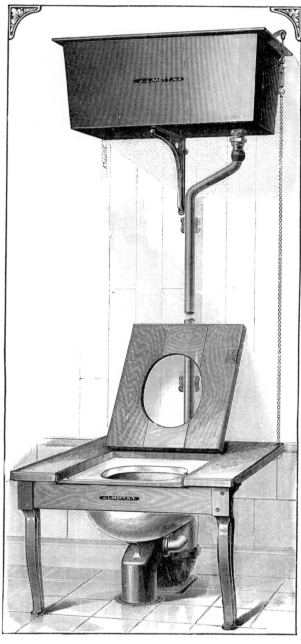

PLATE 118-G.

THE "PURITA,"

With No. 11 After-wash Waste-preventing Cistern, Enameled Cast
or Wrought Iron Slop Safe, Cherry, Black Walnut or Ash
Seat with Iron Legs, Bracket and Chain.

This Water Closet apparatus is automatic in action; when the
seat is relieved about 2½ gallons of water descend and thoroughly
flush the closet.

THE "Purita" is shown with Trap to caulk into Hub of Soil Pipe, but it is furnished with Trap for Lead Pipe Connection as shown by
Plate 91-G, if so ordered.

For sectional view and description of "Purita" see page 54.

The "Dolphin" Front-Outlet Wash-Out Ventilating Water Closet.

PATENTED.

IT is now a general practice in all fine plumbing work, both for private and public buildings, to have the various appliances set up open, dispensing as far as possible with cabinet work, so that they may be readily accessible on all sides for cleaning.

The "Dolphin," put up as illustrated on the following pages, represents not only the perfection of cleanliness but is an ornament to any bath room. It is efficient in operation and without any moving or mechanical parts liable to get out of order. The "Dolphin" is made in England and guaranteed not to craze or discolor. The Flushing Rim is designed to give the greatest wash-out force with the least amount of water, and to insure that all parts of the bowl are flushed. The sectional cuts show the "Dolphin" with and without Local or Bowl Vent: this Vent is rarely used unless where it can be readily connected with a Hot Flue.

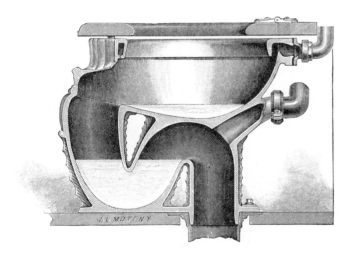

PLATE 119-G.

Section of the "Dolphin."

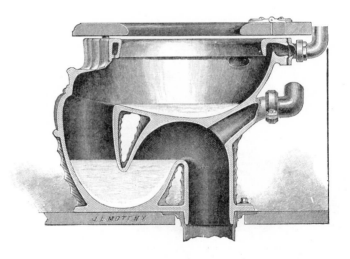

PLATE 120-G.

Section of the "Dolphin" with 2 inch Local or Bowl Vent.

The "Dolphin" is furnished with Patent Brass Inlet and Vent Coupling, and Brass Lag Bolts and Washers.

THE "DOLPHIN."

DESIGN PATENTED.

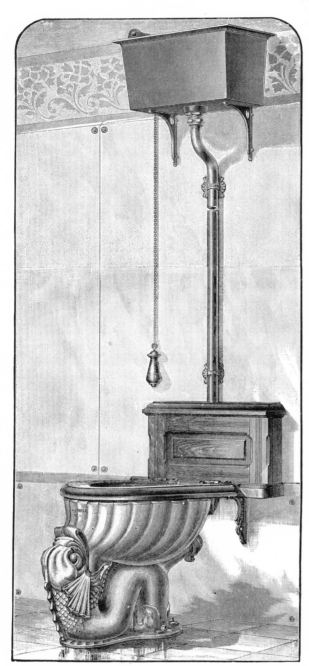

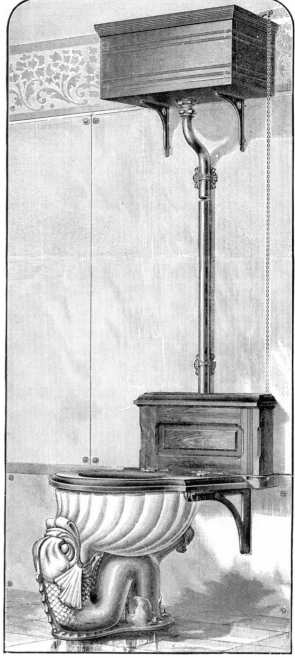

PLATE 121-G.

PLATE 122-G.

THE "DOLPHIN," IVORY-TINTED AND WHITE PORCELAIN,
With Open Seat and Back, No. 4½ Cistern, Nickel-plated or Polished
Brass Flush Pipe, Brackets, Chain and Pull.

With the No. 4½ Cistern the Syphon is started by drawing down
the Pull and releasing it at once, when the contents of Cistern (about
three gallons) descend rapidly and with force to the closet. Dimensions, 18 × 9 × 10 inches deep.

THE "DOLPHIN," IVORY-TINTED AND WHITE PORCELAIN,
With Automatic Open Seat and Back, Bronzed or Brass-plated Iron
Seat Brackets, No. 11 Copper-lined Stained Wood After-wash
Cistern, Nickel-plated or Polished Brass Flush
Pipe, Cistern Brackets, and Chain.

This Water Closet apparatus is automatic in action ; when the seat
is relieved about 2½ gallons of water descend and flush the closet.
A novel feature is the combination of Bracket, Lever and Roller ;
the Seat rests on the Roller, and when depressed operates the lever
without loss of power and without friction.

THE Seat may be of Cherry, Ash, Black Walnut or Mahogany ; when ordering it will be necessary to state which is desired. The Brass Flush Pipe
(patent applied for) is an important feature and adds greatly to the appearance of the apparatus, while its cost does not exceed that of lead pipe, taking
into consideration the expense of bending, fitting and encasing the latter. With each Brass Flush Pipe is furnished the Offset as shown and an
Adjustable Bottom Bend and Coupling, which enables the plumber to make the connection quickly and easily.
Our Stained Cisterns are made of seasoned White-wood, stained to represent Cherry or Black Walnut, and unless examined closely it is difficult to
discover that they are not the real wood. Being neat in appearance and costing but a trifle more than a plain wood cistern, they are adapted for use in
Hotels, Government and Public Buildings, where water closets are frequently put up under such conditions that the Stained Cisterns will answer as well as
Cabinet-finished.
For sectional view and description of the "Dolphin" see page 69.

THE "DOLPHIN."

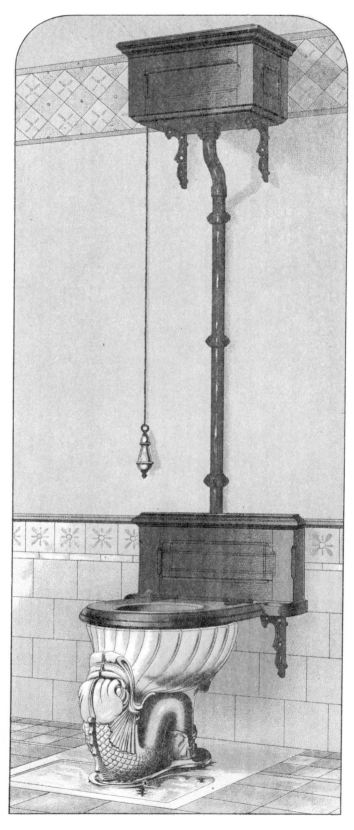

Plate 123-G.   Plate 124-G.

For description, see opposite page.

THE "DOLPHIN."

DESIGN PATENTED.

PLATE 123-G.

THE "DOLPHIN," IVORY-TINTED PORCELAIN,

With Open Seat and Back, No. 4½ Cabinet-finish Copper-lined Cistern (Design B), Nickel-plated or Polished Brass Flush Pipe, Nickel-plated or Polished Brass Brackets for Seat and Cistern, Pull and Chain.

This Closet is also furnished White, instead of Ivory-tinted.

PLATE 124-G.

THE "DOLPHIN," IVORY-TINTED PORCELAIN AND TURQUOISE,

With Open Seat and Back, No. 4½ Cabinet-finish Copper-lined Cistern (Design B), Nickel-plated or Polished Brass Flush Pipe, Nickel-plated or Polished Brass Brackets for Seat and Cistern, Pull and Chain.

The Seat and Cistern may be of Cherry, Ash, Black Walnut or Mahogany ; when ordering, it will be necessary to state which is desired.

THE Brass Flush Pipe (patent applied for,) is an important feature, and adds greatly to the appearance of the apparatus, while its cost does not exceed that of lead, taking into consideration the expense of bending, fitting and encasing the latter. With each Brass Flush Pipe is furnished the Offset as shown and an Adjustable Bottom Bend and Coupling which enables the plumber to make the connection quickly and easily. For illustration and description see page 66.

With the No. 4½ Cistern the Syphon is started by drawing down the Pull and releasing it at once, when the contents (about 3 gallons) descend and flush the Closet.

The illustrations represent the "Dolphin" placed upon a Counter-sunk Marble Floor Slab, which is well adapted for the purpose and heightens the general neat and attractive appearance of the apparatus.

Floor Connections for "Dolphin" are illustrated on page 66.

For sectional view and description of the "Dolphin" see page 69.

THE "DOLPHIN."

DESIGN PATENTED.

PLATE 125-G.	PLATE 126-G.
THE "DOLPHIN," IVORY-TINTED PORCELAIN, TURQUOISE AND GOLD,	THE "DOLPHIN," IVORY-TINTED PORCELAIN AND GOLD,
With Carved Open Seat and Back, No. 21½ Cabinet-finish Copper-lined Cistern (Design B), Nickel–plated or Polished Brass Flush Pipe, Nickel-plated or Polished Brass Brackets for Seat and Cistern, Pull and Chain.	With Carved Open Seat and Back, No. 21½ Cabinet-finish Copper-lined Cistern, Nickel-plated or Polished Brass Flush Pipe, Nickel-plated or Polished Brass Brackets for Seat and Cistern, Pull and Chain.

The Seat and Cistern may be of Cherry, Ash, Black Walnut or Mahogany ; when ordering, it will be necessary to state which is desired.

THE Brass Flush Pipe is an important feature, and adds greatly to the appearance of the apparatus, while its cost does not exceed that of lead, taking into consideration the expense of bending, fitting and encasing the latter. With each Flush Pipe is furnished the Offset as shown and an Adjustable Bottom Bend and Coupling which enables the plumber to make the connection quickly and easily. For illustration and description see page 66.

The illustrations represent the "Dolphin" placed upon a Counter-sunk Marble Floor Slab, which is well adapted for the purpose and heightens the general neat and attractive appearance of the apparatus.

With the No. 21½ Cistern a momentary retention of Pull will insure a thorough and forcible flush of the Closet and Trap. The capacity is 8 gallons. Dimensions, 24 × 14 × 10 inches deep.

Floor Connections for "Dolphin" are illustrated on page 66.

For sectional view and description of the "Dolphin" see page 69.

THE "DOLPHIN."

Plate 125-G.

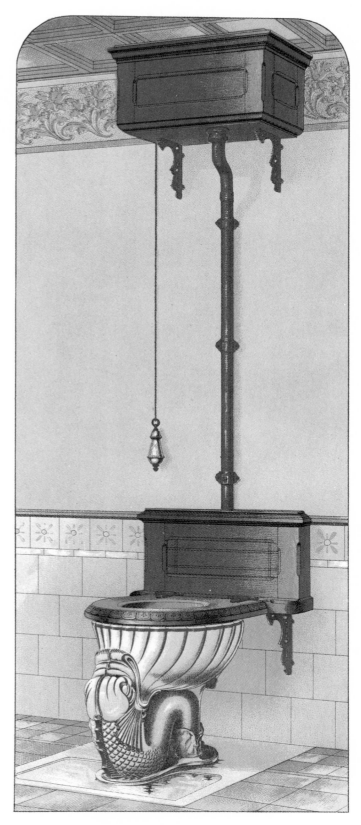

Plate 126-G.

Reproduced in color on Plate H following page 26.

For description, see opposite page.

THE "UNDINE" FRONT-OUTLET WASH-OUT VENTILATING WATER CLOSET.

PATENTED.

THE "Undine" is a strictly first-class Front-outlet Wash-out Water Closet similar in principle to the "Dolphin." It is efficient in operation and without any moving or mechanical parts liable to get out of order. The "Undine" is of the best English ware and warranted not to craze or discolor. The Flushing Rim is designed to give the greatest wash-out force with the least amount of water and to insure that all parts of the Bowl are flushed.

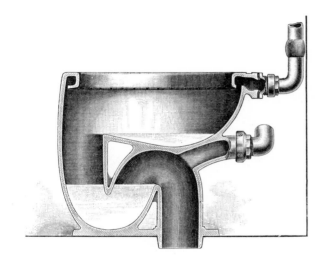

PLATE 127-G.

Section of the "Undine."

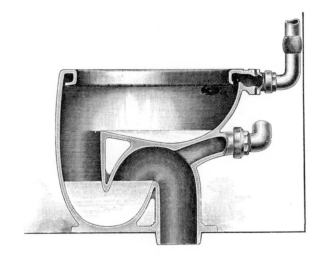

PLATE 128-G.

Section of the "Undine" with Local or Bowl Vent.

The "Undine" is furnished with Patent Brass Inlet and Vent Coupling, and Brass Lag Bolts and Washers.

THE "UNDINE," ALL-PORCELAIN.

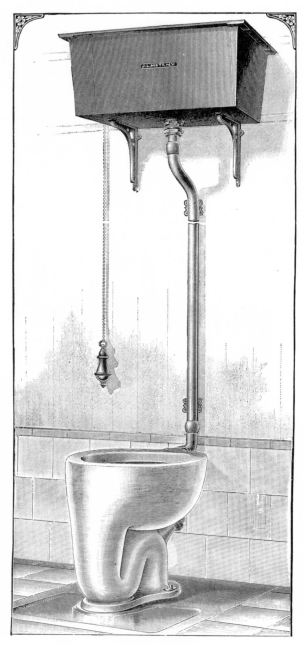

PLATE 129-G.

THE "UNDINE," IVORY-TINTED OR WHITE PORCELAIN,

With No. 21½ Cistern, Brackets, Pull and Chain.

With the No. 21½ Cistern a momentary retention of Pull will insure a thorough and forcible flush of the Closet and Trap. The capacity is 8 gallons and the dimensions, 24 × 14 × 10 inches deep.

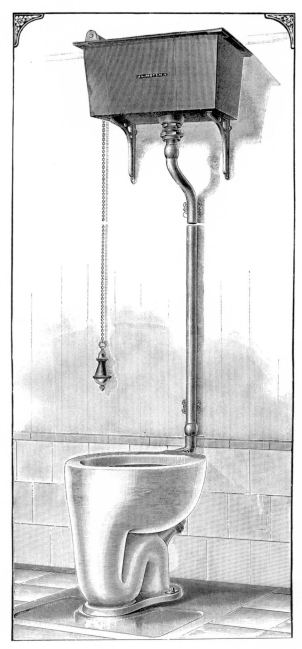

PLATE 130-G.

THE "UNDINE," IVORY-TINTED OR WHITE PORCELAIN,

With No. 4½ Cistern, Brackets, Chain and Pull.

With the No. 4½ Cistern the Syphon is started by drawing down the Pull and releasing it at once, when the contents of the Cistern (about 3 gallons) descend rapidly and forcibly to the Closet.

The Cisterns may be Painted, Galvanized or Porcelain-lined Iron, or Wood Copper-lined.

Floor Connections for "Undine" are illustrated on page 66.

For sectional view and description of "Undine" see page 77.

The "Undine" All-Porcelain.

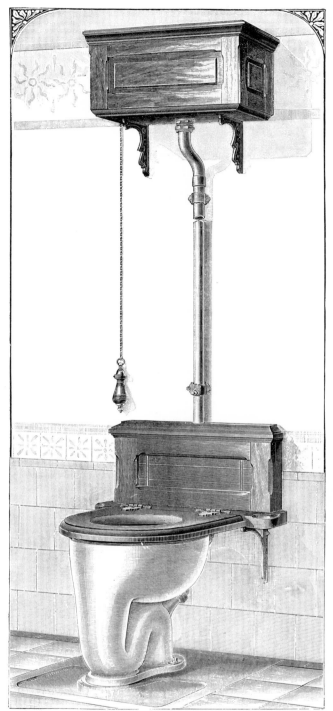

PLATE 131-G.

The "Undine" Ivory-tinted or White Porcelain,

With No. 4½ or No. 21½ Cabinet-finish Copper-lined Cistern, (Design B,)
Open Seat and Back, Nickel-plated or Polished Brass Flush
Pipe, Nickel-plated or Polished Brass Brackets
for Seat and Cistern, Pull and Chain.
Seat and Cistern may be of Cherry, Black Walnut, Ash or Mahogany.

PLATE 132-G.

The "Undine" Ivory-tinted or White Porcelain,

With No. 4½ or No. 21½ Stained Wood Copper lined Cistern, Hardwood
Open Seat and Back, Nickel-plated or Polished Brass
Flush Pipe, Japanned Seat and Cistern
Brackets, Pull and Chain.
Seat may be of Cherry or Black Walnut and Cistern stained to match.

THE Brass Flush Pipe is an important feature and adds greatly to the appearance of the apparatus, while its cost does not exceed that of lead pipe, taking into consideration the expense of bending, fitting and encasing the latter. With each Flush Pipe is furnished the Offset as shown, and an Adjustable Bottom Bend and Coupling, which enables the plumber to make the connection quickly and easily. For illustration and description, see page 66.

Our Stained Cisterns are made of seasoned White-wood, stained to represent Cherry or Black Walnut, and unless examined closely it is difficult to discover that they are not the real wood. Being neat in appearance and costing but a trifle more than a plain wood cistern, they are adapted for use in Hotels, Government and Public Buildings, where water closets are frequently put up under such conditions that the Stained Cisterns will answer as well as Cabinet finished.

For description of No. 4½ and No. 21½ Cistern see page 78.

Floor Connections for "Undine" are illustrated on page 66. For sectional view and description of the "Undine" see page 77.

THE "UNDINE."

PLATE 133-G.

THE "UNDINE," IVORY-TINTED OR WHITE PORCELAIN,

With No. 11 After-wash Stained Wood Copper-lined Cistern, Open Seat and Back with Bronzed or Brass Plated Iron Brackets, Polished or Nickel plated Brass Flush Pipe, Japanned Cistern Brackets, and Chain ; also furnished with Iron or Plain Wood Cistern.

This Water Closet apparatus is automatic in action ; when the seat is relieved about 2½ gallons of water descend and thoroughly flush the Closet. A novel feature is the combination of Bracket, Lever and Roller. The Seat rests on the Roller and when depressed operates the Lever without loss of power and without friction.

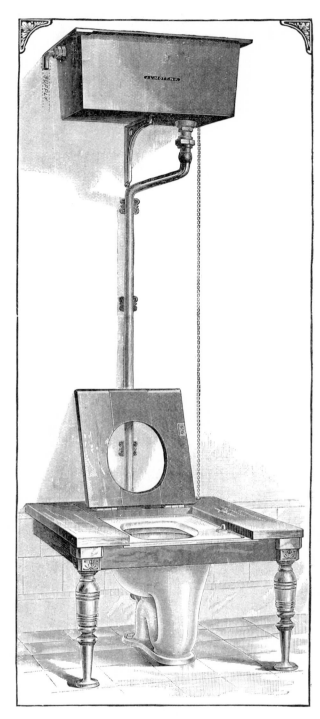

PLATE 134-G.

THE "UNDINE," IVORY-TINTED OR WHITE PORCELAIN,

With No 11 After-wash Cistern, Black Walnut, Cherry or Ash Seat with Bronzed Iron Legs, Enameled Cast or Wrought Iron Slop Safe, Japanned Cistern Brackets, and Chain ; also furnished with Plain or Stained Wood Copper-lined Cistern.

This Water Closet apparatus is automatic in action ; when the seat is relieved about 2½ gallons of water descend and thoroughly flush the Closet.

Floor Connections for "Undine" are illustrated on page 66.

For description of Brass Flush Pipe see page 66; for description of Stained Cisterns see page 79; for sectional view and description of the "Undine" see page 77.

The "Triplex" Side-Outlet Wash-Out Ventilating Water Closet.

B Y those who prefer a Side-outlet the "Triplex" will be found ahead of any Wash-out Closet in the market. In the first place it is of the very best imported ware; it is washed by our Patent "Triplex" Fan, which does the work most effectually, washing all parts of the Closet with great force. Its simplicity also insures the working of all closets equally well. The Vent on Trap is 2 inches, and the Local Vent (which need not be used unless desired, as we send a porcelain plug or cap with each closet,) is 2¼ inches. This Closet is intended for 1¼ inch supply pipe from cistern.

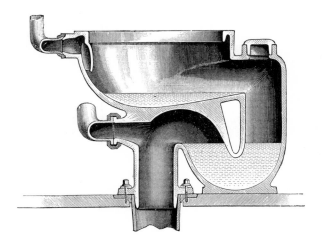

PLATE 135-G.

Section of "Triplex" All-Porcelain.

The "Triplex" All-Porcelain is furnished with Patent Brass Inlet and Vent Coupling, and Brass Lag Bolts and Washers.

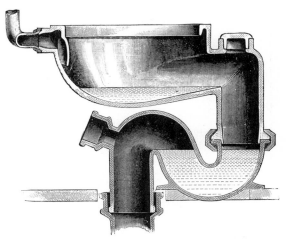

PLATE 136-G.

Section of "Triplex" Iron Trap.

The above is in all respects the same as the All-Porcelain, only the Trap is Cast Iron and is made to caulk into hub of soil pipe. This makes a very desirable Closet for hotels and public buildings. The Trap can be enameled if desired. It can also be furnished with flange for lead waste pipe connection.

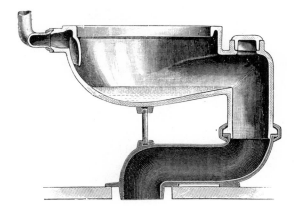

PLATE 137-G.

Section of "Triplex" Iron Offset.

This Closet is intended for use where it takes the place of an old closet having the Trap below the floor, which cannot conveniently be removed.

THE "TRIPLEX," ALL-PORCELAIN.

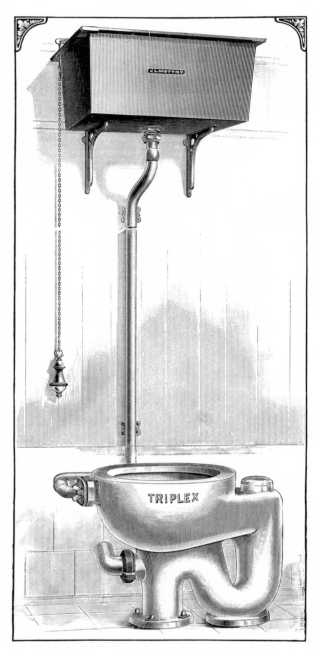

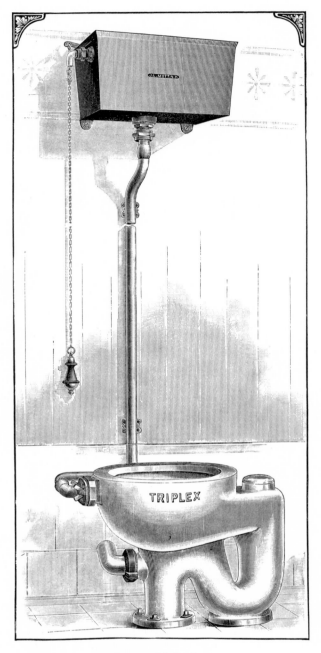

PLATE 138-G.

PLATE 139-G.

THE "TRIPLEX," ALL-PORCELAIN,

With No. 21½ Cistern, Nickel-plated Chain, Ebony Pull and Brackets.

With the No. 21½ Cistern, a momentary retention of Pull will insure a thorough and forcible flush of the Closet and Trap. The capacity is 8 gallons, and the dimensions, 24 × 14 × 10 inches deep.

THE "TRIPLEX," ALL-PORCELAIN,

With No. 15½ or 4½ Cistern, Nickel-plated Chain and Ebony Pull.

With the No 15½ Cistern a momentary retention of Pull will insure a thorough flush of the Closet and Trap. Dimensions, 18 × 9 × 10 inches deep.

With the No, 4½ Cistern the Syphon is started by drawing down the Pull and releasing it at once and when the contents (about 3 gallons) descend and flush the Closet. Dimensions, 18 × 9 × 10 inches deep.

The Cisterns may be Painted, Galvanized or Porcelain-lined Iron, or Wood Copper-lined.

Floor Connections for "Triplex" All-porcelain are illustrated on page 66.

For sectional view and description of the "Triplex" see page 81.

The "Triplex," All-Porcelain.

PATENTED.

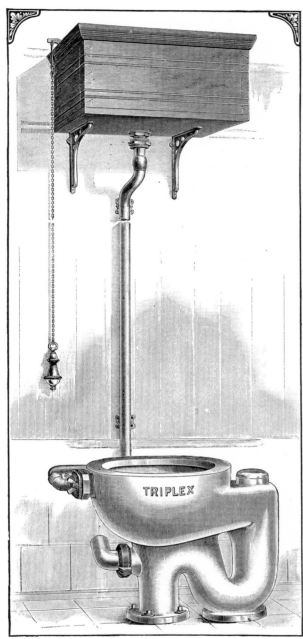

Plate 140-G.

The "Triplex," All-Porcelain,

With No. 21½, 4½ or 15½ Copper-lined Stained Wood Cistern, Brackets, Chain and Pull.

For description of Nos. 21½, 4½ and 15½ Cisterns see previous page.

Our Stained Cisterns are made of seasoned White-wood stained to represent Cherry or Black Walnut, and unless closely examined, it is difficult to distinguish them from the real wood. Being neat in appearance and costing but a little more than a plain wood Cistern, they are adapted for use in Public and Private Buildings, where water closets are frequently put up under such conditions that the Stained Cisterns would answer as well as Cabinet-finished.

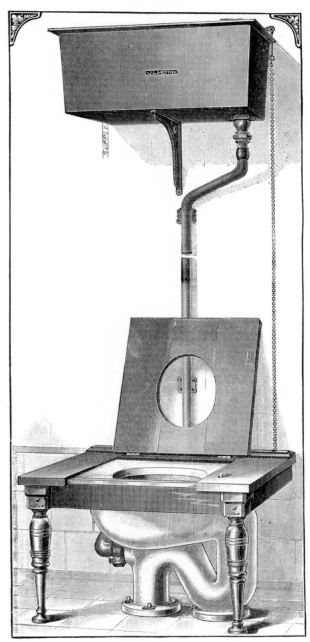

Plate 141-G.

The "Triplex," All-Porcelain,

With No. 11 After-wash Cistern, Porcelain Slop Safe, Black Walnut Seat with Bronzed Iron Legs, Bracket and Chain.

This Water Closet Apparatus is automatic in action. When the Seat is relieved about 2½ gallons of water descend and flush the closet

The Cistern may be Painted, Galvanized or Porcelain-lined Iron, or Wood Copper-lined.

The Seat may be of Cherry or Ash if so ordered.

For sectional view and description of the "Triplex" see page 81

THE "TRIPLEX," IRON TRAP.

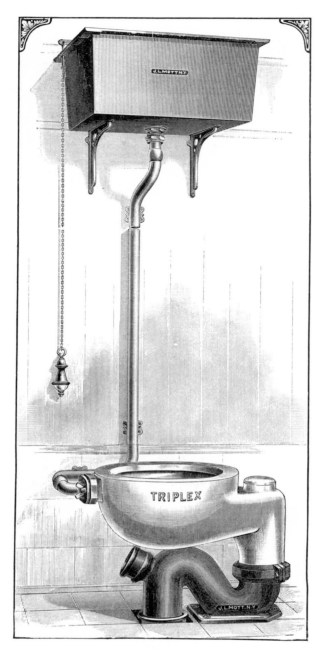

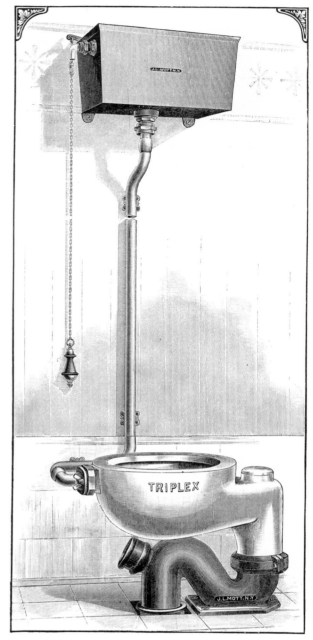

PLATE 142-G.

THE "TRIPLEX," IRON TRAP,

With No. 21½ Cistern, Brackets, Nickel-plated Chain and Pull.

With the No. 21½ Cistern a momentary retention of Pull insures a thorough and forcible flush of the Closet and Trap. The capacity is eight gallons and the dimensions 24 × 14 × 10 inches deep.

PLATE 143-G.

THE "TRIPLEX," IRON TRAP,

With No. 15½ or No. 4½ Cistern, Nickel-plated Chain and Pull.

With the No. 15½ Cistern a momentary retention of Pull will insure a thorough flush of the Closet. Dimensions, 18 × 9 × 10 inches deep.

With the No. 4½ Cistern the Syphon is started by drawing down the Pull and releasing it at once when the contents (about three gallons) descend and flush the Closet. Dimensions, 18 × 9 × 10 inches deep.

THE "Triplex" is shown with Trap having Spigot End to be caulked into hub of soil pipe; it can be furnished with Trap having Flange for lead waste pipe connection, if so ordered. It can also be furnished with Offset as shown by Plate 137–G, if so ordered.

For sectional view and description of the "Triplex," Iron Trap, see page 81

THE "TRIPLEX," IRON TRAP.

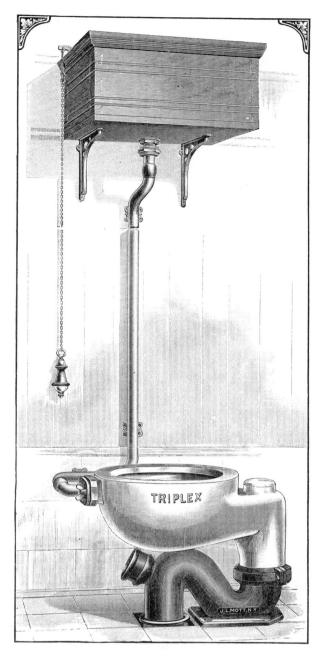

PLATE 144-G.

THE "TRIPLEX," IRON TRAP,

With No. 21½, 4½ or 15½ Copper-lined Stained Wood Cistern, Brackets, Chain and Pull.

For description of Nos. 21½, 4½ and 15½ Cisterns see previous page.

For description of Stained Wood Cisterns see page 83.

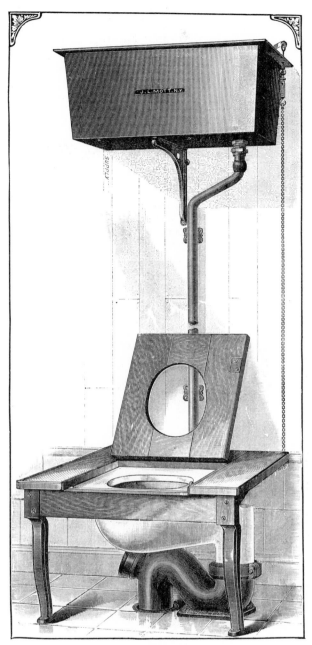

PLATE 145-G.

THE "TRIPLEX," IRON TRAP,

With No. 11 After-wash Cistern, Enameled Cast Iron Slop Safe, Black Walnut Seat with Iron Legs, Bracket and Chain.

This Water Closet Apparatus is automatic in action. When the Seat is relieved, about 2½ gallons of water descend and flush the Closet.

The Seat we can furnish of Cherry or Ash, if so ordered. Size, 24 × 24 inches.

THE illustrations show the Trap having Spigot End to be caulked into hub of soil pipe; it can be furnished with Trap having Flange for lead waste pipe connection if so ordered.

For sectional view and description of the "Triplex," Iron Trap, see page 81.

The "Triplex," Porcelain-Lined Iron Side-Outlet Wash-Out Water Closet.

PATENTED

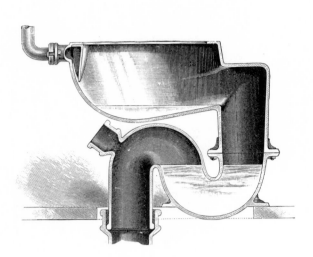

PLATE 146-G

Sectional view of the "Triplex," Porcelain lined Iron.

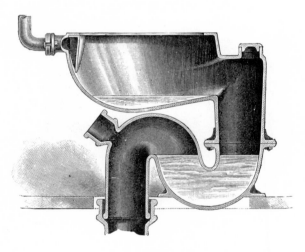

PLATE 147-G.

Sectional view showing Local Vent.

The "Triplex," Porcelain-lined Iron, is designed for use in Asylums and similar institutions, where a Porcelain "Triplex" or other Wash-Out Closet might be exposed to danger of breaking. As shown by Plate 146–G, there is always water in bowl; the "Triplex," Porcelain-lined Iron, may therefore be considered quite a step in advance of the Enameled Iron Hopper, while its cost is but little more.

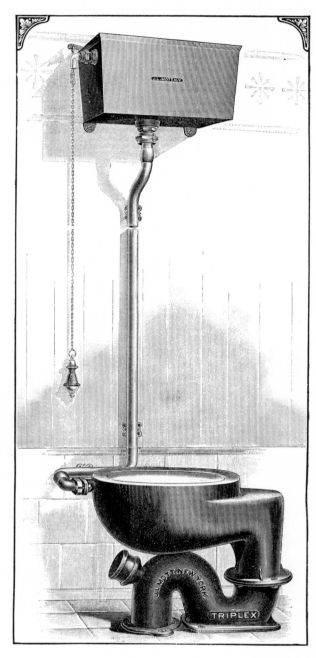

PLATE 148-G.

The "Triplex," Porcelain-Lined Iron,

With No 15½ or No. 4½ Cistern, Chain and Pull

The illustration shows the "Triplex" with Trap having flange for lead waste-pipe connection; it can be furnished with Trap having spigot end to be caulked into hub of soil pipe, as shown by Plates 146–G and 147–G. We also furnish the "Triplex" with Offset instead of Trap, to order.

For description of No. 15½ and No. 4½ Cisterns see page 84.

THE "TRIPLEX," PORCELAIN-LINED IRON.

PATENTED.

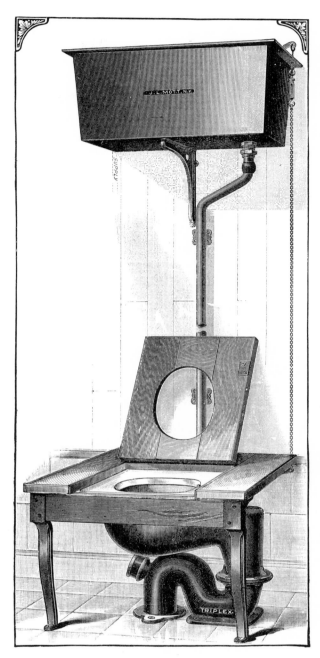

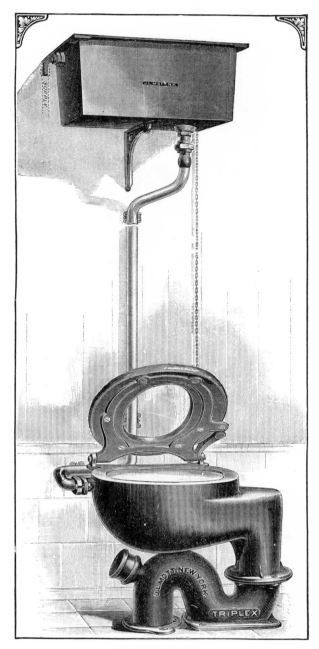

PLATE 149-G.

THE "TRIPLEX," PORCELAIN-LINED IRON,

With No. 11 After-wash Cistern, Enameled Iron Slop Safe, Black
Walnut, Cherry or Ash Seat with Painted Iron
Legs, Bracket and Chain.

This Water Closet Apparatus is automatic in action. When Seat
is relieved, about 2½ gallons of water descend and thoroughly flush
the Closet.

PLATE 150-G.

THE "TRIPLEX," PORCELAIN-LINED IRON,

With Self-raising Seat, No. 11 After-wash Cistern,
Bracket, Chain and Pulley.

The above is a desirable Water Closet Apparatus for Factory
use. The Seat being Self raising, it cannot be soiled or wetted
by the workmen using the Closet as a Urinal, nor can it be used
without operating the Cistern.

THE illustrations show the "Triplex" with Trap having Flange for lead waste pipe connection; it can be furnished with Trap having Spigot
to be caulked into hub of soil pipe, as shown by Plate 146-G, if so ordered.

The "Hygeia," Side-Outlet Flushing-Rim Water Closet.

PATENTED.

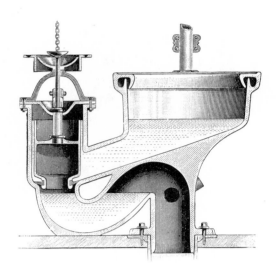

PLATE 151-G.

Sectional view of the "Hygeia," All-Porcelain.

·The Plunger is of Galvanized Iron; the Inlet and Vent Couplings are of Brass.

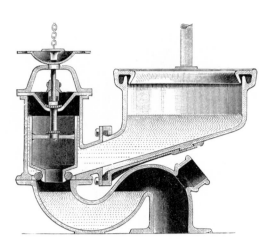

PLATE 152-G.

Sectional view of the "Hygeia," Porcelain Bowl.

The Plunger is of Galvanized Cast Iron, the Plunger Section Porcelain-lined; the Trap is also furnished Porcelain-lined to order. The Inlet Coupling is of Brass.

FOR perfect cleanliness and simplicity of construction we invite comparison of the "Hygeia" with any Cistern Plunger Closet ever made on the Side-Outlet principle, which is preferred by many for fine work, as it shows no outlet and retains a larger body of water in the Bowl than any other form of Water Closet. As will be apparent by reference to sectional view, it combines with the utmost simplicity all the best points of a strictly first-class Water Closet—the Flushing Rim, supplied from Cistern by inch and a quarter pipe, insuring a quick and thorough wash of all parts of the Closet, and the space (about one-eighth of an inch) around the Plunger, for overflow, being washed out with great force every time the Closet is operated. The operation of Plunger and Lever, though simple, is very ingenious, the cup-shaped or concave cover giving full stroke to the Lever, and the Pull Rod being attached to the middle of the Plunger allows the top of same to be raised to the top of the section. The workmanship of this Closet is of the best possible kind, the Porcelain being specially made for us in Staffordshire, England, by the very best makers; in short, nothing has been spared to make this Closet a strictly first-class one in every respect.

PLATE 153-G.

The "Hygeia," All-Porcelain,

With Local or Bowl Vent to be connected with Hot Flue.

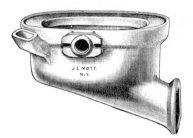

PLATE 154-G.

Porcelain Bowl for "Hygeia,"

With Local Vent to be connected with Hot Flue.

The Closet with Local Vent is rarely used, unless it can be connected readily with a Hot Flue.

THE "HYGEIA," ALL-PORCELAIN.

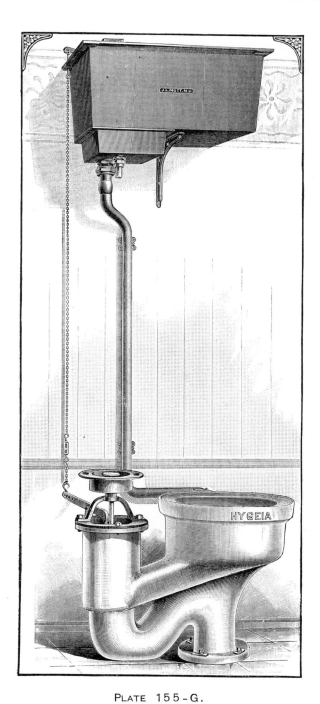

PLATE 155-G.

THE "HYGEIA," ALL-PORCELAIN, NO. 1 (TRAP),

With No. 2 Cistern, Bracket and Chain

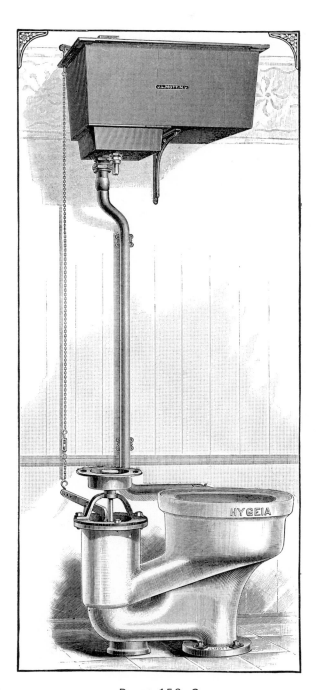

PLATE 156-G.

THE "HYGEIA," ALL-PORCELAIN, NO. 2 (OFFSET),

With No 2 Cistern, Bracket and Chain.

THE No. 2 Cistern is $24 \times 14 \times 10$ inches deep and the capacity is eight gallons, sufficient for two to three successive flushes. It may be Painted, Galvanized or Porcelain-lined Iron, or Wood Copper-lined.

Floor Connections as illustrated on page 66 may be used with the "Hygeia," All-Porcelain.

For sectional view and description of the "Hygeia," All-Porcelain, see page 88.

THE "HYGEIA," WITH PORCELAIN BOWL.

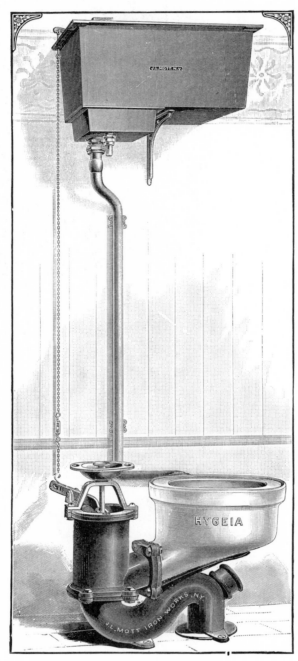

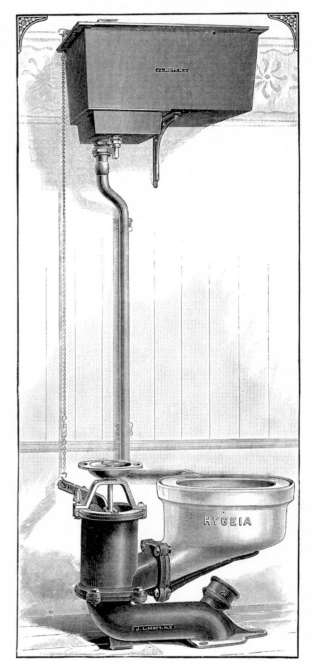

PLATE 157-G.

THE "HYGEIA," PORCELAIN BOWL, No. 1 (TRAP),

With No. 2 Cistern, Bracket and Chain.

PLATE 158-G.

THE "HYGEIA," PORCELAIN BOWL, No. 2 (OFFSET),

With No 2 Cistern, Bracket and Chain.

THE No. 2 Cistern is 24 x 14 x 10 inches deep and the capacity is eight gallons, sufficient for two to three successive flushes.   It may be Painted, Galvanized or Porcelain-lined Iron, or Wood Copper-lined.

For sectional view and description of the "Hygeia," Porcelain Bowl, see page 88.

THE "HYGEIA," WITH PORCELAIN BOWL.

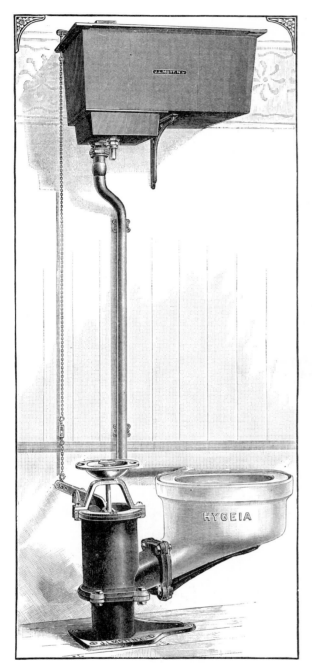

PLATE 159-G.

THE "HYGEIA," PORCELAIN BOWL, No. 3 (STRAIGHTWAY),

With No. 2 Cistern, Bracket and Chain.

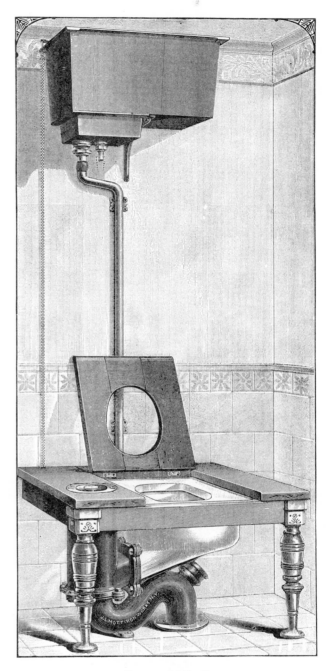

PLATE 160-G.

THE "HYGEIA," PORCELAIN BOWL, No. 1 (TRAP),

With No 2 Cistern, Bracket, Chain, Black Walnut, Cherry or Ash
Seat with Bronzed Iron Legs, and Slop Safe.

The dimensions of the No. 2 Cistern are $24 \times 14 \times 10$ inches deep and the capacity eight gallons, sufficient for two to three
successive flushes.

For sectional view and description of the "Hygeia," Porcelain Bowl, see page 88.

The "Simplex," Side-Outlet Cistern Water Closet.

PATENTED.

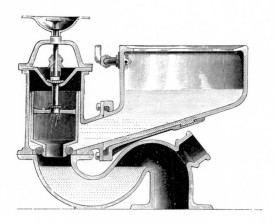

PLATE 161-G.

Sectional view of the "Simplex."

WE take pleasure in calling the attention of our customers and the trade generally to our Cistern Closet, the "Simplex." It is without doubt, taking the price into consideration, one of the most desirable Cistern Closets that has yet been produced. The workmanship is in all respects first-class; the principle and operation are of the simplest kind, as can be seen by reference to sectional cut, while the Porcelain Bowl is the same as used in our famous Valve Closet, the "Demarest." The Cistern has a 4 inch Valve and large Service Box, with a ¾ inch Coupling, yet, in connection with the Fan or Water Spreader used on this Closet it gives a very thorough and satisfactory flush.

The "Simplex" cannot fail to commend itself to all desiring a really first-class article at an extremely moderate price.

PLATE 162-G.

PORCELAIN BOWL FOR "SIMPLEX," WITH SIDE VENT.

PLATE 163-G.

PORCELAIN BOWL FOR "SIMPLEX," WITH BACK VENT.

The Porcelain Bowl with Local or Bowl Vent is rarely used, unless when it can be connected with a Hot Flue.

THE "SIMPLEX," SIDE-OUTLET CISTERN WATER CLOSET.

PATENTED.

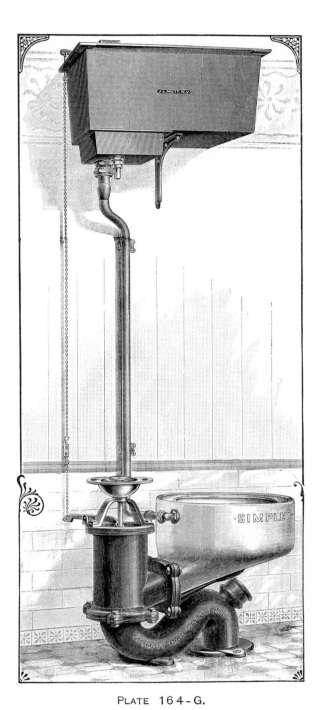

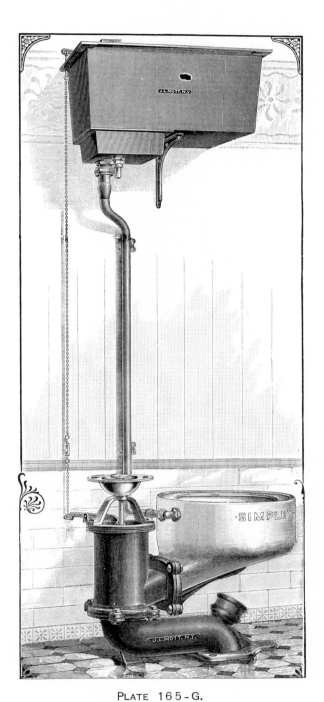

PLATE 164-G.

THE "SIMPLEX," No. 1–A (TRAP),

With Cistern, Bracket and Chain.

PLATE 165-G.

THE "SIMPLEX," No. 2–A (OFFSET),

With Cistern, Bracket and Chain.

The Cistern is $24 \times 14 \times 10$ inches deep and the capacity eight gallons.

For sectional view and description of the "Simplex" see page 92.

Mott's All-Porcelain or Enameled Cast or Wrought Iron Slop Safes may be used with the "Simplex."

THE "SIMPLEX," SIDE-OUTLET CISTERN WATER CLOSET.

PATENTED.

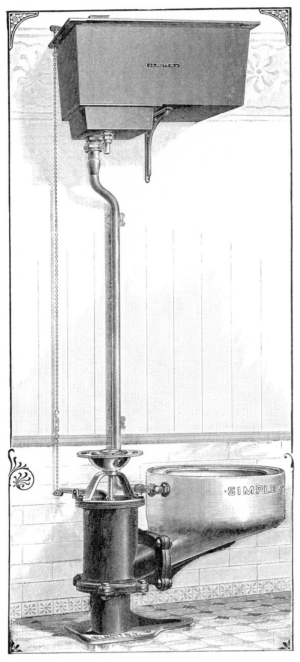

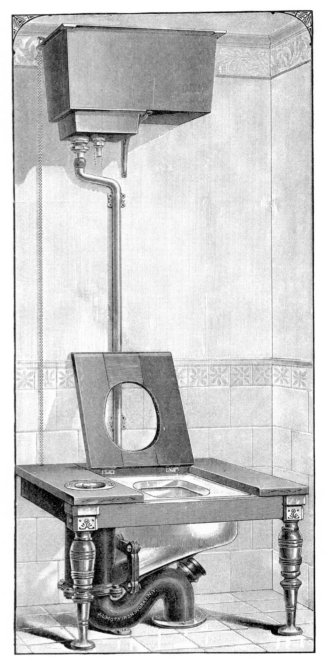

PLATE 166-G.

THE "SIMPLEX," NO. 3-A (STRAIGHTWAY),

With Cistern, Bracket and Chain.

PLATE 167-G.

THE "SIMPLEX," NO. 1-A (TRAP)

With Cistern, Bracket, Chain, Cherry, Black Walnut or Ash Seat
with Bronzed Iron Legs, and Slop Safe.

THE "Simplex" Cistern is 24 × 14 × 10 inches deep, and the capacity eight gallons. The size of Flush Pipe used with this Closet is only ¾ inch, yet gives a very thorough and satisfactory flush.

For description and sectional view of the "Simplex" see page 92.

MOTT'S CABINET-FINISH COPPER-LINED CISTERNS FOR WATER CLOSETS.

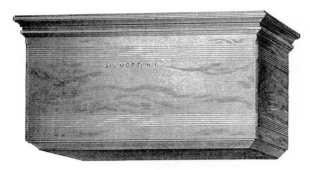

PLATE 168-G.

CABINET-FINISH COPPER-LINED CISTERN, DESIGN A.

Cherry, Black Walnut or Ash.

PLATE 169-G.

CABINET-FINISH COPPER-LINED CISTERN, DESIGN B.

Black Walnut, Cherry, Ash or Mahogany.

PLATE 170-G.

CABINET-FINISH COPPER-LINED CISTERN, DESIGN C.

Mahogany; Carved Mouldings.

PLATE 171-G.

CABINET-FINISH COPPER-LINED CISTERN   DESIGN D.

Mahogany; Carved Panels and Mouldings.

The Cisterns we furnish in the above designs are:

No. $4\frac{1}{2}$, for Wash-Out Water Closets; outside dimensions, $21 \times 11 \times 11$ inches.
" $21\frac{1}{2}$, "   "   "   "   " $26 \times 14 \times 13$ "
" 10,   "   "   "   "   " $26 \times 14 \times 15$ "
" 2,   for "Hygeia" and "Simplex" Closets; outside dimensions, $26 \times 14 \times 15$ inches.

OUR Cabinet-finish, Copper-lined Cisterns, being neat and compact in appearance, remove in a great measure the objection entertained by many to Water Closets put up with an iron or plain wood Cistern having a large and more or less cumbersome outside casing, more especially where the apartment is of limited dimensions. On the score of economy they also commend themselves, as their cost is less than that of a plain Cistern, taking into consideration the expense of casing same, in fact, by using our Cabinet-finish Cistern in conjunction with the Open Seats illustrated on previous pages, Water Closets can be put up without requiring the services of a carpenter.

These Cisterns are made in the best manner of thoroughly seasoned wood, well put together, and carved and finished by hand.

NOTE.—Our Cisterns are so constructed that they are comparatively noiseless in operation.

THE "DEMAREST," SIDE-OUTLET VALVE WATER CLOSET.

PATENTED.

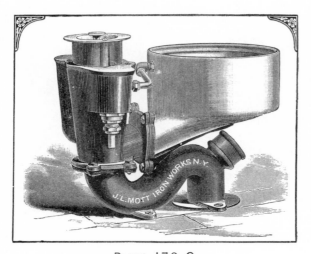

PLATE 172-G.

Nos. 1, 1–A and 1–B Closets (Trap),

With No. 4 Valve.

No. 1.   Painted Valve Section and Porcelain-lined Iron Bowl.
No. 1–A. Painted Valve Section and Porcelain Bowl.
No. 1–B. Porcelain-lined Valve Section and Porcelain Bowl.

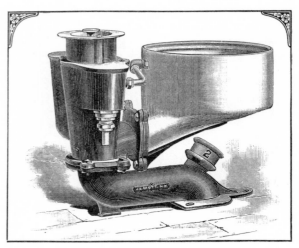

PLATE 173-G.

Nos. 2, 2–A and 2–B Closets (Offset),

With No. 4 Valve.

No. 2.   Painted Valve Section and Porcelain-lined Iron Bowl.
No. 2–A. Painted Valve Section and Porcelain Bowl.
No. 2–B. Porcelain-lined Valve Section and Porcelain Bowl.

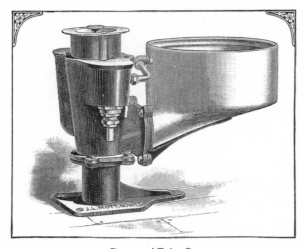

PLATE 174-G.

Nos. 3, 3–A and 3–B Closets (Straightway),

With No. 4 Valve.

No. 3.   Painted Valve Section and Porcelain-lined Iron Bowl.
No. 3–A. Painted Valve Section and Porcelain Bowl.
No. 3–B. Porcelain-lined Valve Section and Porcelain Bowl.

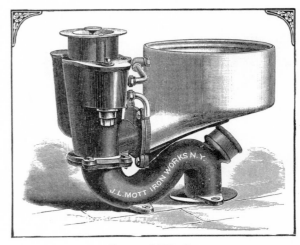

PLATE 175-G.

Nos. 1, 1–A and 1–B Closets (Trap),

With No. 1 Valve.

No. 1.   Painted Valve Section and Porcelain-lined Iron Bowl.
No. 1–A. Painted Valve Section and Porcelain Bowl.
No. 1–B. Porcelain-lined Valve Section and Porcelain Bowl.

ANY remarks relative to the "Demarest" might seem superfluous, from the fact that it is more widely known and has been more generally used in the last eight years than any other Water Closet in the market. That they have given very general satisfaction is most conclusively proved by the largely increased demand from year to year. It is also well known to our many customers that we have carefully watched the manufacture of this Closet, and lost no opportunity to improve it when convinced that an improvement could be made in any of its parts; the result is that *the Closet as manufactured by us to-day might almost be looked upon as a perfect one, and an article altogether beyond experiment.*

The Closets are generally sent out with No. 4 Valve, which is simple, easily repaired and well suited for use on all pressures; still, we can furnish the Closets with No. 1 Valve—as shown by Plate 175-G—to those who may prefer it.

In calling attention to the thorough manner in which this Closet is made, we would particularly mention the quality of the Bowls, which are *specially manufactured for us in Staffordshire, England, by the very best makers.* The quality of the earthen ware, as every one knows, is a most important feature in a Water Closet, as inferior ware is likely to craze, discolor, and become offensive to the eye.

Mott's All-Porcelain or Enameled Wrought or Cast Iron Slop Safes may be used with the "Demarest."

The "Demarest."

PLATE 176-G.

PORCELAIN BOWL WITH BACK VENT.

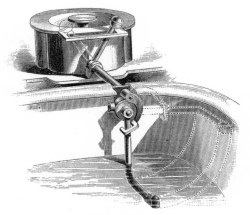

PLATE 178-G.

"DEMAREST" CLOSET WITH PATENT BIDET ATTACHMENT.

PLATE 177-G.

PORCELAIN BOWL WITH SIDE VENT.

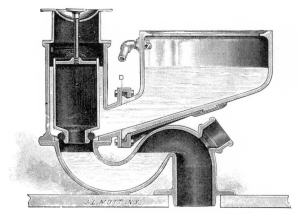

PLATE 179-G.

Section showing Bowl, Plunger Section and Trap.

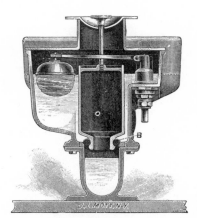

PLATE 180-G.

Section showing No. 4 Valve, Plunger and Float.

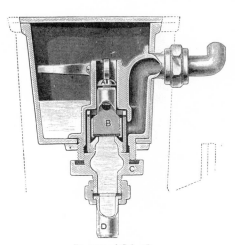

PLATE 181-G.

Section showing No. 4 Valve with ½ inch Couplings.

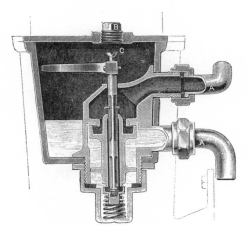

PLATE 182-G.

Section of No. 1 Valve with ½ inch Couplings

THE No. 4 VALVE is now being most generally used on account of its simplicity and adaptability to all pressures and to any kind of water; as regularly sent out, it works satisfactorily on all pressures from 20 to 100 pounds; when it is required for pressures of over 100 pounds, or less than 20 pounds, it is necessary to state the exact amount of pressure when ordering the Closets. To regulate the Depth of Water in Bowl, turn Regulating Screw A to the Right *to increase* the water, and to the Left *to decrease* it; the Regulating Screw is reached by removing Part C, to which Supply Coupling D is attached, when moving Part B can be taken out. The small hole in Part B is for the Plumber to put the leg of his compasses through while turning the Screw. This Valve is very easily repaired; it is also interchangeable with No. 1 Valve—shown by Plate 182-G—which is of course familiar to all who have been using the "Demarest," and is still furnished with the Closets to those who may prefer it, only when ordering, it should be stated that Closet is wanted with No. 1 Valve. When regulating this Valve it is only necessary to unscrew Plug B, when the Screw C can be turned to the right or left, as required.

THE "PREMIER," SIDE-OUTLET FLUSHING-RIM VALVE WATER CLOSET.

FOR PRESSURE OR TANK USE.

PATENTED.

PLATE 183-G.

THE "PREMIER." NO. 1 (TRAP).

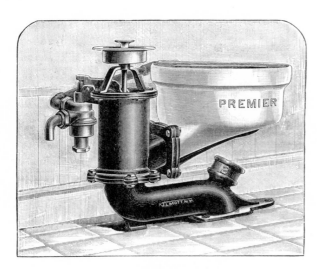

PLATE 184-G.

THE "PREMIER," NO. 2 (OFFSET).

PLATE 185-G.

THE "PREMIER," NO. 3 (STRAIGHTWAY).

For sectional view and description of the "Premier" see following page.

Mott's All-Porcelain and Enameled Wrought and Cast Iron Slop Safes are adapted for use with the "Premier."

THE "PREMIER," SIDE-OUTLET FLUSHING-RIM VALVE WATER CLOSET.

PATENTED.

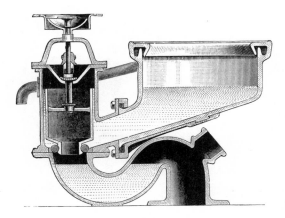

PLATE 186-G.

Sectional view of the "Premier."

The Bowl is of Porcelain ; the Plunger Section is Porcelain lined.

The Trap, Offset or Straightway will be furnished Porcelain-lined if so ordered.

THE "Premier" is fitted with a large Valve (one inch waterway) suited to all pressures, and which under ordinary pressure charges the Flushing-rim and flushes the Closet almost, if not equal, to the wash of a Cistern ; this, heretofore, has been the great desideratum, namely, a Valve that would be capable of supplying a Flushing rim Bowl and thereby washing every part of same ; moreover, this is accomplished almost entirely without noise, which we apprehend will be acknowledged by every one to be a most important feature. Regarding construction of Closet we have only to repeat that it is the same as our "Hygeia," and made with no idea of cheapness whatever, our object being to produce a strictly first-class article, not only from a sanitary point of view, but one that would be durable and efficient in every way ; the Valve and all its Pipes and Couplings are of heavy Brass ; in its construction it is of the simplest kind, very durable, and can be readily understood and repaired.

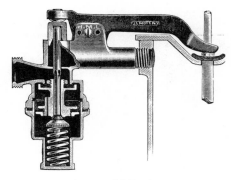

PLATE 187-G.

Cross Section showing "Premier" Leather-seated, Cup Leather
Valve and mode of working same by Lever, the stroke
being regulated by passing Screw through hole nearest
Valve marked H for high pressure ; through the
one marked M for medium pressure, and
through the one marked L for low
pressure.

PLATE 188-G.

PORCELAIN BOWL FOR "PREMIER,"

With Local or Bowl Vent to be connected with Hot Flue.

CABINET WORK FOR CISTERN AND VALVE CLOSETS

PLATE 189-G.

PLAIN PANEL DESIGN.

We furnish the above in Cherry and Veneered or Plain Black Walnut and Ash.

Length, 30 inches; Width, 20 inches.

PLATE 190-G.

"ELIZABETHAN" DESIGN.

Furnished in Mahogany.

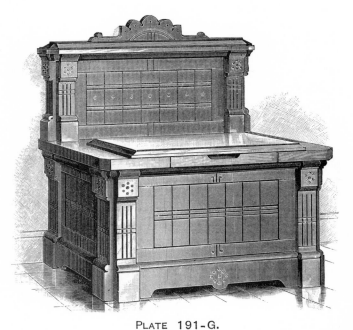

PLATE 191-G.

"EASTLAKE" DESIGN.

Furnished in Black Walnut, Ash or Cherry

NOTE.—When ordering it is necessary to state for which Closet the Case is required: also, whether it is to be fitted for Enameled Iron or Porcelain Slop Safe.

Cabinet Work for Cistern and Valve Closets.

PLATE 192-G.

Cherry, Black Walnut or Ash Case

Dimensions: Length, 30 inches; Width, 20 inches.

PLATE 193-G.

FRONT AND TOP.

Furnished in Cherry and Plain and Veneered Black Walnut
and Ash.

The above is made 33 inches long, but can be cut down to suit
any opening not under 28 inches. Special sizes made to order.

PLATE 194-G.

CUP AND PULL WITH SEAT LEVER

For operating Cistern Water Closet.

NOTE.—When ordering it is necessary to state for which Closet the Case is desired; also, whether it is to be fitted for All-Porcelain or
Enameled Iron Slop Safe.

CABINET WORK FOR WATER CLOSETS.

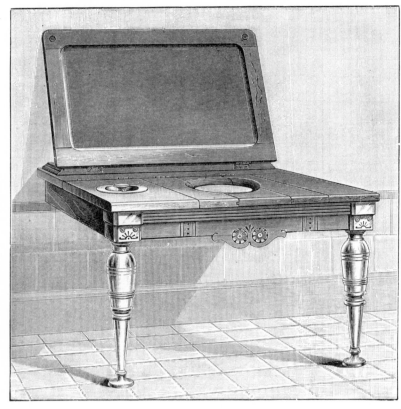

PLATE 195-G.

Open Seat with Bronzed Iron, Polished or Nickel-plated Brass Legs for use with "Hygeia," "Simplex," "Demarest" or "Premier" Water Closets; also, with Hopper and Cistern Combinations by using Seat Lever as shown by Plate 194-G.
Furnished in Black Walnut, Ash, Cherry and Mahogany.   Size, 30 inches long by 24 inches wide.

PLATE 196-G.

Open Seat with Bronzed Iron, Polished or Nickel-plated Brass Legs for use with Water Closets operated by Pull.
Furnished in Black Walnut, Cherry, Ash or Mahogany.   Size, 30 inches long by 24 inches wide.

NOTE.—When ordering it will be necessary to state for which Closet the Seat is desired; also, whether Enameled Cast or Wrought Iron or Porcelain Slop Safe is to be used.

CABINET WORK FOR CISTERN AND VALVE CLOSETS.

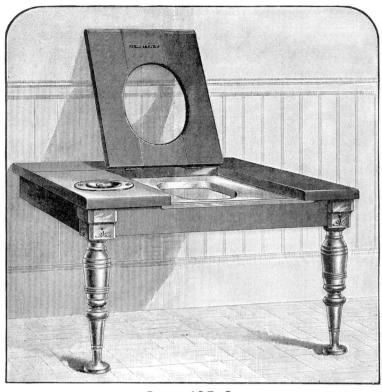

PLATE 197-G.

Open Seat with Bronzed Iron Legs for use with "Hygeia," "Simplex," "Demarest" or "Premier" Water Closets; also with Hopper and Cistern Combinations by using Seat Lever as shown by Plate 194-G.
Furnished in Cherry, Black Walnut or Ash.　　　Size, 30 inches long by 24 inches wide.

PLATE 198-G.

Open Seat with Bronzed Iron Legs for use with Water Closet operated by Pull.
Furnished in Cherry, Black Walnut or Ash.　　　Size, 27 inches long by 24 inches wide.

NOTE.—When ordering it will be necessary to state for which Closet the Seat is desired; also, whether Enameled Cast or Wrought Iron or Porcelain Slop Safe is to be used.

DEMAREST'S PATENT WATER CLOSET APPARATUS.

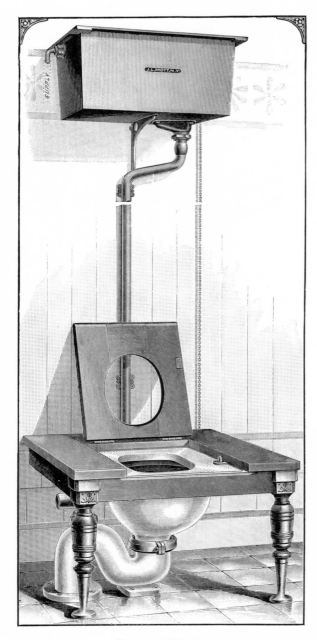

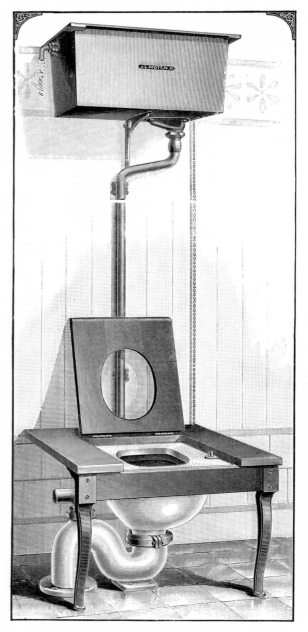

PLATE 199-G.

WATER CLOSET APPARATUS,

Comprising

Porcelain Flushing-rim Oval Hopper and Trap, No. 11½ Fore-and-
after-wash Waste-preventing Cistern, Enameled Cast Iron
Slop Safe, Black Walnut Seat with Bronzed Iron
Legs, Bracket and Chain

This Seat is 27 inches long by 24 inches wide

PLATE 200-G.

WATER CLOSET APPARATUS,

Comprising

Porcelain Flushing-rim Oval Hopper and Trap, No. 11½ Fore-and-
after-wash Waste-preventing Cistern, Enameled Cast Iron
Slop Safe, Black Walnut Seat with Painted Iron
Legs, Bracket and Chain.

This Seat is 24 inches long by 24 inches wide.

The Seat will be furnished of Cherry or Ash if so ordered.

The Cistern may be Painted, Galvanized or Porcelain-lined Iron, or Wood Copper-lined.

THE above are Automatic in action; when the Seat is depressed, one-half gallon of water descends and wets the Hopper so that nothing
will adhere; when the Seat is relieved 2½ gallons of water descend and thoroughly flush the Hopper and Trap. The Cistern and Seat
Lever are simple in construction, positive in action and not liable to get out of order; the Porcelain Hopper and Trap are of the best
English ware, which will not craze or discolor. We guarantee every Apparatus to be efficient in operation.
     This form of Water Closet is adapted for use in Public and Private Buildings, etc., where persons using cannot be trusted to flush
the Closet by drawing down a Pull or raising a Handle.

For sectional view of Cistern, and separate view of Hopper, see subsequent pages of this Catalogue.

Demarest's Patent Water Closet Apparatus.

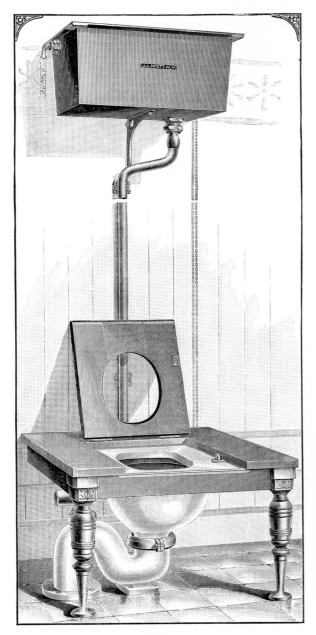

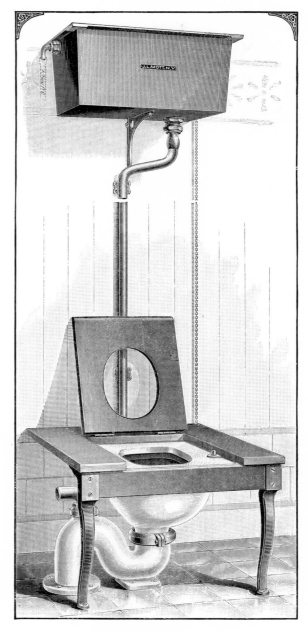

PLATE 201-G.

Water Closet Apparatus,

Comprising

Porcelain Flushing-rim Oval Hopper and Trap, No. 11 After-wash
Waste-preventing Cistern, Enameled Cast Iron Slop Safe,
Black Walnut Seat with Bronzed Iron Legs,
Bracket and Chain.

This Seat is 27 inches long by 24 inches wide.

PLATE 202-G.

Water Closet Apparatus,

Comprising

Porcelain Flushing-rim Oval Hopper and Trap, No. 11 After-wash
Waste-preventing Cistern, Enameled Cast Iron Slop Safe,
Black Walnut Seat with Painted Iron Legs,
Bracket and Chain.

This Seat is 24 inches long by 24 inches wide.

The Seat will be furnished of Cherry or Ash if so ordered.

The Cistern may be Painted, Galvanized or Porcelain-lined Iron, or Wood Copper-lined.

THE above are automatic in action; when the Seat is relieved, about 2½ gallons of water descend and thoroughly flush the Hopper and Trap. The Cistern and Seat Lever are simple in construction, positive in action and not liable to get out of order; the Porcelain Hopper and Trap are of the best English ware which will not craze or discolor. We guarantee every Apparatus to be efficient in operation.
This form of Water Closet is adapted for use in Public and Private Buildings, Factories, etc., where persons using cannot be trusted to flush the Closet by drawing down a Pull or raising a Handle.

For sectional view of Cistern, and separate view of Hopper, see subsequent pages of this Catalogue.

DEMAREST'S PATENT WATER CLOSET APPARATUS.

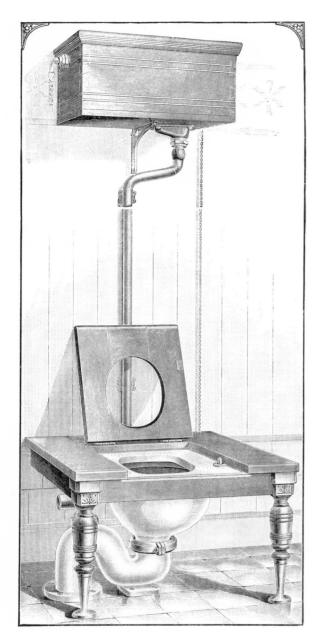

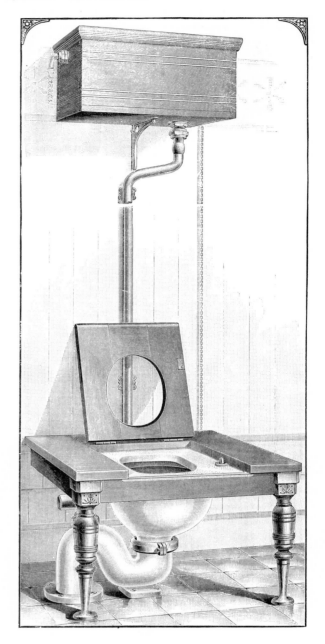

PLATE 203-G.

WATER CLOSET APPARATUS,

Comprising

Porcelain Flushing-rim Oval Hopper and Trap, No. 11½ Fore-and-after-wash Waste-preventing Copper-lined Stained Wood Cistern, Enameled Cast Iron Slop Safe, Cherry or Black Walnut Seat with Bronzed Iron Legs, Bracket and Chain.

Plate 203-G is Automatic in action; when the Seat is depressed, one-half gallon of water descends and wets the Hopper so that nothing will adhere; when the Seat is relieved, 2½ gallons of water descend and thoroughly flush the Hopper and Trap.

PLATE 204-G.

WATER CLOSET APPARATUS,

Comprising

Porcelain Flushing-rim Oval Hopper and Trap, No. 11 After-wash Waste-preventing Copper-lined Stained Wood Cistern, Enameled Cast Iron Slop Safe, Cherry or Black Walnut Seat with Bronzed Iron Legs, Bracket and Chain.

Plate 204-G is Automatic in action; when the Seat is relieved about 2½ gallons of water descend and thoroughly flush the Hopper and Trap.

The Seat is 27 inches long by 24 inches wide.

THE Nos. 11 and 11½ Cisterns, also the Seat Lever, are simple in construction, positive in action and not liable to get out of order; the Porcelain Hopper and Trap are of the best English ware which will not craze or discolor. We guarantee every Apparatus to be efficient in operation.

Our Stained Wood Cisterns are made of seasoned White-wood stained to represent Cherry or Black Walnut and unless closely examined it is difficult to distinguish them from the real wood.

For sectional view of Cisterns, and separate view of Hopper, see subsequent pages of this Catalogue.

Demarest's Patent Water Closet Apparatus.

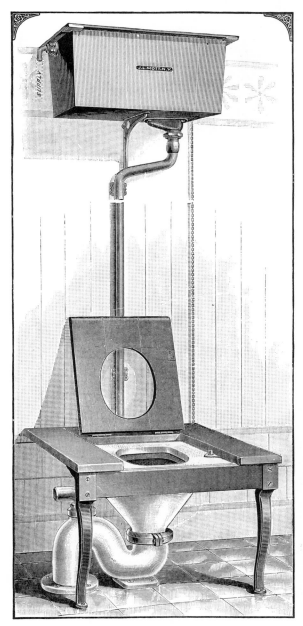

Plate 205-G.

Water Closet Apparatus,

Comprising

Porcelain Flushing-rim Round Hopper and Trap, No. 11½ Fore-
and-after-wash Waste-preventing Cistern, Enameled Cast
Iron Slop Safe, Black Walnut Seat with Painted
Iron Legs, Bracket and Chain.

Plate 205–G is Automatic in action; when the Seat is depressed, one-half gallon of water descends and wets the Hopper
so that nothing will adhere; when the Seat is relieved, 2½ gallons of water descend and thoroughly flush the Hopper and Trap.

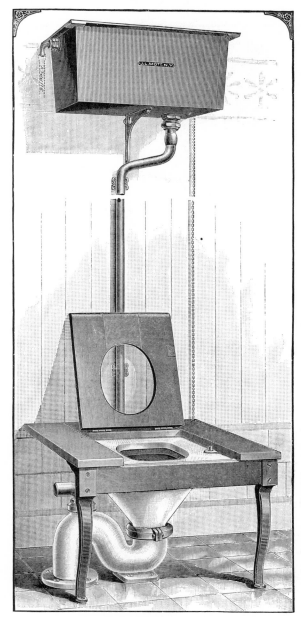

Plate 206-G.

Water Closet Apparatus,

Comprising

Porcelain Flushing-rim Round Hopper and Trap, No. 11 After-
wash Waste-preventing Cistern, Enameled Cast Iron Slop
Safe, Black Walnut Seat with Painted Iron Legs,
Bracket and Chain.

Plate 206–G is Automatic in action; when the Seat is relieved, 2½ gallons of water descend and thoroughly flush the
Hopper and Trap.

The Seats are 24 inches long by 24 inches wide.   The Seats will be furnished of Cherry or Ash if so ordered.

The Traps may be Porcelain-lined Iron instead of Porcelain, or the Hoppers and Traps both may be Porcelain-lined Iron.

The Cistern may be Painted, Galvanized or Porcelain-lined Iron, or Wood Copper-lined.

THE Nos. 11 and 11½ Cisterns, also the Seat Lever, are simple in construction, positive in action and not liable to get out of order. The
Porcelain Hopper and Trap are of the best English ware, which will not craze or discolor. We guarantee every Apparatus to be efficient
in operation.
The above form of Water Closet Apparatus is adapted for use in Public and Private Buildings where parties using cannot be trusted
to flush the Closet by drawing down a Pull or raising a Handle.

For sectional view of Cisterns, and separate view of Hoppers and Traps, see subsequent pages of this Catalogue.

Demarest's Patent Water Closet Apparatus.

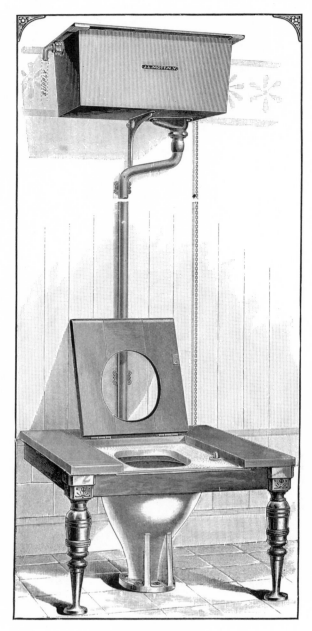

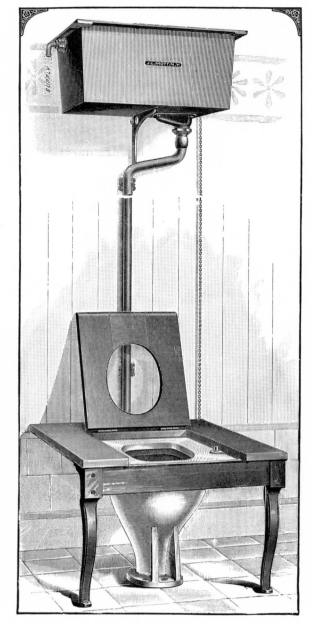

PLATE 207-G.

WATER CLOSET APPARATUS,

Comprising

Porcelain Flushing-rim Long Oval Hopper, No. 11½ Fore-and-after-wash Waste-preventing Cistern, Enameled Cast Iron Slop Safe, Black Walnut Seat with Bronzed Iron Legs, Bracket and Chain.

This Seat is 27 inches long by 24 inches wide.

PLATE 208-G.

WATER CLOSET APPARATUS,

Comprising

Porcelain Flushing-rim Long Oval Hopper, No. 11½ Fore-and-after-wash Waste-preventing Cistern, Enameled Cast Iron Slop Safe, Black Walnut Seat with Painted Iron Legs, Bracket and Chain.

This Seat is 24 inches long by 24 inches wide.

The Seats will be furnished of Cherry or Ash if so ordered.

The Cistern may be Painted, Galvanized or Porcelain-lined Iron, or Wood Copper-lined.

PLATES 207–G and 208–G are Automatic in action; when the Seat is depressed, one-half gallon of water descends and wets the Hopper so that nothing will adhere; when the Seat is relieved, 2½ gallons of water descend and thoroughly flush the Hopper. The Cistern and Seat Lever are simple in construction, positive in action and not liable to get out of order. The Porcelain Hopper is of the best English ware, which will not craze or discolor. We guarantee every Apparatus to be efficient in operation.

The above form of Water Closet is adapted for use in Public and Private Buildings where parties using cannot be trusted to flush the Closet by drawing down a Pull or raising a Handle.

For sectional view of Cisterns, and separate view of Hopper, see subsequent pages of this Catalogue.

DEMAREST'S PATENT WATER CLOSET APPARATUS.

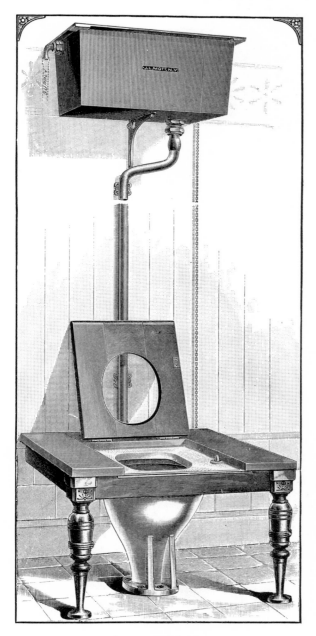

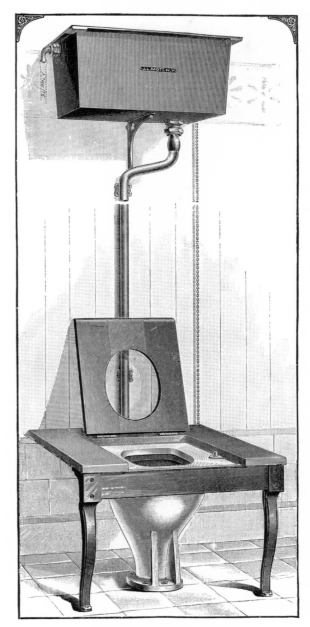

<table>
<tr><td align="center">

PLATE 209-G.

WATER CLOSET APPARATUS,

Comprising

Porcelain Flushing-rim Long Oval Hopper, No. 11 After-wash
Waste-preventing Cistern, Enameled Cast Iron Slop
Safe, Black Walnut Seat with Bronzed
Iron Legs, Bracket and Chain.

This Seat is 27 inches long by 24 inches wide.

</td><td align="center">

PLATE 210-G.

WATER CLOSET APPARATUS,

Comprising

Porcelain Flushing-rim Long Oval Hopper, No. 11 After-wash
Waste-preventing Cistern, Enameled Cast Iron Slop
Safe, Black Walnut Seat with Painted
Iron Legs, Bracket and Chain.

This Seat is 24 inches long by 24 inches wide.

</td></tr>
</table>

The Seats will be furnished of Cherry or Ash if so ordered.

The Cistern may be Painted, Galvanized or Porcelain-lined Iron, or Wood Copper-lined.

PLATES 209-G and 210-G are Automatic in action; when the Seat is relieved, 2½ gallons of water descend and thoroughly flush the Hopper. The Cistern and Seat Lever are simple in construction, positive in action and not liable to get out of order. The Porcelain Hopper is of the best English ware which will not craze or discolor. We guarantee every Apparatus to be efficient in operation. This form of Water Closet is adapted for use in Public and Private Buildings where parties using cannot be trusted to flush the Closet by drawing down a Pull or raising a Handle.

For sectional view of Cistern, and separate view of Hopper, see subsequent pages of this Catalogue.

DEMAREST'S PATENT WATER CLOSET APPARATUS.

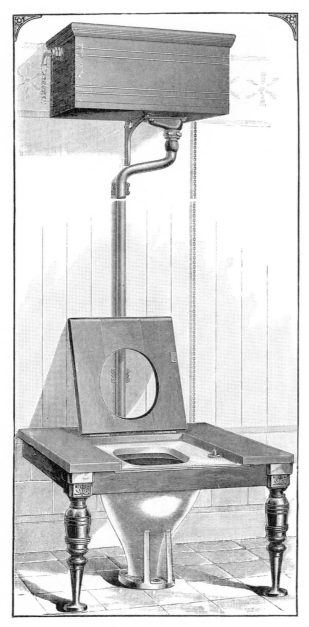 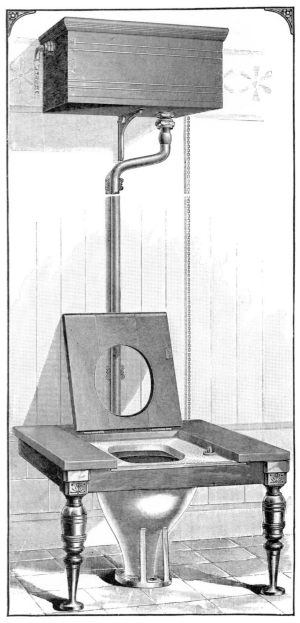

PLATE 211-G.

WATER CLOSET APPARATUS,

Comprising

Porcelain Flushing-rim Long Oval Hopper, No. 11½ Fore-and-after-wash Waste-preventing Stained Wood Copper-lined Cistern, Enameled Cast Iron Slop Safe, Cherry or Black Walnut Seat with Bronzed Iron Legs, Bracket and Chain.

Plate 211–G is Automatic in action; when the Seat is depressed, one-half gallon of water descends and wets the Hopper so that nothing will adhere; when the Seat is relieved, 2½ gallons of water descend and thoroughly flush the Hopper.

PLATE 212-G.

WATER CLOSET APPARATUS,

Comprising

Porcelain Flushing-rim Long Oval Hopper, No. 11 After-wash Waste-preventing Stained Wood Copper-lined Cistern, Enameled Cast Iron Slop Safe, Cherry or Black Walnut Seat with Bronzed Iron Legs, Bracket and Chain.

Plate 212–G is Automatic in action; when the Seat is relieved, about 2½ gallons of water descend and thoroughly flush the Hopper.

The Seats are 27 inches long by 24 inches wide.

THE Nos. 11 and 11½ Cisterns, also the Seat Lever, are simple in construction, positive in action and not liable to get out of order. The Porcelain Hopper is of the best English ware, which will not craze or discolor. We guarantee every Apparatus to be efficient in operation.

Our Stained Wood Cisterns are made of seasoned White-wood stained to represent Cherry or Black Walnut and unless closely examined cannot be distinguished from the real wood.

For sectional view of Cisterns, and separate view of Hoppers, see subsequent pages of this Catalogue.

DEMAREST'S PATENT WATER CLOSET APPARATUS.

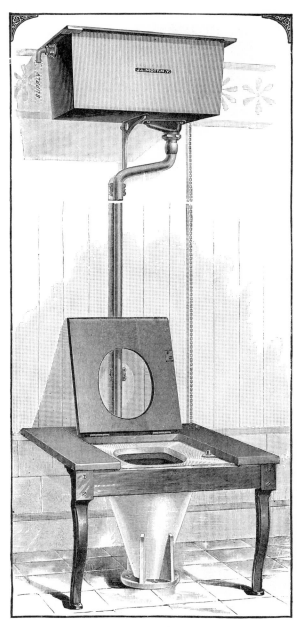

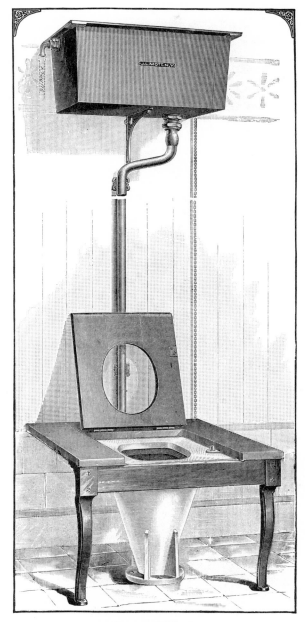

PLATE 213-G.

WATER CLOSET APPARATUS,

Comprising

Porcelain Flushing-rim Long Round Hopper, No. 11½ Fore-and-
after-wash Waste-preventing Cistern, Enameled Cast Iron
Slop Safe, Black Walnut Seat with Painted Iron
Legs, Bracket and Chain.

Plate 213-G is Automatic in action; when the Seat is depressed, one-half gallon of water descends and wets the Hopper
so that nothing will adhere; when the Seat is relieved, 2½ gallons descend and thoroughly flush the Hopper.

PLATE 214-G.

WATER CLOSET APPARATUS

Comprising

Porcelain Flushing-rim Long Round Hopper, No. 11 After-wash
Waste-preventing Cistern, Enameled Cast Iron Slop
Safe, Black Walnut Seat with Painted
Iron Legs, Bracket and Chain.

Plate 214-G is Automatic in action; when the Seat is relieved, about 2½ gallons of water descend and thoroughly flush
the Hopper.

The Seats are 24 inches long by 24 inches wide.   The Seats will be furnished of Cherry or Ash if so ordered.

The Cistern may be Painted, Galvanized or Porcelain-lined Iron, or Wood Copper-lined.

THE No. 11 and No. 11½ Cisterns, also the Seat Lever, are simple in construction, positive in action and not liable to get out of order.
The Porcelain Hopper is of the best English ware, which will not craze or discolor. We guarantee every Apparatus to be efficient in
operation.
The above form of Water Closet is adapted for use in Public and Private Buildings where parties using cannot be trusted to flush
the Closet by drawing down a Pull or raising a Handle.

For sectional view of Cisterns, and separate view of Hoppers, see subsequent pages of this Catalogue.

DEMAREST'S PATENT WATER CLOSET APPARATUS.

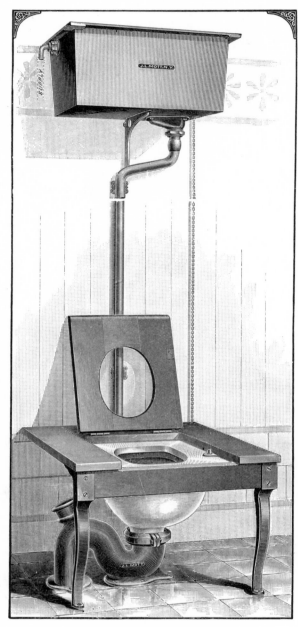

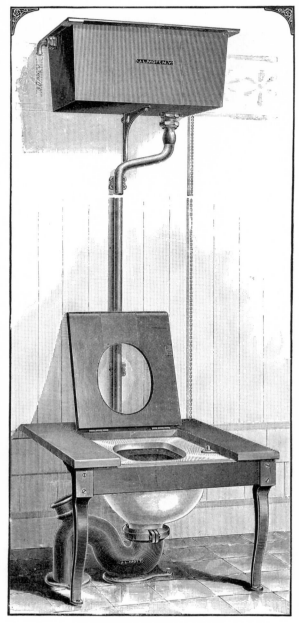

PLATE 215-G.

WATER CLOSET APPARATUS,

Comprising

Porcelain Flushing-rim Oval Hopper with Porcelain-lined Iron Trap, No. 11½ Fore-and-after-wash Waste-preventing Cistern, Enameled Cast Iron Slop Safe, Black Walnut Seat with Painted Iron Legs, Bracket and Chain.

Plate 215–G is Automatic in action; when the Seat is depressed, one-half gallon of water descends and wets the Hopper so that nothing will adhere; when the Seat is relieved, 2½ gallons descend and thoroughly flush the Hopper and Trap.

PLATE 216-G.

WATER CLOSET APPARATUS.

Comprising

Porcelain Flushing-rim Oval Hopper with Porcelain-lined Iron Trap, No. 11 After wash Waste-preventing Cistern, Enameled Cast Iron Slop Safe, Black Walnut Seat with Painted Iron Legs, Bracket and Chain.

Plate 216–G is Automatic in action; when the Seat is relieved, about 2½ gallons of water descend and thoroughly flush the Hopper and Trap.

The Seats are 24 inches long by 24 inches wide.   The Seats will be furnished of Cherry or Ash if so ordered.

The illustrations show Trap with Flange for Lead Waste Pipe Connection, but it can be furnished with Spigot End to caulk into Hub of Soil Pipe.   Can also be furnished with ½ S or ¾ S Traps as shown on subsequent pages of this Catalogue.

The Cistern may be Painted, Galvanized or Porcelain-lined Iron, or Wood Copper-lined.

THE No. 11 and No. 11½ Cisterns, also the Seat Lever, are of simple construction, positive in action and not liable to get out of order. The Porcelain Hopper is of the best English ware, which will not craze or discolor.   We guarantee every Apparatus to be efficient in operation.

For sectional view of Cisterns, and separate view of Hoppers and Traps, see subsequent pages of this Catalogue.

DEMAREST'S PATENT WATER CLOSET APPARATUS.

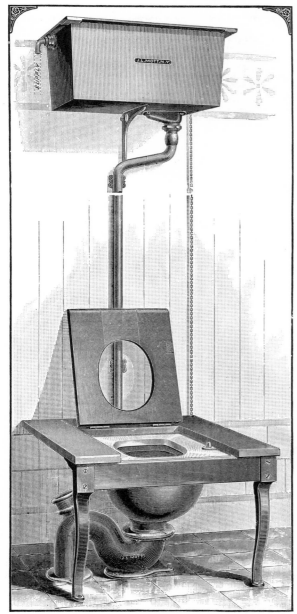

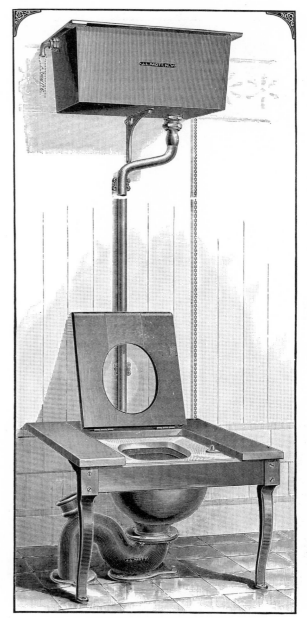

PLATE 217-G.

WATER CLOSET APPARATUS,

Comprising

Porcelain-lined Iron Flushing-rim Oval Hopper and Trap, No. 11½
Fore-and-after wash Waste-preventing Cistern, Enameled
Cast Iron Slop Safe, Black Walnut Seat with
Painted Iron Legs, Bracket and Chain.

Plate 217-G is Automatic in action; when the Seat is depressed, one-half gallon of water descends and wets the Hopper
so that nothing will adhere; when the Seat is relieved, 2½ gallons descend and thoroughly flush the Hopper and Trap.

PLATE 218-G.

WATER CLOSET APPARATUS,

Comprising

Porcelain-lined Iron Flushing-rim Oval Hopper and Trap, No. 11
After-wash Waste-preventing Cistern, Enameled Cast Iron
Slop Safe, Black Walnut Seat with Painted Iron
Legs, Bracket and Chain.

Plate 218-G is Automatic in action; when the Seat is relieved, about 2½ gallons of water descend and thoroughly flush
the Hopper and Trap.

The Seats are 24 inches long by 24 inches wide.

The Seats will be furnished of Cherry or Ash if so ordered.

The illustrations show Trap with Flange for Lead Waste Pipe Connection, but it can be furnished with Spigot End to caulk into Hub of Soil
Pipe. Can also be furnished with ½ S or ¾ S Traps as shown on subsequent pages of this Catalogue.

The Cistern may be Painted, Galvanized or Porcelain-lined Iron, or Wood Copper lined.

THE Nos. 11 and 11½ Cisterns, also the Seat Lever, are simple in construction, positive in action and not liable to get out of order. We
guarantee every Apparatus to be efficient in operation.
The above form of Water Closet is adapted for use in Public and Private Buildings where parties using cannot be trusted to
flush the Closet by drawing down a Pull or raising a Handle.

For sectional view of Cisterns, and separate view of Hoppers and Traps, see subsequent pages of this Catalogue.

DEMAREST'S PATENT WATER CLOSET APPARATUS.

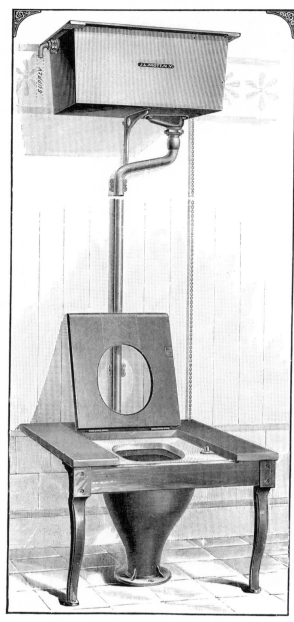

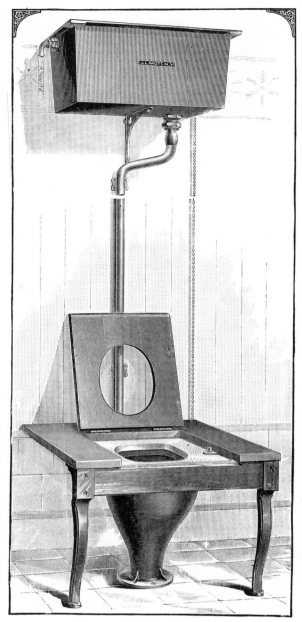

PLATE 219-G.   PLATE 220-G.

WATER CLOSET APPARATUS,   WATER CLOSET APPARATUS,

Comprising   Comprising

Porcelain-lined Iron Flushing-rim Long Oval Hopper, No. 11½ Fore-and-after-wash Waste-preventing Cistern, Enameled Cast Iron Slop Safe, Black Walnut Seat with Painted Iron Legs, Bracket and Chain.

Plate 219-G is Automatic in action; when the Seat is depressed, one-half gallon of water descends and wets the Hopper so that nothing will adhere; when the Seat is relieved, 2½ gallons descend and thoroughly flush the Hopper.

Porcelain-lined Iron Flushing-rim Long Oval Hopper, No. 11 After-wash Waste-preventing Cistern, Enameled Cast Iron Slop Safe, Black Walnut Seat with Painted Iron Legs, Bracket and Chain.

Plate 220-G is Automatic in action; when the Seat is relieved, about 2½ gallons of water descend and thoroughly flush the Hopper

The Seats are 24 inches long by 24 inches wide.   The Seats will be furnished of Cherry or Ash if so ordered.

The Cistern may be Painted, Galvanized or Porcelain-lined Iron, or Wood Copper-lined.

THE Nos. 11 and 11½ Cisterns, also the Seat Lever, are simple in construction, positive in action and not liable to get out of order. We guarantee every Apparatus to be efficient in operation.

The above form of Water Closet is adapted for use in Public and Private Buildings where parties using cannot be trusted to flush the Closet by drawing down a Pull or raising a Handle.

For sectional view of Cisterns, and separate view of Hoppers, see subsequent pages of this Catalogue.

Demarest's Patent Water Closet Apparatus.

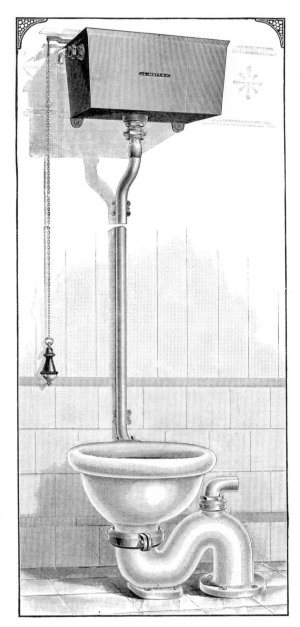

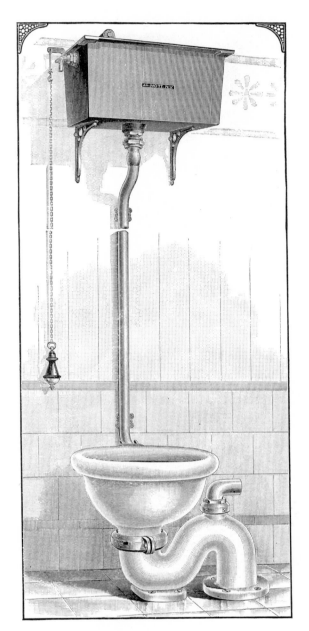

PLATE 221-G.

Water Closet Apparatus,

Comprising

Porcelain Flushing-rim Oval Hopper and Trap, No. 15 Cistern, Nickel-plated Chain and Pull.

With the No. 15 Cistern, a momentary retention of Pull will insure a thorough flush of the Hopper and Trap. Dimensions, 18 × 9 × 10 inches deep; capacity, four gallons.

PLATE 222-G.

Water Closet Apparatus,

Comprising

Porcelain Flushing-rim Oval Hopper and Trap, No. 4 Syphon Cistern, Brackets, Nickel-plated Chain and Pull.

With the No. 4 Cistern the Syphon is started by drawing down the Pull and releasing it at once, when the contents (about three gallons) descend and thoroughly flush the Hopper and Trap. Dimensions, 18 × 9 × 10 inches deep.

The Cistern may be Painted, Galvanized or Porcelain-lined Iron, or Wood Copper-lined.

For sectional view of Cisterns, and separate view of Hoppers and Traps, see subsequent pages of this Catalogue.

DEMAREST'S PATENT WATER CLOSET APPARATUS.

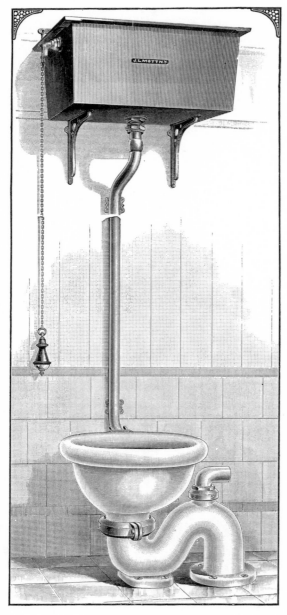 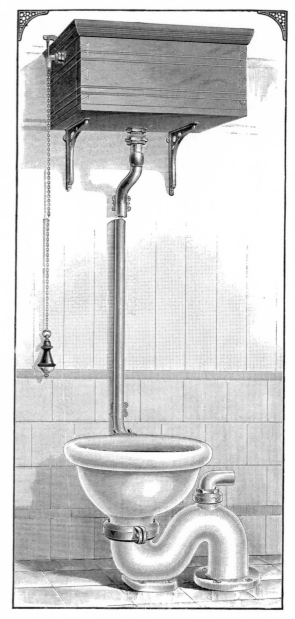

PLATE 223-G.

WATER CLOSET APPARATUS,

Comprising

Porcelain Flushing-rim Oval Hopper and Trap, No. 21 Cistern,
Brackets, Nickel-plated Chain and Pull.

PLATE 224-G.

WATER CLOSET APPARATUS,

Comprising

Porcelain Flushing-rim Oval Hopper and Trap, No. 21 Copper-lined
Stained Wood Cistern, Japanned Brackets, Nickel-
plated Chain and Pull.   Also furnished
with No. 4 or No. 15 Cistern.

With the No. 21 Cistern a momentary retention of Pull insures a thorough flush of the Hopper and Trap.   Dimensions, 24×14×10 inches deep,
and capacity eight gallons.   For description of Nos. 4 and 15 Cisterns see previous page.

OUR Stained Cisterns are made of seasoned White-wood stained to represent Cherry or Black Walnut, and unless closely examined cannot
be distinguished from the real wood.   Their cost is but a trifle more than that of a plain Wood Cistern.

For sectional view of Cisterns, and separate view of Hoppers and Traps, see subsequent pages of this Catalogue.

Demarest's Patent Water Closet Apparatus.

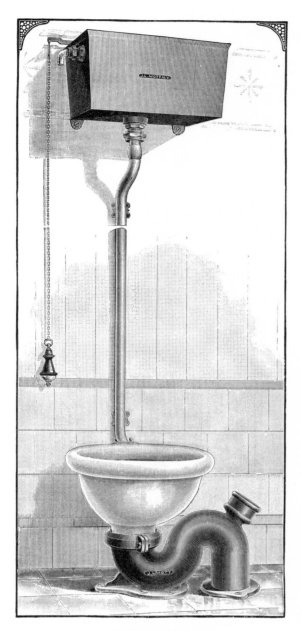

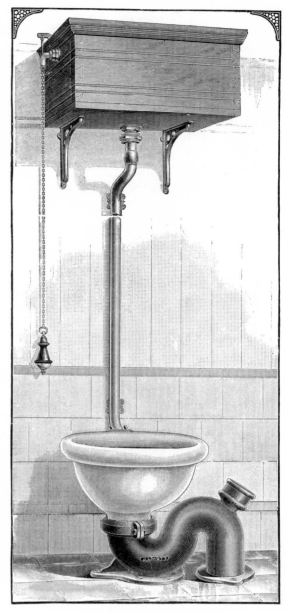

PLATE 225-G.

WATER CLOSET APPARATUS,

Comprising

Porcelain Flushing-rim Oval Hopper and Porcelain-lined Iron Trap, No. 15 Cistern, Nickel-plated Chain and Pull.   Also furnished with No. 4 or No. 21 Cistern.

The Cistern may be Painted, Galvanized or Porcelain-lined Iron, or Wood Copper-lined.

PLATE 226-G.

WATER CLOSET APPARATUS,

Comprising

Porcelain Flushing-rim Oval Hopper and Porcelain-lined Iron Trap, No. 21 Copper-lined Stained Wood Cistern, Brackets, Nickel plated Chain and Pull.   Also furnished with No. 4 or No. 15 Stained Wood Cistern.

When ordering it is necessary to state whether Trap is to be for Lead Waste Pipe Connection, as shown, or with Spigot End to caulk into Soil Pipe.   Can also be furnished with ½ S or ¾ S Traps, as shown on subsequent pages.

With the Nos. 15 and 21 Cisterns a momentary retention of Pull will insure a thorough flush of Hopper and Trap.   Dimensions of No. 15, 18×9×10 inches deep, and capacity four gallons.   Dimensions of No. 21, 24×14×10 inches deep, and capacity eight gallons.

With the No. 4 Cistern the Syphon is started by drawing down the Pull and releasing it at once, when the contents (about three gallons) descend and flush the Hopper and Trap.   Dimensions, 18 × 9 × 10 inches deep.

OUR Stained Cisterns are made of seasoned White-wood stained to represent Cherry or Black Walnut, and unless closely examined cannot be distinguished from the real wood.

DEMAREST'S PATENT WATER CLOSET APPARATUS.

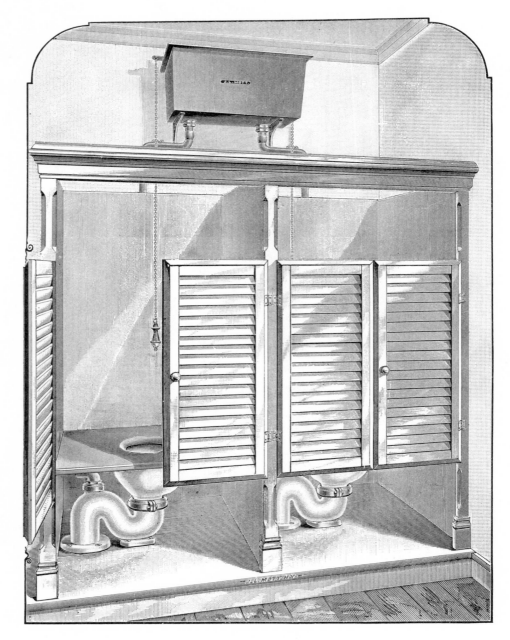

PLATE 227-G.

PORCELAIN FLUSHING-RIM OVAL HOPPERS AND TRAPS,

With No. 23 Double Cistern, Brackets, Nickel-plated Chains and Pulls.

Any of the Flushing-rim Porcelain or Porcelain-lined Iron Hoppers illustrated on subsequent pages may be used instead of those shown above.

The Cistern may be Painted, Galvanized or Porcelain-lined Iron, or Wood Copper-lined.

When two Hoppers can be put up as indicated by the illustration, economy is effected by using the No. 23 Double Cistern, as shown.

For sectional view of No. 23 Cistern see subsequent page of this Catalogue.

DEMAREST'S PATENT WATER CLOSET APPARATUS.

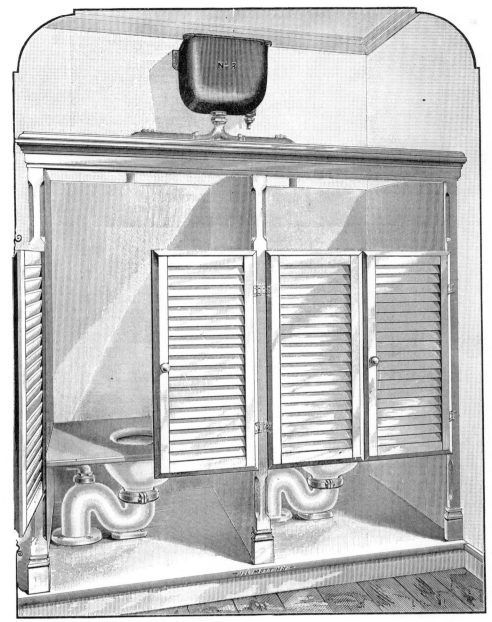

PLATE 228-G.

PORCELAIN FLUSHING-RIM OVAL HOPPERS AND TRAPS,

With Demarest's Patent Automatic Flushing Cistern.

The Automatic Flushing Cisterns suitable for use over Hoppers are furnished in the following sizes:

No. 2, (2 gallon), Single Coupling.   No. 5, (5 gallon), Double Coupling.   No. 8, (8 gallon), Triple Coupling.
"   3, (3 gallon), Double   "   "   5, (5 gallon), Triple   "   " 10, (10 gallon), Triple   "
"   4, (4 gallon), Double   "

The Cistern may be Painted or Porcelain-lined Iron, or Wood Copper-lined.

Any of the Flushing-rim Hoppers illustrated on the following pages may be used instead of those shown above.

HOPPERS flushed by our Patent Automatic Cisterns are well adapted for use in Railroad Depots, Factories, and Prisons, where the water supply is not limited. The Cisterns can be regulated to flush at desired intervals and, as the water is in constant motion, they are anti-freezing.
  The illustration shows a No. 3 (3 gallon) Flushing Cistern set over two Hoppers. Any number of Hoppers may be placed in a row and flushed from one or more of the Automatic Flushing Cisterns, the quantity of water for each Hopper being governed by local conditions, still the wash should never be less than say from one and one-half to two gallons.

For sectional view and description of Patent Automatic Flushing Cisterns see subsequent pages of this Catalogue.

DEMAREST'S PATENT WATER CLOSET APPARATUS.

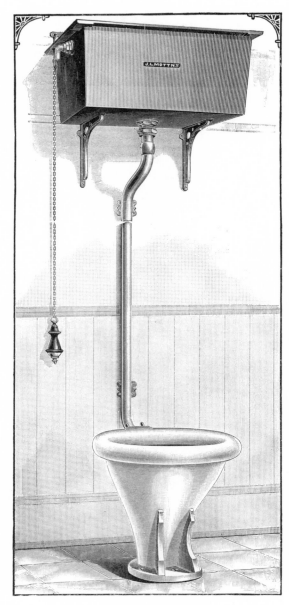

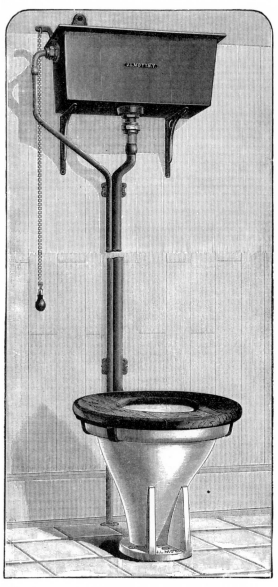

PLATE 229-G.

WATER CLOSET APPARATUS,

Comprising

Porcelain Flushing-rim Long Oval Hopper, with No. 21 Cistern,
Brackets, Nickel-plated Chain and Pull.   Also furnished
with No. 4 or No. 15 Cistern.

With the No. 21 or No. 15 Cistern, a momentary retention of
Pull insures a thorough flush of the Hopper.   Dimensions of
No. 21, 24 × 14 × 10 inches deep, and capacity, eight gallons.
Dimensions of No. 15, 18 × 9 × 10 inches deep, and capacity,
four gallons.

PLATE 230-G.

WATER CLOSET APPARATUS,

Comprising

Porcelain Flushing-rim Long Oval Hopper, with Cherry, Black
Walnut or Ash Rim, No. 4 Syphon Cistern, Brackets,
Nickel-plated Chain and Pull.

With the No. 4 Cistern the Syphon is started by drawing
down the Pull and releasing it at once, when the contents
(about three gallons). descend and flush the Hopper.   Dimensions, 18 × 9 × 10 inches deep.

The Cistern may be Painted, Galvanized or Porcelain-lined Iron, or Wood Copper-lined.

For sectional view of Cisterns, and separate view of Hoppers, see subsequent pages of this Catalogue.

DEMAREST'S PATENT WATER CLOSET APPARATUS.

PLATE 231-G.

PORCELAIN FLUSHING-RIM LONG OVAL HOPPERS,

With No. 23 Double Cistern, Brackets, Nickel-plated Chains and Ebony Pulls.

Any of the Flushing-rim Porcelain or Porcelain-lined Iron Hoppers illustrated on subsequent pages may be used instead of those shown above.

The Cistern may be Painted, Galvanized or Porcelain-lined Iron, or Wood Copper-lined.

When two Hoppers can be put up as indicated by the illustration, economy is effected by using the No. 23 (Double) Cistern, as shown.

For sectional view of No. 23 Cistern, and separate view of Hoppers, see subsequent pages of this Catalogue.

DEMAREST'S PATENT WATER CLOSET APPARATUS.

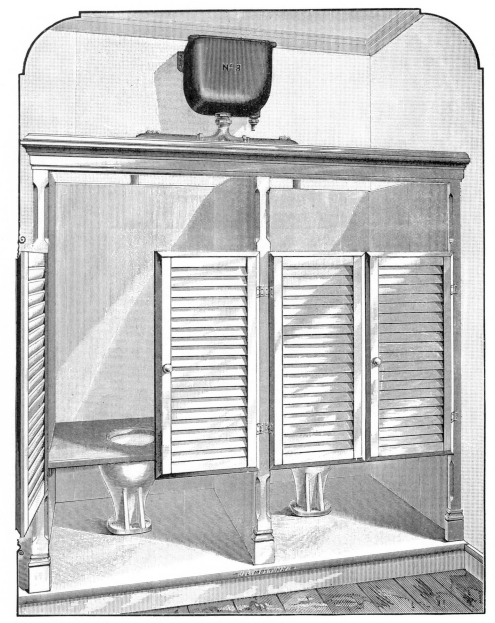

PLATE 232-G.

PORCELAIN FLUSHING-RIM LONG OVAL HOPPERS,

With Demarest's Patent Automatic Flushing Cistern.

The Automatic Flushing Cisterns suitable for use over Hoppers are furnished in the following sizes:

No. 2, (2 gallon), Single Coupling.   No. 5, (5 gallon), Double Coupling.   No. 8, (8 gallon), Triple Coupling.
" 3, (3 gallon), Double "   " 5, (5 gallon), Triple "   " 10, (10 gallon), Triple "
" 4, (4 gallon), Double "

The Cisterns may be Painted or Porcelain-lined Iron, or Wood Copper-lined.

Any of the Flushing-rim Hoppers illustrated on subsequent pages may be used instead of those shown above.

HOPPERS flushed by our Automatic Cisterns are well adapted for use in Railway Depots, Factories and Prisons, where the water supply is not limited. The interval of flushing may be regulated as desired, and as the water is in constant motion, the Cisterns are anti-freezing.

The illustration shows a No. 3 (3 gallon) Flushing Cistern set over two Hoppers. Any number of Hoppers may be placed in a row and flushed from one or more of the Automatic Flushing Cisterns, the quantity of water for each Hopper being governed by local conditions, still the wash should never be less than say from one and one-half to two gallons.

For sectional view of Automatic Flushing Cisterns see subsequent pages of this Catalogue.

DEMAREST'S PATENT WATER CLOSET APPARATUS.

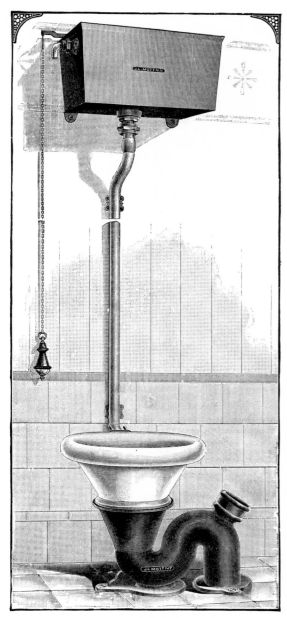

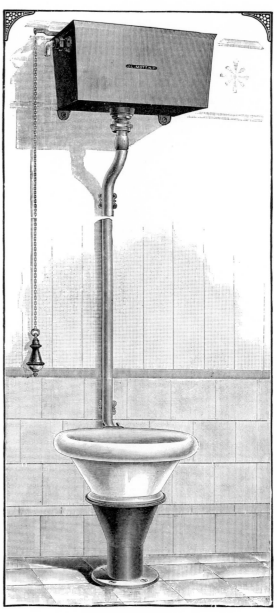

PLATE 233-G.   PLATE 234-G.

PORCELAIN FLUSHING-RIM OVAL BOWL,   PORCELAIN FLUSHING-RIM OVAL BOWL,

With Combined Hopper Stand and Trap, No. 15 Cistern, Nickel-plated Chain and Pull.

With Hopper Stand, No. 15 Cistern. Nickel-plated Chain and Pull.

The Trap can be furnished for Iron Waste Pipe Connection as shown by Plate 249-G if so ordered.

The Hopper Stand can be furnished with Vent if so ordered.

With the No. 15 Cistern a momentary retention of Pull insures a thorough flush of the Closet.   Dimensions, $18 \times 9 \times 10$ inches deep, and capacity four gallons.   When a Cistern of greater capacity is desired we can furnish our No. 21 which holds eight gallons;   Dimensions, $24 \times 14 \times 10$ inches deep.

Plates 233-G and 234-G represent a good, durable and very inexpensive style of Water Closet.

DEMAREST'S PATENT WATER CLOSET APPARATUS.

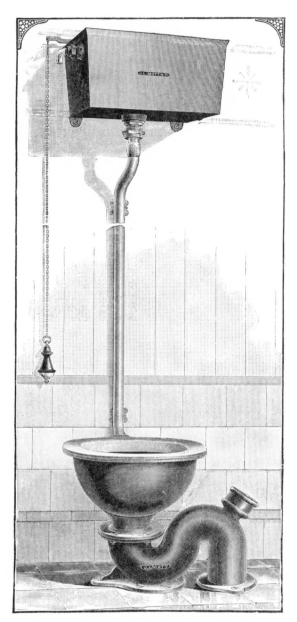

PLATE 235-G.

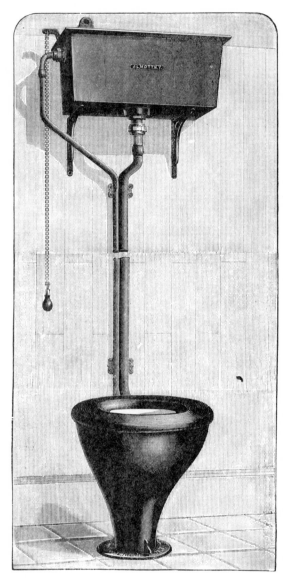

PLATE 236-G.

PORCELAIN-LINED IRON FLUSHING-RIM HOPPER AND TRAP,

With No. 15 Cistern, Nickel-plated Chain and Pull.

With the No. 15 Cistern a momentary retention of Pull insures a thorough flush of Hopper and Trap. Dimensions, 18×9×10 inches deep; capacity, 4 gallons.

When a cistern of greater capacity is desired, we can furnish our No. 21, which holds 8 gallons; dimensions, 24 × 14 × 10 inches deep.

PORCELAIN-LINED IRON FLUSHING-RIM LONG OVAL HOPPER,

With Hardwood Rim, No. 4 Syphon Cistern, Brackets, Nickel-plated Chain and Pull. Also furnished without Hardwood Rim.

With the No. 4 Cistern the Syphon is started by drawing down the pull and releasing it at once, when the contents (about 3 gallons) descend and flush the Hopper. Dimensions, 18 × 9 × 10 inches deep.

The Cisterns may be Painted, Galvanized or Porcelain-lined Iron, or Wood Copper-lined.

Demarest's Patent Water Closet Apparatus.

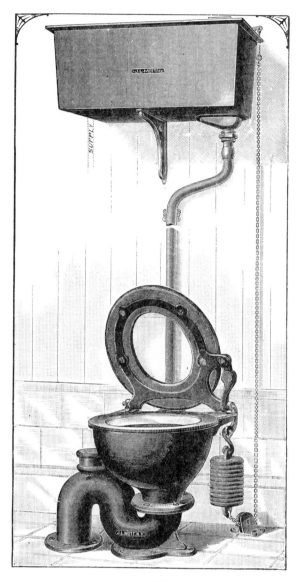

PLATE 237-G.

PORCELAIN LINED IRON FLUSHING-RIM HOPPER AND TRAP,

With No. 11½ Fore-and-after-wash Waste-preventing Cistern, Bracket,
Chain and Pulley.

This Water Closet Apparatus is automatic in action; when
the seat is depressed ½ gallon of water descends and wets the
Hopper so that nothing will adhere; when the seat is relieved
2½ gallons descend and flush the Hopper and Trap.

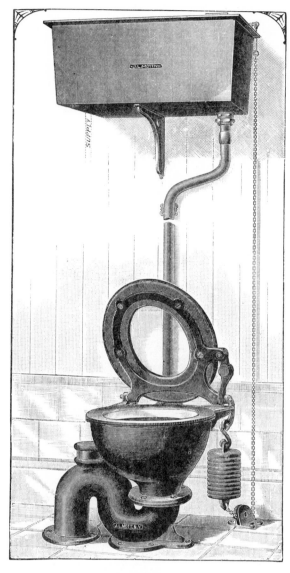

PLATE 238-G.

PORCELAIN-LINED IRON FLUSHING-RIM HOPPER AND TRAP,

With No. 11 After-wash Waste-preventing Cistern, Bracket, Chain
and Pulley.

This Water Closet Apparatus is automatic in action; when
the seat is relieved about 2½ gallons of water descend and flush
the Hopper and Trap.

Plates 237–G and 238–G represent a desirable form of Water Closet Apparatus for Factory use.   The seat being self-raising cannot be dirtied
or wet by the men using the Hoppers as Urinals.

DEMAREST'S PATENT WATER CLOSET APPARATUS.

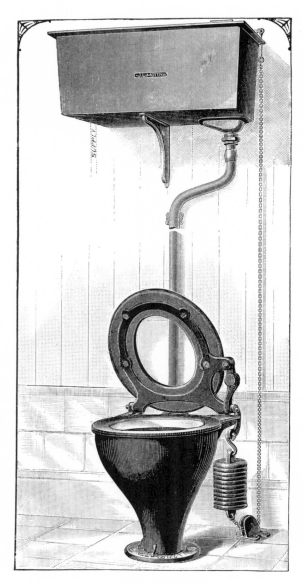

PLATE 239-G.

PORCELAIN-LINED IRON FLUSHING-RIM LONG OVAL HOPPER,

With No. 11½ Fore-and after-wash Waste-preventing Cistern, Bracket, Chain and Pulley.

This Water Closet Apparatus is Automatic in action; when the Seat is depressed, one-half gallon of water descends and wets the Hopper so that nothing will adhere; when the Seat is relieved, 2½ gallons descend and flush the Hopper.

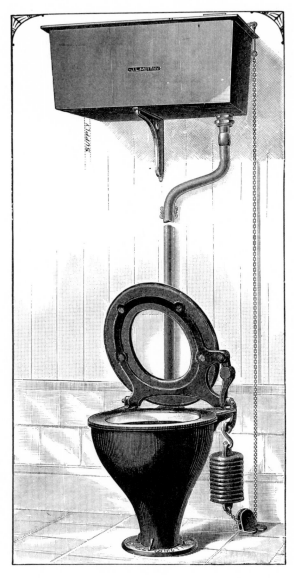

PLATE 240-G.

PORCELAIN-LINED IRON FLUSHING-RIM LONG OVAL HOPPER,

With No. 11 After-wash Waste-preventing Cistern, Bracket, Chain and Pulley.

This Water Closet Apparatus is Automatic in action; when the Seat is relieved about 2½ gallons of water descend and flush the Hopper.

Plates 239-G and 240-G represent a desirable Water Closet Apparatus for Factory use.   The Seat being Self-raising cannot be soiled when the Hopper is used as a Urinal.

DEMAREST'S PATENT WATER CLOSET APPARATUS.

PLATE 241-G.

WATER CLOSET APPARATUS.

Comprising

Porcelain Flushing-rim Long Oval Hopper, with No. 4 Syphon Cistern to operate by Door Attachment.

Any of the Flushing-rim Hoppers illustrated on subsequent pages may be used instead of that shown above.

PLATE 241-G is Automatic in action, and is a very complete arrangement where the supply of water is unlimited, as it gives a full flush every time the Door is opened.

The illustration shows Right-hand Door Attachment; when ordering it will be necessary to state whether Right or Left-hand Door Attachment is desired.

DEMAREST'S PATENT WATER CLOSET APPARATUS.

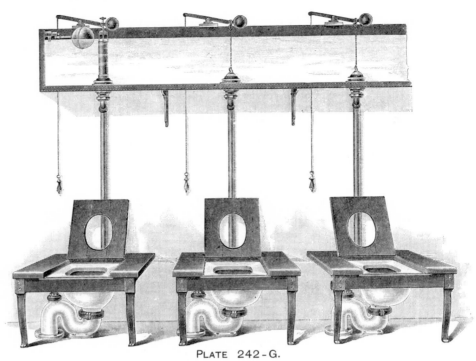

PLATE 242-G.

WATER CLOSET APPARATUS,

Comprising

Continuous Copper-lined Wood Cistern with Valves, Ball Cock, Chains, Pulls, Brackets, Porcelain Flushing-rim Oval Hoppers and Traps, Black Walnut, Cherry or Ash Seat with Iron Legs and Enameled Iron Slop Safe.

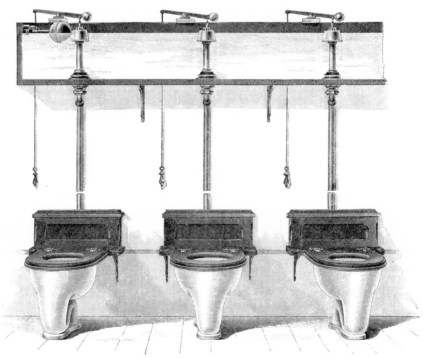

PLATE 243 G.

WATER CLOSET APPARATUS,

Comprising

Continuous Copper-lined Wood Cistern with Valves having Combined Refill and Noiseless Attachment, Ball Cock, Chains, Pulls, Brackets, and the "Undine" Front-outlet Wash out Water Closet with Cherry, Black Walnut or Ash Open Seat and Back.

THE illustrations represent a Continuous Copper-lined Wood Cistern, 14 inches wide and 12 inches deep, with a distance of 30 inches from centre to centre of Valves; we can furnish the Cistern, however, of any desired length, width and depth, and can place the Valves at a greater or less distance apart. Demarest's Combined Refill and Noiseless Valve is not only the simplest, but is without doubt away ahead of anything yet devised for use in a Continuous Tank; a very slight retention of the Pull gives all the wash desired, and the refill is always ample.

Any of our Flushing rim Hoppers and Wash-out Closets may be used with the above apparatus. The Cistern may be plain as shown, or stained to represent Cherry or Black Walnut as shown and described on page 106.

Demarest's Patent Water Closet Apparatus.

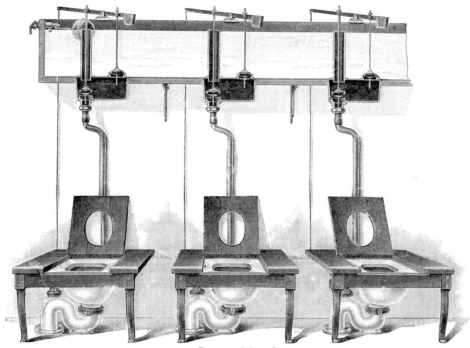

Plate 244-G.
Water Closet Apparatus.
Comprising

Continuous Copper-lined Wood After-wash Waste-preventing Cistern with Porcelain Flushing-Rim Oval Hopper and Trap, Black Walnut Seat with Painted Iron Legs and Enameled Cast Iron Slop Safe.

This Apparatus is automatic in action; when the seat is relieved 2½ gallons of water descend and flush the Hopper and Trap.

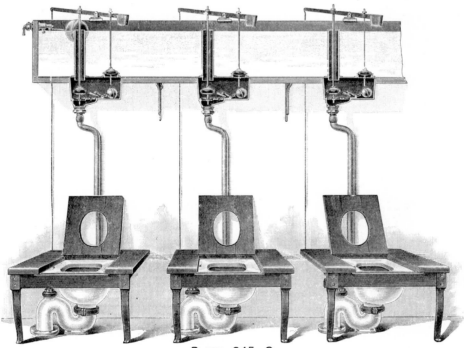

Plate 245-G.
Water Closet Apparatus.
Comprising

Continuous Copper-lined Wood Fore-and-after-wash Waste-preventing Cistern with Porcelain Flushing-rim Oval Hopper and Trap, Black Walnut Seat with Painted Iron Legs and Enameled Cast Iron Slop Safe.

This Apparatus is automatic in action; when the seat is depressed ½ gallon of water descends and wets the Hopper so that nothing will adhere; when the seat is relieved 2½ gallons descend and flush the Hopper and Trap.

The seats are 24 inches long by 24 inches wide; if so ordered they will be furnished of Cherry or Ash.

Any of our Flushing-rim Hoppers illustrated on the following pages may be used instead of those shown above; also with Plate 244-G, Wash-out Closets can be used.

THE illustrations represent a Continuous Copper-lined Wood Cistern 14 inches wide by 12 inches deep, with a distance of 30 inches from centre to centre of valves. We can, however, furnish the Cistern of any desired width and depth, and can place the valves at a greater or less distance apart. When parties desire to build and line their own Cistern we will furnish the necessary Fittings.

PATENT FLUSHING-RIM HOPPERS.

PLATE 246-G.

PORCELAIN OVAL FLUSHING-RIM HOPPER AND TRAP,

With Brass Vent Coupling.

PLATE 247-G.

PORCELAIN OVAL FLUSHING-RIM HOPPER AND TRAP,

With Local or Bowl Vent; Brass Vent Coupling.

We can furnish the Hopper with Bowl Vent to the Right of Inlet if so ordered.

PLATE 248-G.

PORCELAIN OVAL FLUSHING-RIM HOPPER AND PORCELAIN-LINED IRON S TRAP FOR LEAD WASTE PIPE CONNECTION.

PLATE 249-G.

PORCELAIN OVAL FLUSHING-RIM HOPPER AND PORCELAIN-LINED IRON S TRAP FOR IRON WASTE PIPE CONNECTION.

PLATE 250-G.

PORCELAIN OVAL FLUSHING-RIM HOPPER AND PORCELAIN-LINED IRON ¾ S TRAP.

PLATE 251-G.

PORCELAIN OVAL FLUSHING-RIM HOPPER AND PORCELAIN-LINED IRON ½ S TRAP.

The Traps we can furnish without Vent, or with Hand Hole instead of Vent, if so ordered.

Dimensions of above Hoppers and Traps: Height, 15½ inches; Outlet, 4 inches; Vent, 2 inches; Inlet for 1¼ inch Lead Pipe. Each Hopper is furnished with our Patent Inlet by means of which an effective and durable connection between Flush Pipe and Hopper is quickly made.

If so ordered we furnish the Hoppers with Inlet Coupling tapped for Iron Pipe.

NOTE.—Our Porcelain Ware is the very best *imported*, warranted not to craze or discolor.

FLUSHING-RIM HOPPERS AND TRAPS.
PATENTED.

PLATE 252-G.
PORCELAIN FLUSHING-RIM LONG OVAL HOPPER.

Height, 15½ inches; Outlet, 4 inches; Inlet for 1¼ inch Lead Pipe Connection.

PLATE 253-G.
PORCELAIN FLUSHING-RIM LONG OVAL HOPPER,
With 2 inch Vent.

Height, 15½ inches; Outlet, 4 inches; Inlet for 1¼ inch Lead Pipe Connection.

PLATE 254-G.
PORCELAIN FLUSHING-RIM ROUND HOPPER AND TRAP,
With Brass Vent Coupling.

Also furnished with Porcelain-lined Iron Trap, S, ¾ S or ½ S as shown on previous page.

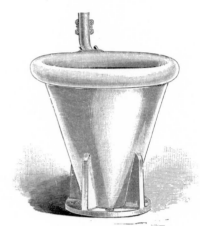

PLATE 255-G.
PORCELAIN FLUSHING-RIM LONG ROUND HOPPER.

Height, 15½ inches; Outlet, 4 inches; Inlet for 1¼ inch Lead Pipe Connection.

PLATE 256-G.
PORCELAIN FLUSHING-RIM OVAL BOWL,
With Combined Hopper Stand and Trap.

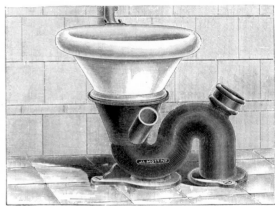

PLATE 257-G.
PORCELAIN FLUSHING-RIM OVAL BOWL,
With Combined Vented Hopper Stand and Trap.

The Trap can be furnished with Spigot for Iron Waste Pipe, and with Hand Hole instead of Vent, if so ordered.

The above Hoppers and Bowls are furnished with our Patent Inlet by means of which an effective and durable connection between Hopper and Flush Pipe is quickly made.

If so ordered we furnish the Hoppers and Bowls with Inlet Coupling tapped for Iron Pipe.

NOTE.— Our Porcelain Ware is the very best *imported*, warranted not to craze or discolor.

PORCELAIN FLUSHING-RIM OVAL BOWLS AND IRON HOPPER STANDS.

PLATE 258-G.

PORCELAIN FLUSHING-RIM OVAL BOWL WITH HOPPER STAND.

Height, 16 inches; Outlet, 4 inches; Inlet for 1¼ inch Lead Pipe.

PLATE 259-G.

PORCELAIN FLUSHING-RIM OVAL BOWL WITH VENTED HOPPER STAND.

Height, 16 inches; Outlet, 4 inches; Vent, 2 inches; Inlet for 1¼ inch Lead Pipe.

Each Bowl is furnished with our Patent Inlet by means of which an effective and durable connection is quickly made. If so ordered we can tap the Inlet Coupling for Iron Pipe Supply.

PLATE 260-G.

PORCELAIN FLUSHING-RIM OVAL BOWL WITH DEMAREST'S PATENT INLET.

PLATE 261-G.

HOPPER STAND.

PLATE 262-G.

HOPPER STAND WITH VENT.

PLATE 263-G.

COMBINED HOPPER STAND AND TRAP.

PLATE 264-G.

COMBINED VENTED HOPPER STAND AND TRAP.

The Trap can be furnished for Iron Waste Pipe Connection instead of for Lead, and with Hand Hole instead of Vent, if so ordered; or it can be ¾ or ½ S.

NOTE.—Our Porcelain Ware is the very best *imported*, warranted not to craze or discolor.

SHORT OVAL FLUSHING-RIM PORCELAIN-LINED IRON HOPPERS AND TRAPS.

PLATE 265-G.

HOPPER WITH VENTED S TRAP FOR LEAD WASTE PIPE CONNECTION.

PLATE 266-G

HOPPER WITH S TRAP FOR LEAD WASTE PIPE CONNECTION.

PLATE 267-G.

HOPPER WITH VENTED S TRAP FOR IRON WASTE PIPE CONNECTION.

PLATE 268-G.

HOPPER WITH S TRAP FOR IRON WASTE PIPE CONNECTION.

PLATE 269-G.

HOPPER WITH VENTED ¾ S TRAP.

PLATE 270-G.

HOPPER WITH ¾ S TRAP.

PLATE 271-G.

HOPPER WITH VENTED ½ S TRAP.

PLATE 272-G.

HOPPER WITH ½ S TRAP.

Dimensions of above Hoppers and Traps: Height, 15½ inches; Outlet, 4 inches; Vent, 2 inches; Inlet for 1¼ inch Lead Pipe. If so ordered we furnish the Hoppers with Inlet Coupling tapped for Iron Pipe Supply.

Short Round Flushing-Rim Porcelain-Lined Iron Hoppers and Traps.

Plate 273-G.

Hopper with Vented S Trap for Lead Waste Pipe Connection.

Plate 274-G.

Hopper with S Trap for Lead Waste Pipe Connection.

Plate 275-G.

Hopper with Vented S Trap for Iron Waste Pipe Connection.

Plate 276-G.

Hopper with S Trap for Iron Waste Pipe Connection.

Plate 277-G.

Hopper with Vented ¾ S Trap.

Plate 278-G.

Hopper with ¾ S Trap.

Plate 279-G.

Hopper with Vented ½ S Trap.

Plate 280-G.

Hopper with ½ S Trap.

Dimensions of above Hoppers and Traps: Height, 16½ inches; Outlet, 4 inches; Vent, 2 inches; Inlet for 1¼ inch Lead Pipe. If so ordered we furnish the Hoppers with Inlet tapped for Iron Pipe.

Each Hopper is furnished with our Patent Inlet by means of which an effective and durable connection is quickly made.

LONG OVAL AND ROUND FLUSHING-RIM PORCELAIN-LINED IRON HOPPERS.

PLATE 281-G.

LONG OVAL FLUSHING-RIM HOPPER.

PLATE 282-G.

LONG OVAL FLUSHING-RIM HOPPER,

With Black Walnut, Cherry or Ash Rim.

Height, 15½ in.; Outlet, 4 in.; Inlet for 1¼ in. Lead Pipe.   Also furnished with Inlet for 1¼ inch Iron Pipe and with 2¼ inch Outlet, if so ordered.

PLATE 283-G.

LONG ROUND FLUSHING-RIM HOPPER.

PLATE 284-G.

LONG ROUND FLUSHING-RIM HOPPER,

With Black Walnut, Cherry or Ash Rim.

Height, 16 inches; Outlet, 4 inches: Inlet for 1¼ inch Lead Pipe.   Also furnished with Inlet for 1¼ inch Iron Pipe, if so ordered.

PLATE 285-G.

STRAIGHT BACK LONG OVAL FLUSHING-RIM HOPPER
FOR HOSPITAL AND ASYLUM USE.

Height, 15 in.; Outlet, 2¼ in.; Inlet for 1¼ inch Iron Pipe.
Also furnished with Hardwood Rim, as Plate 282-G.

PLATE 286-G.
Section of Plate 287-G.

PLATE 287-G.

DEMAREST'S PATENT COMBINED IRON SEAT AND FLUSHING-RIM
HOPPER FOR PRISONS, STATION HOUSES, ETC.

Height, 16 inches; Outlet, 4 inches: Inlet for 1¼ inch
Iron Pipe.

Each Hopper is furnished with our Patent Inlet by means of which an effective and durable connection is quickly made.

DEMAREST'S PATENT SYPHON CISTERNS FOR WATER CLOSETS.

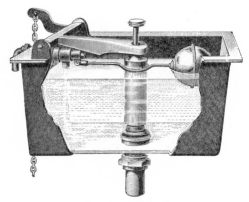

PLATE 288-G.

No. 4 IRON CISTERN, PAINTED, GALVANIZED OR PORCELAIN-LINED.

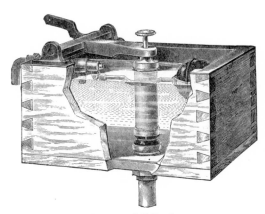

PLATE 289-G.

No. 4 COPPER-LINED WOOD CISTERN.

Dimensions, 18 × 9 × 10 inches deep.

To be operated by Pull, and for use over any form of Flushing-rim Hopper or Bowl. The Syphon is started by drawing down the Pull and releasing it at once, when the contents of Cistern (about three gallons) descend and flush the Closet.

PLATE 290-G.

No. 4½ IRON CISTERN, PAINTED, GALVANIZED OR PORCELAIN-LINED.

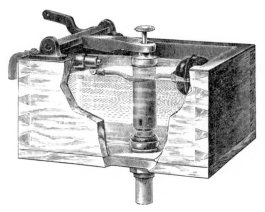

PLATE 291-G.

No. 4½ COPPER-LINED WOOD CISTERN.

Dimensions, 18 × 9 × 10 inches deep.

To be operated by Pull, and for use over any form of Wash-out Water Closet. Drawing down the Pull and releasing it at once starts the Syphon, when the contents of Cistern descend and flush the Closet. The re-fill to Bowl is obtained by the Slot in lower end of Syphon Tube which causes the Syphon to break gradually.

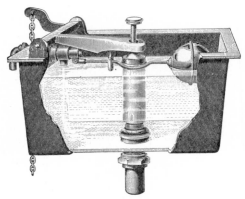

PLATE 292-G.

No. 5 WASTE-PREVENTING SYPHON CISTERN, PAINTED, GALVAN-IZED OR PORCELAIN-LINED.

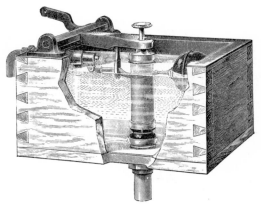

PLATE 293-G.

No. 5 COPPER-LINED WOOD CISTERN.

Dimensions, 18 × 9 × 10 inches deep.

No. 5 Cistern is the same as No. 4, with the addition of a Loop to hold up Ball Cock so it will remain closed as long as Pull is held, thereby preventing any waste of water should anyone feel disposed to hold the Pull.

DEMAREST'S PATENT CISTERNS FOR WATER CLOSETS.

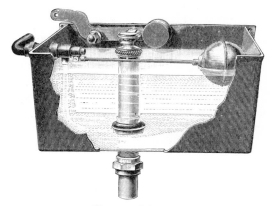

PLATE 294-G.

No. 15 Iron Cistern, Painted, Galvanized or Porcelain-lined.

PLATE 295-G.

No. 15 Copper-lined Wood Cistern.

Dimensions, 18×9×10 inches deep; capacity, four gallons.

To be operated by Pull, and for use over any form of Flushing-rim Hopper or Bowl.

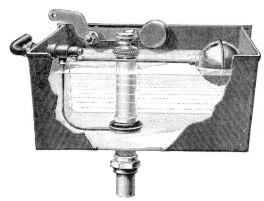

PLATE 296-G.

No. 15½ Iron Cistern, Painted, Galvanized or Porcelain-lined.

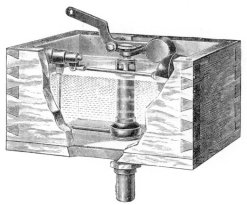

PLATE 297-G.

No. 15½ Copper-lined Wood Cistern.

Dimensions, 18 × 9 × 10 inches deep; capacity, four gallons.

To be operated by Pull, and for use over any form of .Wash-out Water Closet.　After Closet has been flushed, the re-fill to Bowl is obtained by the Tube which extends from Ball Cock to below the seat of Valve.

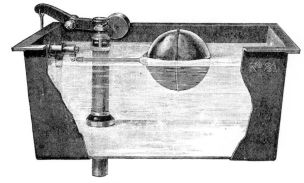

PLATE 298-G.

No. 21 Iron Cistern, Painted, Galvanized or Porcelain-lined.

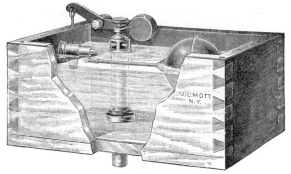

PLATE 299-G.

No. 21 Copper-lined Wood Cistern.

No. 21.　　　　Dimensions, 24 × 14 × 10 in. deep; capacity, 8 gallons.　　No. 21.　Size 3, Dimensions, 40 × 13 × 14 in. deep; capacity, 25 gallons.
"　　Size 2,　　"　　　30 × 13 × 14　"　　"　18　"　　　"　　"　4,　　"　　45 × 13 × 14　"　　"　30　"

To be operated by Pull, and for use over any form of Flushing-rim Hopper or Bowl.

DEMAREST'S PATENT CISTERNS FOR WATER CLOSETS.

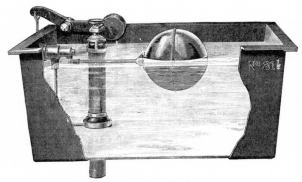

PLATE 300-G.

No. 21½ IRON CISTERN, PAINTED, GALVANIZED OR PORCELAIN-LINED.

No. 21½.   Dimensions, 24 × 14 × 10 in. deep; capacity, 8 gallons.
   "   Size 2,   "   30 × 13 × 14   "   "   18   "
   "   " 3,   "   40 × 13 × 14   "   "   25   "
   "   " 4,   "   45 × 13 × 14   "   "   30   "

To be operated by Pull, and for use over any form of Wash-out Water Closet.

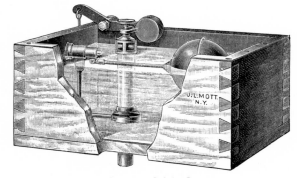

PLATE 301-G.

No. 21½ COPPER-LINED WOOD CISTERN.

Dimensions, 24 × 14 × 10 inches deep; capacity, eight gallons.

Can be made any size required to order.

After Closet has been flushed, the re-fill to Bowl is obtained by the Tube which extends from Ball Cock to below the seat of Valve.

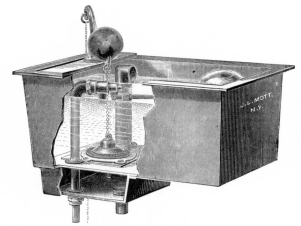

PLATE 302-G.

No. 10 IRON CISTERN, PAINTED, GALVANIZED OR PORCELAIN-LINED.

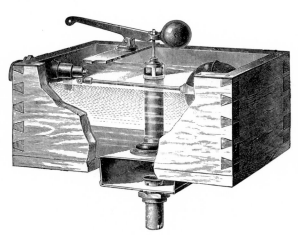

PLATE 303-G.

No. 10 COPPER-LINED WOOD CISTERN.

No. 10.   Dimensions, 24 × 14 × 10 inches deep; capacity, 8 gallons.
  " 10½.   "   30 × 13 × 14   "   "   18   "

To be operated by Pull, and for use over Wash-out Water Closets. After Closet is flushed, the re-fill to Bowl is obtained by the Perforated Stand Pipe in bottom of Service Box.

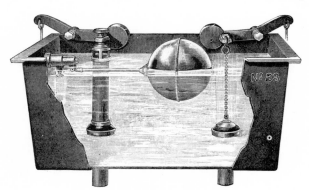

PLATE 304-G.

No. 23 IRON CISTERN, PAINTED, GALVANIZED OR PORCELAIN-LINED.

No. 23.   Dimensions, 24 × 14 × 10 in. deep; capacity, 8 gallons.
   "   Size 2,   "   30 × 13 × 14   "   "   18   "
   "   " 3,   "   40 × 13 × 14   "   "   25   "
   "   " 4,   "   45 × 13 × 14   "   "   30   "

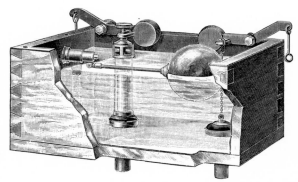

PLATE 305-G.

No. 23 COPPER-LINED WOOD CISTERN.

Dimensions, 24 × 14 × 10 inches deep; capacity, eight gallons.

Can be made any size required to order.

To be operated by Pull, and for use over any form of Flushing-rim Hopper or Bowl.

DEMAREST'S PATENT CISTERNS FOR WATER CLOSETS.

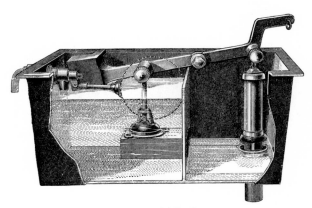

PLATE 306-G.

No. 11 AFTER-WASH WASTE-PREVENTING IRON CISTERN, PAINTED
GALVANIZED OR PORCELAIN-LINED.

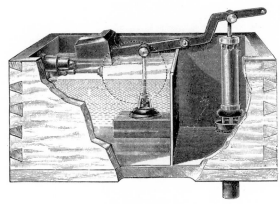

PLATE 307-G.

No. 11 AFTER-WASH WASTE-PREVENTING COPPER-LINED WOOD
CISTERN.

Dimensions, $24 \times 14 \times 11$ inches deep.

To be operated by Seat Action, and for use over Wash-out Closets and Flushing-rim Hoppers.

The illustrations show the Cistern as when the Closet is not in use. When Seat is depressed, water passes from the Left-hand Compartment to the Right until it is on a level in both; when Seat is relieved, the water in Right-hand Compartment descends and flushes the Closet.

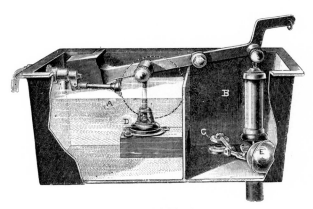

PLATE 308-G.

No. 11½ FORE-AND-AFTER-WASH WASTE-PREVENTING IRON CISTERN,
PAINTED, GALVANIZED OR PORCELAIN-LINED.

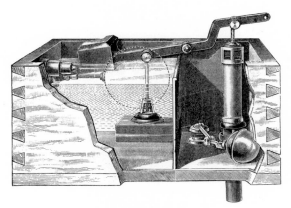

PLATE 309-G.

No. 11½ FORE-AND-AFTER-WASH WASTE-PREVENTING COPPER-LINED
WOOD CISTERN.

Dimensions, $24 \times 14 \times 11$ inches deep.

To be operated by Seat Action, and for use over Flushing-rim Hoppers.

THE illustrations show the Cistern as when Closet is not in use; when Seat is depressed, water passes from Compartment A to Compartment B; a measured quantity of from ½ to 1 gallon then descends to the Hopper, constituting the preliminary wash; as Valve D is larger than Valve C, the water in Compartment B quickly rises and with it the Float E; this closes Valve C and the water in Compartment B rises to the level of that in Compartment A. When Seat is relieved, the water in Compartment B descends and flushes the Closet.

A prejudice has been entertained by many against Automatic Water Closets to be operated by the Seat, on the ground that they are very liable to derangement; this is due in a great measure to the complicated construction of the After-wash and Fore-and-after-wash Cisterns, especially the latter. A glance will show that the Nos. 11 and 11½ Cisterns are exceedingly simple in operation, without any delicate mechanism to get out of order, and they require no nice adjustment of the Chain to insure their working properly; moreover, they are made in the *very best* manner and the result is that among the many thousands sold we have yet to hear of one not giving satisfaction.

DEMAREST'S PATENT CISTERNS FOR WATER CLOSETS.

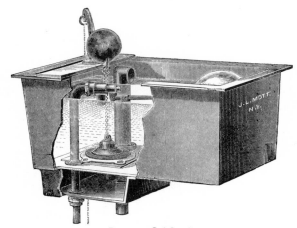

PLATE 310-G.

No. 2 IRON CISTERN, PAINTED, GALVANIZED OR PORCELAIN-LINED.

No. 2 Cistern, 24 × 14 × 10 in. deep; Service Box, 10 × 10 × 3 in. deep.
" 2½ " 30 × 13 × 14 " " 10 × 10 × 3 "

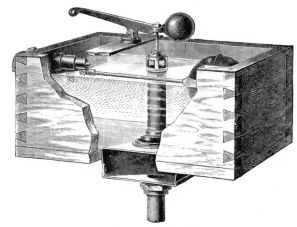

PLATE 311-G.

No. 2 COPPER-LINED WOOD CISTERN.

No. 2 Cistern, 24 × 14 × 10 in. deep; Service Box, 10 × 10 × 3 in. deep.
" 2½ " 30 × 13 × 14 " " 10 × 10 × 3 "

The Nos. 2 and 2½ Cisterns are for use over our Side-outlet Plunger Closets, the "Hygeia" and "Simplex."

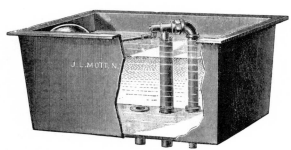

PLATE 312-G.

No. 7 IRON CISTERN, PAINTED, GALVANIZED OR PORCELAIN-LINED.

No. 7. Size, 24 × 14 × 10 inches deep; capacity, 8 gallons.
" 8. " 30 × 13 × 14 " " 18 "

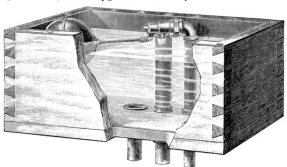

PLATE 313-G.

No. 7 COPPER-LINED WOOD CISTERN.

No. 17. Size, 40 × 13 × 14 inches deep; capacity, 25 gallons.
" 18. " 45 × 13 × 14 " " 30 "

The above Cistern is intended for use over Valve Closets or any fixture where the supply is controlled by Valve attached to the fixture itself.

PLATE 314-G.

COPPER SERVICE BOX WITH 4 INCH VALVE AND OVERFLOW.

Size of Service Box, 9×9×3¼ in. deep, not including Flange; Overflow, 13½ inches high, but can be lengthened or shortened to order.

PLATE 315-G

IRON SERVICE BOX WITH 4-INCH VALVE AND OVERFLOW.

Size of Service Box, 12½ × 11 in., including 1⅛ in. Flange all around, by 3½ in. deep; Height of Overflow, 13½ in., but can be lengthened or shortened to order.

PLATE 316-G.

Section showing Iron or Copper Service Box fitted in Copper lined Wood Cistern. Suited for use with either Plunger or Wash-out Closets.

FITTINGS FOR COPPER OR LEAD LINED WOOD CISTERNS.

PLATE 317-G.

1¼ INCH VALVE, OVERFLOW AND LEVER,
With Patent Noiseless Attachment.
For use over Flushing-rim Hoppers and Bowls.

PLATE 318-G.

1¼ INCH VALVE, COUPLING
AND CHAIN.

PLATE 319-G.

1¼ INCH VALVE, OVERFLOW AND LEVER,
With Combined Re-fill and Noiseless Attachment.
For use over Wash-out Closets.

PLATE 320-G.

FOUR INCH VALVE.
For Cistern with Service Box.

PLATE 321-G.

BALL COCK AND BALL.

Size, ½ inch Ball Cock with 5 inch Ball.
  ''   ½   ''   ''   '' 6 ''   ''
  ''   ⅝   ''   ''   '' 6 ''   ''
  ''   ¾   ''   ''   '' 8 ''   ''

PLATE 322-G.

CAST IRON LEVER.
Painted or Galvanized.

PLATE 323-G.

DEMAREST'S PATENT NO. 4 SYPHON VALVE AND LEVER.
For use over Hoppers.

Drawing down the Pull and releasing it at
once starts the Syphon, and contents of Cistern
pass to Closet.

PLATE 324-G.

FOUR INCH VALVE AND OVERFLOW.

Overflow, 13½ inches long, but can
be lengthened or shortened.
For Cistern with Service Box.

PLATE 325-G.

DEMAREST'S PATENT NO. 4½ SYPHON VALVE AND LEVER.
For use over Wash-out Closets.

Drawing down the Pull and releasing it at once
starts the Syphon, and contents of Cistern descend to
Closet. The re-fill to Bowl is obtained by the Slot in
Syphon, which causes the latter to break gradually.

Valve Hopper Closets, Porcelain-Lined,
WITH DEMAREST'S PATENT DOUBLE OR SINGLE ACTING VALVE.

VALVE HOPPER CLOSETS are comparatively inexpensive and when supplied by a pressure of over twenty pounds give general satisfaction; when the pressure is less than twenty pounds, however, any of the various forms of Cistern Hopper Closets illustrated on previous pages, is preferable.

 The Demarest Patent Valve, as used on the Hopper Closets illustrated on the following pages, is *double acting*, that is, it washes the Hopper when the Seat is pressed down and gives a full wash when the Seat is allowed to rise. If *single action* is required, that is, if it is desired that Valve should run all the time Seat is pressed down, take off the Cap with a pair of plyers, unscrew the Flange Nut inside, and take out the Leather Washer, then replace the Nut and screw down the Cap firmly.

PLATE 326-G
FLUSHING-RIM OVAL HOPPER AND TRAP,
With Self-raising Seat and ¾ inch Double-acting Valve.
Also furnished with Trap having Spigot End to caulk into Hub of Iron Waste Pipe, or with ¾ S or ½ S Trap.

PLATE 327-G.
FLUSHING-RIM LONG OVAL HOPPER,
With Self-raising Seat and ¾ inch Double-acting Valve.

PLATE 328-G.
HOPPER AND TRAP,
With Round Self-raising Seat and ½ inch Double-acting Valve.
Also furnished with Trap having Spigot End to caulk into Hub of Iron Waste Pipe, or with ¾ S or ½ S Trap.

PLATE 329-G.
HOPPER AND TRAP,
With Round Self-raising Seat and ½ inch Double-acting Valve.

Valve Hopper Closets, Porcelain-Lined,

WITH DEMAREST'S PATENT DOUBLE OR SINGLE ACTING VALVE.

PLATE 330-G.

HOPPER AND TRAP,

With Square Self-raising Seat and ½ inch Double-acting Valve.

PLATE 331-G.

HOPPER AND TRAP,

With Square Self-raising Seat and ½ inch Double-acting Valve.

Also furnished with Trap having Spigot End to caulk into Hub of Iron Waste Pipe, or with ¾ S or ½ S Trap.

PLATE 332-G.

LONG HOPPER,

With Round Self-raising Seat and ½ inch Double-acting Valve.

PLATE 333-G.

LONG HOPPER,

With Square Self-raising Seat and ½ inch Double-acting Valve.

VALVE HOPPER CLOSETS, PORCELAIN-LINED AND PAINTED IRON.

PLATE 334-G.

FLUSHING-RIM LONG ROUND HOPPER, WITH HARDWOOD SEAT
AND DOUBLE-ACTING CONCEALED VALVE.

PLATE 335-G.

FLUSHING-RIM OVAL HOPPER AND ¾ S TRAP, WITH HARDWOOD SEAT
AND DOUBLE-ACTING CONCEALED VALVE.

Also furnished with ½ S or Full S Trap.

The Valve of above Closets being arranged at the back and entirely out of sight renders them very desirable for Prison or Hospital use.
The Seat is not self-raising and has only play enough to work Valve.

PLATE 336-G.

HOPPER AND TRAP WITH ROUND SELF-RAISING SEAT, WITHOUT
VALVE, BUT WITH FAN AND COUPLING.

Also furnished with Trap for Iron Waste Pipe Connection, or
with ¾ S or ½ S Trap.

Seat can be furnished Square instead of Round as shown by
Plate 337-G.

PLATE 337-G.

LONG HOPPER WITH SQUARE SELF-RAISING SEAT, WITHOUT VALVE
BUT WITH FAN AND COUPLING.

Seat can be furnished Round instead of Square as shown by
Plate 336-G.

Demarest's Patent Water Closets and Wash Basins for Prisons.

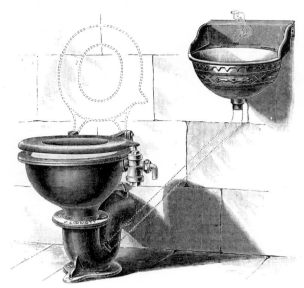

PLATE 338-G.

Porcelain lined Iron Oval Flushing-rim Hopper and Trap,

With ¾ inch Double-acting Valve, Hardwood or Cast Iron Seat, and Porcelain-lined Iron Wash Basin with Brass Plug and Rubber Stopper.

The above is a very desirable and complete apparatus, the extra large Valve and Flushing-rim giving a good large wash under ordinary pressure.

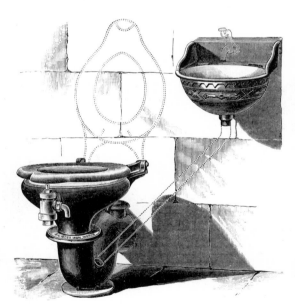

PLATE 339-G.

Porcelain-lined Iron Round Hopper and Trap,

With ½ inch Double-acting Valve, Cast Iron or Hardwood Seat, and Porcelain-lined Iron Wash Basin with Brass Plug and Rubber Stopper.

WE can furnish the Trap on either of above with Outlet End of any desired length where it is desired to run through wall to connect with Soil Pipe; also furnished with ¾ S or S Trap. The Handhole is bolted to Trap so that prisoners cannot remove it. The Trap may be tapped on either right or left side.

With our Double-acting Valve a preliminary flush is obtained when Seat is depressed and the after or main flush when Seat is relieved.

The above cuts show Hopper and Basin as lately put in some of the largest Prisons throughout the country. The dotted line indicates the Wrought Iron Pipe connecting the Wash Basin with Trap of Hopper. Some are used with Telegraph Faucet in Back as shown in above cut; we also furnish them with Hole in Slab, so that any other Self-closing Faucet can be used.

DEMAREST'S PATENT WATER CLOSETS FOR PRISONS.

PLATE 340-G.

INTERIOR OF PRISON CELLS,

Illustrating Hopper Closet and Wash Basin.   The Hopper Closet used may be as shown by Plate 338–G or Plate 339–G, or Long Flushing-rim Hopper
to be flushed by Stop Cock.

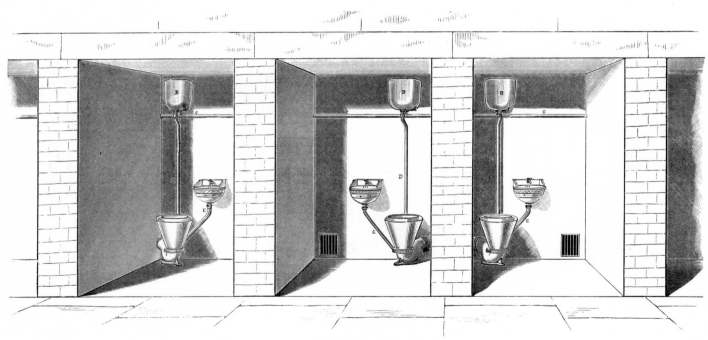

PLATE 341-G.

INTERIOR OF PRISON CELLS,

Illustrating Porcelain-lined Iron Flushing-rim Hopper and Trap with Hardwood Rim, Demarest's Patent Automatic Flushing Cistern, and
Porcelain-lined Wash Basin.

WITH this apparatus the Hoppers are flushed at desired intervals by the jailer, who turns on the supply to Cisterns, which fill to a certain
height and then discharge their contents to the Hoppers; or the Hoppers may be flushed automatically by allowing a small steady
supply to pass to the Cisterns, the intervals of flushing being governed by the size of supply.

PLATE 342-G.

IMPORTED PORCELAIN ROUND CLOSET BOWL.

FLATE 343-G.

IMPORTED PORCELAIN PHILADELPHIA HOPPER.

Height, 14½ inches; diameter on top, 13¼ inches;
outlet, 4 inches; diameter across flange, 6½ inches.

PLATE 344-G.

IRON CLOSET BOWL,

Plain, Painted and Porcelain-lined.

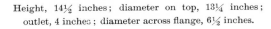

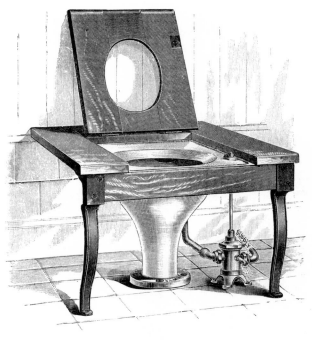

PLATE 345-G.

IMPORTED PORCELAIN PHILADELPHIA HOPPER,

With Double-acting Valve, Black Walnut Seat with Painted Legs,
and Enameled Cast Iron Slop Safe.

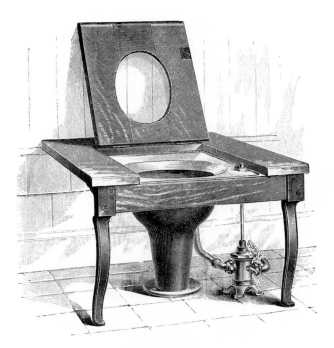

PLATE 346-G.

PORCELAIN-LINED IRON PHILADELPHIA HOPPER,

With Double-acting Valve, Black Walnut Seat with Painted Legs,
and Enameled Cast Iron Slop Safe.

The Seat is 24 inches square; it will be furnished of either Cherry or Ash, if so ordered.

THE Double-acting Valve gives a preliminary wash when seat is depressed, and the main wash when seat is relieved. The Valve can be placed underground away from the frost by using a longer rod; the drip pipe will allow the water in Supply Pipe between Valve and Hopper to pass out. When Slop Safe is not used a guide for the rod is attached to the seat.

Supplied under a good pressure the above makes a cheap and effective Water Closet.

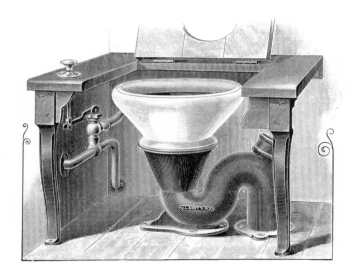

PLATE 347-G.

ROUND CLOSET BOWL ON COMBINED HOPPER STAND AND S TRAP,

With Self-closing Hopper Cock.

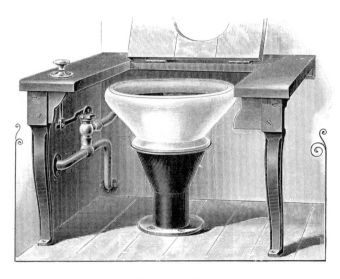

PLATE 348-G.

ROUND CLOSET BOWL ON HOPPER STAND,

With Self-closing Hopper Cock.

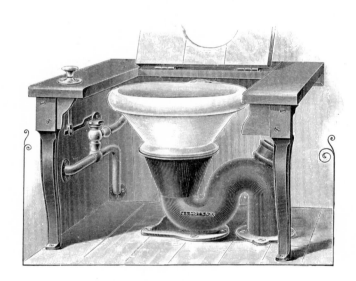

PLATE 349-G.

OVAL FLUSHING RIM CLOSET BOWL ON COMBINED HOPPER STAND AND S TRAP,

With Self-closing Hopper Cock.

PLATE 350-G.

OVAL FLUSHING RIM CLOSET BOWL ON HOPPER STAND,

With Self-closing Hopper Cock.

The Hopper Stand can be furnished with Vent if so ordered.

The Trap of Plates 349-G and 347-G can be furnished with Spigot End for Iron Pipe Connection if so ordered.

Supplied under a good pressure the above make a cheap and effective Water Closet.

HOPPER TRAPS, PLAIN, PAINTED OR PORCELAIN-LINED IRON.

PLATE 351-G.

SHORT HOPPER AND S TRAP,

For Iron Pipe Connection.

Can be furnished with Trap for Lead Pipe Connection as Plate 352-G
if so ordered, or with ¾ or ½ S Trap.

PLATE 352-G.

OVAL CLOSET BOWL AND S TRAP,

For Lead Pipe Connection.

Can be furnished with Trap for Iron Pipe Connection as Plate 351-G,
if so ordered or with ¾ or ½ S Trap.

PLATE 353-G.

S HOPPER TRAP FOR LEAD PIPE CONNECTION.
4-inch.

PLATE 354-G.

S HOPPER TRAP FOR IRON PIPE CONNECTION.
4-inch.

PLATE 355-G.

¾ S HOPPER TRAP.
4-inch.

PLATE 356-G.

½ S HOPPER TRAP.

4-inch.

PLATE 357-G.

S HOPPER TRAP FOR LEAD PIPE CONNECTION.

With 2-inch Inlet on right or left side ; 4-inch.

Can be furnished for Iron Pipe Connection as
Plate 354–G, if so ordered.

PLATE 358-G.

S HOPPER TRAP FOR LEAD PIPE CONNECTION.

With 2-inch Inlet in Heel : 4-inch.

Can be furnished for Iron Pipe Connection, as
Plate 354–G, if so ordered.

The above Traps can be furnished with Hub for Vent, instead of Hand Hole, if so ordered.

HOPPERS.

PLATE 359-G.

PHILADELPHIA HOPPER,

Plain, Painted and Porcelain-lined.

Height, 16 inches; diameter on top, 14 inches; outlet, 4 inches.

PLATE 360-G.

PHILADELPHIA HOPPER,

Plain, Painted and Porcelain-lined.

With Lugs for Seat Attachment and Guide for Valve Rod.

PLATE 361-G.

MOTT HOPPER,

With Side or Straight Arm; Plain, Painted and Porcelain-lined.

Height, 16½ inches; diameter on top, 14 inches; outlet, 4 inches.

PLATE 362-G

ENGLISH HOPPER,

Straight Arm; Plain, Painted and Porcelain-lined.

Height, 17 inches; diameter on top, 14 inches; outlet, 4 inches.

PLATE 363-G.

CAR HOPPER,

Springfield Pattern, Plain, Painted and Porcelain-lined.

Height, 16 inches; diameter on top, 12½ × 11½ inches; outlet, 6 × 4 inches.

PLATE 364-G.

OLD PATTERN HOPPER,

Straight Arm; Plain, Painted and Porcelain-lined.

Height, 16 inches; diameter on top, 12½ inches; outlet, 4 inches.

MOTT'S SLOP SAFES FOR WATER CLOSETS.

PLATE 365-G.

PORCELAIN OVAL SLOP SAFE.

PLATE 366-G.

PORCELAIN ROUND SLOP SAFE.

The above is of the finest Imported Ware, and the only one to use in really fine work.

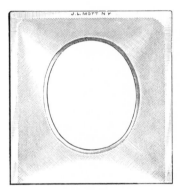

PLATE 367-G.

ENAMELED WROUGHT IRON OVAL SLOP SAFE.

PLATE 368-G.

ENAMELED WROUGHT IRON ROUND SLOP SAFE.

We present the above as far superior in every way to any Wrought Iron Slop Safe in the market. The enameling is perfect and cannot be cracked or broken off; it is also made to dip towards the Closet same as in the Porcelain and Cast Iron.

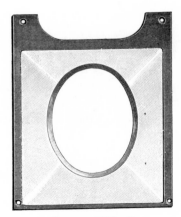

PLATE 369-G.

ENAMELED CAST IRON OVAL SLOP SAFE.

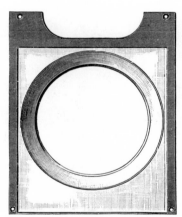

PLATE 370-G.

ENAMELED CAST IRON ROUND SLOP SAFE.

The above is so well known that no remarks are necessary; suffice it to say that in all work where strength and durability are desired it is without an equal.

Mott's Patent Latrines.

Plate 371-G.

Latrines with Valve Section.

T HE Valve Section contains the Supply Valve and Discharge Plug, which is also the Overflow.   When Plug is raised to allow the Soil to
      pass off, the Supply is opened by the dropping of the Float, and each Latrine is washed the same as in a Water Closet.   When the Plug
is dropped in its seat, after the discharge, the Latrines are again filled with water, as shown by Plate 372-G.   Outlet of Valve Section, 6 inches.

      Each Latrine is cast in one piece, and is furnished Painted or Porcelain-lined throughout.   Any number can be used together in a row,
one Valve Section being required for one Latrine, or any number from one to eight.

      If necessary the Valve Section can be put in, so that it can be locked up, and be accessible only to the janitor or person in charge,
who can let off the soil daily or oftener if necessary.

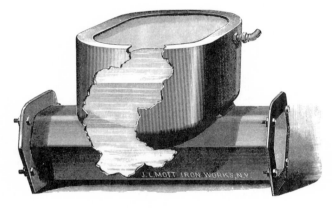

Plate 372-G.

Sectional View of Latrine.

Showing amount of water carried in each Latrine.

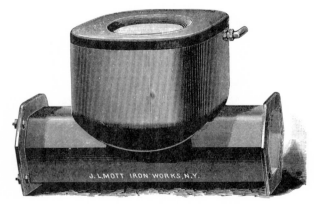

Plate 373-G.

Latrine with Black Walnut, Cherry or Ash Seat.

The above makes a very complete finish without any further wood-work.

L ATRINES are 24 inches from flange to flange, or 24 inches from center to center, but can be increased to any length by using Extension
      Pieces, as shown on next page.   Latrine is $18 \times 14\frac{1}{2}$; this gives a large water surface, and when hole is cut in wood seat, say 10×8,
      no soil can strike the sides of Latrine.   Hole should be kept well to front, say $5\frac{1}{2}$ inches from back and $2\frac{1}{2}$ inches from front.   Height
of Latrine from floor, 17 inches.

Mott's Patent Latrines.

PLATE 374-G.

Latrine with Iron Seat and Cover.

For Prison use.

The hole in Seat is 10×5 inches.

PLATE 375-G.

Blank End.

A Blank End is required for every row of Latrines.

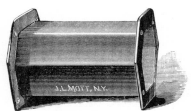

PLATE 376-G.

Extension Piece.

6, 9, 12, 15, 18, 21, 24, 27, 30, 36 inches long. Any other length made to order.

PLATE 377-G.

Blank End with Coupling.

For use when the discharge of contents of Latrines is to be aided by a separate stream of water entering at end of line.

PLATE 378-G.

Quarter Bend.

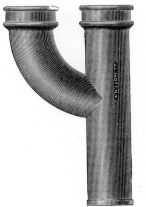

PLATE 379-G.

H Branch.

To connect Latrine Valve Section to Vertical Pipe. Sizes, 6×6 and 8×6.

When a number of Latrines, say eight or more, are to be connected with one Valve Section, it is necessary to facilitate the outgo of contents of Latrines by means of a separate Supply Pipe entering the Blank End at end of line—see Plate 377-G. This Supply Pipe may be ¾-inch, 1-inch, or 1¼-inch, depending upon the pressure and the number of Latrines; it is operated by a Stop Cock, which is opened by the janitor every time he flushes the Latrines.

Note.—When ordering be sure to state whether the Valve Section is on the right or left hand side as you look at Latrines.

MOTT'S PRIVY SINKS.

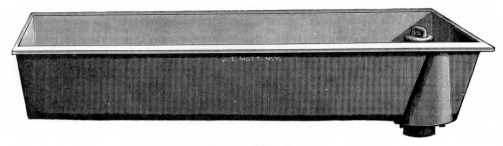

PLATE 380-G.

No. 1 Privy Sink with Patent Overflow Plug.

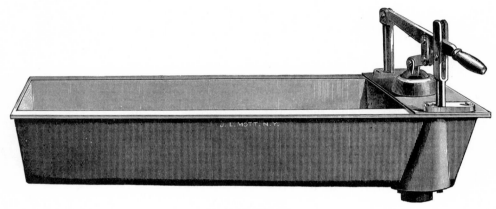

PLATE 381-G.

No. 1 Privy Sink with Patent Overflow Plug and Lever Attachment.

DIMENSIONS OF NO. 1 PRIVY SINKS.

2 feet 3 inches, one section.		13 feet, two sections.		24 feet, three sections.	
4 "	"	14 "	"	25 "	"
4½ "	"	15 "	"	26 "	"
5 "	"	16 "	"	27 "	"
6 "	"	17 "	"	28 "	"
7 "	"	18 "	"	29 "	"
8 "	"	19 "	"	30 "	"
9 "	"	20 "	"	31 "	"
10 "	"	21 "	"	32 "	"
11 "	"	22 "	"	33 "	"
12 "	"	23 "	"	34 "	"
		23½ "	"	35 "	"
				36 "	"

Width, including Flange, 16 inches; depth at plug end, 13 inches; outlet 4 inches, but can be made 6 inches to order.

The above Privy Sinks will be furnished with Strainer in front of Plug if so ordered.

Mott's Privy Sinks.

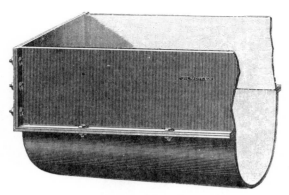

PLATE 382-G.

SECTIONAL EXTENSION PLATES FOR NOS. 1, 2 AND 3 PRIVY SINKS.

Height, 18 inches.

PLATE 383-G.

No. 2 AND No. 3 PRIVY SINKS WITH PATENT OVERFLOW PLUG.

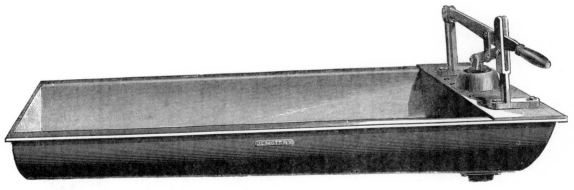

PLATE 384-G.

No. 2 AND No. 3 PRIVY SINKS WITH PATENT OVERFLOW PLUG AND LEVER ATTACHMENT.

DIMENSIONS OF No. 2 AND No. 3 PRIVY SINKS

Length, 6 feet, one section.	Length, 13 feet, two sections.
" 7 " "	" 14 " "
" 8 " "	" 15 " "
" 9 " "	" 16 " "
" 10 " "	" 17 " "
" 11 " "	" 18 " "
" 12 " "	

No. 2.— Width including Flange, 31 inches ; depth at Plug end, 12 inches ; outlet 4 inches, but can be made 6 inches to order.

No. 3.— " " " 28 " " " 12 " " 4 " " " 6

Demarest's Wash-out Water Closet Range.

PATENT APPLIED FOR.

With Patent Automatic or Ready-Supply Cistern.

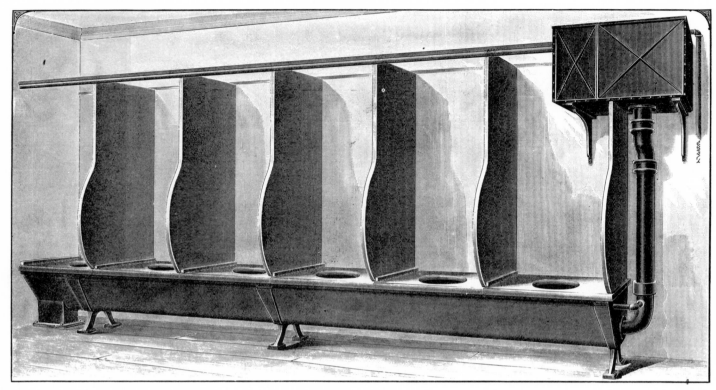

PLATE 385-G.

ILLUSTRATION represents the Wash-out Water Closet Range set up with Automatic Cistern and Wood-work complete. The Wood-work can be modified or changed in any way to suit circumstances, by parties putting up; for instance, if more seclusion is desired, the partitions can be carried to the floor and each compartment furnished with a door same as in the ordinary water closet. The width of seat, *i. e.* from centre of partition to centre of partition, is 2 feet, but can be furnished wider if desired, say 2 feet 3 inches, or 2 feet 6 inches. Of course, the wider the seats the fewer there will be on the same length of Range. The extreme length of Range is ten 2-feet seats, which give a total length of 20 feet; nine 2-feet 3-inch seats, which give a total of 20 feet 3 inches; or eight 2-feet 6-inch seats, giving a total of 20 feet. These lengths do not include, say, 9 inches required at end for Flush-pipe. The Range can be furnished any less length required.

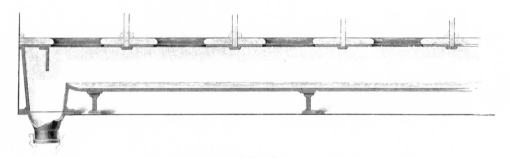

PLATE 386-G.

The above longitudinal section shows the Outlet, which is furnished to connect with 6-inch Soil Pipe. Water covers the entire bottom to depth of about 1½ inches.

PLATE 387-G.

The above cross section shows the auxiliary Flushing-pipe, which thoroughly washes the front of Range every time Cistern operates.

AS shown by the above sectional cuts, the Range is entirely of cast iron and is furnished painted or porcelain-lined throughout. The cover or seat, upon which is laid the wood seat, is cast iron, painted or porcelain-lined underneath, so that all parts of the inside of the Range which comes in any way in contact with the water are non-absorbent. This is a very important feature, and when taken in connection with the perfect and thorough flush renders this one of the most desirable sanitary apparatus in the market for use in schools, factories and other public places. The patent automatic Flushing Cistern, which can be regulated to go off at any stated interval, is of great power and will thoroughly cleanse the Range every time; the Flushing-pipe placed immediately under the seat, as shown by Section Plate 387-G, washes the front of Range so that no urine or other matter can adhere. For six seats, or over, the size of Flush Tank is 27 × 18 inches, under six seats 18 × 18 inches; this Tank is very simple and wonderfully effective, and will be found fully described on subsequent pages of this Catalogue, under heading "Demarest's Patent Flush Tanks." If preferred, we can furnish the Range with a Ready-supply Cistern, *i. e.* a Cistern with Ball-cock Supply, also subsequently described, and to be operated by janitor or person in charge at such intervals as may be deemed necessary. Of course, this Cistern being supplied with a Ball Cock will always be full of water, and ready to be discharged at any time.

Mott's All-Porcelain Open Bidet.

PATENT APPLIED FOR.

PLATE 388-G.

THE above illustration shows the All-porcelain Bidet with fittings for hot and cold supply, also hardwood seat and cover with marble floor slab. It can be furnished complete, or with the supply fittings only, *i. e.* without the wood-work or floor slab.

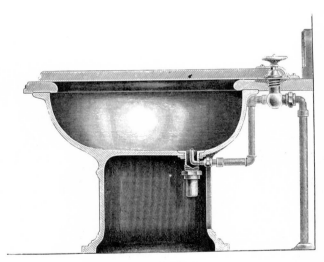

PLATE 389-G.

SHOWING SECTION OF ALL-PORCELAIN BIDET.

NO well appointed private Bath room is complete without a Bidet, and the only reason, we imagine, why it has been in so many instances left out, is because of the difficulty and expense of fitting up the ordinary Bidet Pan in cabinet work to make it a sightly, cleanly and handsome fixture. The above is one piece of porcelain ware, and can be furnished either pure white or tinted a delicate ivory. It can also be decorated in gold, the fittings can be furnished in polished, nickel or silver-plated brass, or with ivory-celluloid handles. In short, it is a most complete and handsome fixture, and, as we have already remarked, should be a prominent feature in all fine private work.

BIDETS.

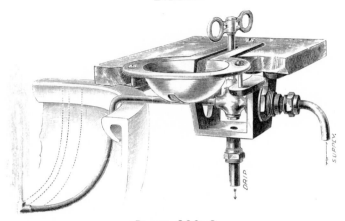

PLATE 390-G.

MOTT'S PATENT BIDET.

For use with any Water Closet.

The illustration shows the Bidet turned down into the Bowl ready for use.   The cup and all exposed parts are nickel or silver-plated.

PLATE 391-G.

IMPORTED PORCELAIN BIDET PAN.

To be used with fittings as per Plate 392-G.   When it is desired to retain
water in the Pan we furnish Standing Overflow Plug to order.

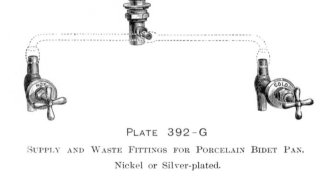

PLATE 392-G

SUPPLY AND WASTE FITTINGS FOR PORCELAIN BIDET PAN.

Nickel or Silver-plated.

PLATE 393-G.

CASE FOR BIDET PAN.

Black Walnut. Cherry or Ash.

PLATE 394-G.

CASE FOR BIDET PAN.   EASTLAKE DESIGN.

Black Walnut, Cherry or Ash.

WASH BASINS.

PLATE 395-G.

OVAL WASH BASIN, NO OVERFLOW.

Three sizes: 17 × 14, 19 × 15 and 21 × 16, outside the flange.

PLATE 396-G.

OVAL WASH BASIN WITH COMMON OVERFLOW.

Three sizes: 17 × 14, 19 × 15 and 21 × 16, outside the flange.

Marbleized, White or Ivory-tinted.

PLATE 397-G.

COMMON OVERFLOW ROUND BASIN.

Sizes: 12, 13, 14, 15 and 16 inches.

Marbleized or White.

PLATE 398-G.

PATENT OVERFLOW ROUND BASIN.

Sizes: 12, 13, 14, 15 and 16 inches.

Marbleized.

PLATE 399-G.

PATENT OVERFLOW ROUND BASIN FOR RUBBER PLUG.

Sizes: 12, 13, 14, 15 and 16 inches.

Marbleized.

All our Wash Basins are of the finest imported ware, warranted not to craze or discolor.

THE "UNIQUE" BASIN WASTE.

FOR NO-OVERFLOW AND COMMON OVERFLOW BASIN.

PATENTED.

PLATE 400-G.

THE "UNIQUE" WASTE, FOR NO-OVERFLOW BASIN.

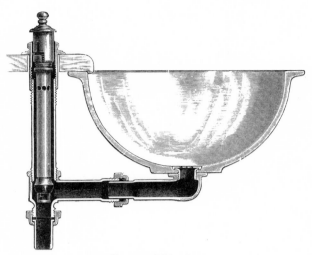

PLATE 401-G.

SECTION SHOWING "UNIQUE" WASTE FITTED TO NO-OVERFLOW BASIN, WITH STAND PIPE RAISED, AS WHEN WATER IS BEING LET OUT OF BASIN.

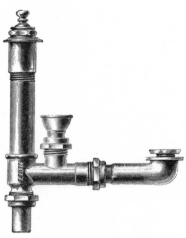

PLATE 402-G.

THE "UNIQUE" WASTE, FOR COMMON OVERFLOW BASIN.

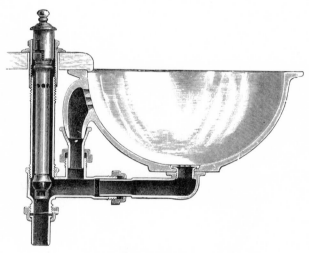

PLATE 403-G

SECTION SHOWING "UNIQUE" WASTE FITTED TO COMMON OVERFLOW BASIN, AND WITH STAND PIPE RAISED, AS WHEN WATER IS BEING LET OUT OF BASIN.

T H E "Unique" Waste is without doubt the most complete, the simplest, the cleanliest, and the very best device ever made for connecting and controlling the overflow and waste of a Wash Basin. As shown by the above cuts, the "Unique" is adjustable in all its parts, that is, it can be used with any thickness of marble, and adjusted to overcome any variation in size of Wash Basins. *The Stand Pipe can be taken out and cleaned with the same facility as an open Standing Waste, and without the use of any tool whatever.*

THE "DUPLEX" BASIN WASTE.

PATENTED.

PLATE 404-G.

THE "DUPLEX" WASTE, FOR COMMON OVERFLOW BASIN.

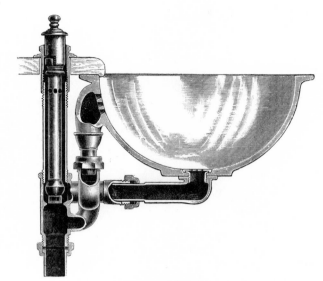

PLATE 405-G.

SECTION SHOWING "DUPLEX" WASTE FITTED TO COMMON OVERFLOW BASIN,
WITH STAND PIPE RAISED, AS WHEN WATER IS BEING LET OUT OF BASIN.

THE "Duplex" is essentially the same as the "Unique" for Common Overflow Basin, only, in the "Duplex" the connection with the overflow of Basin is carried under, and enters the Waste Pipe beneath the plug seat of "Unique" Waste, virtually making a double overflow. The water-way is also enlarged, in order to take care of both overflows. It is well known that, under a heavy pressure, the water entering a basin from two faucets, carelessly turned on, will not be carried off by an overflow of ordinary capacity. Of course, this rarely, if ever, happens in private work, but might occur in hotels or other large public buildings. The "Duplex" is intended to be used where it is desired to guard against an overflow under the circumstances described, and for that purpose is unequalled.

MOTT'S FLUSHING-RIM BASINS.

PATENT APPLIED FOR.

PLATE 406-G.

THE "CAMBRIDGE" OVAL FLUSHING-RIM BASIN WITH SUPPLY
FITTINGS AND "UNIQUE" WASTE.

One size, 19×15 inches outside the flange; marbleized or ivory-tinted.

In the "Cambridge" Basin the hot and cold water must mix before entering the basin, where it is distributed over the interior by the Flushing rim. The "Cambridge" has the advantage of doing away with the protruding shanks of the ordinary basin faucets. It is very attractive in appearance, and the Flushing-rim makes it self-cleansing.

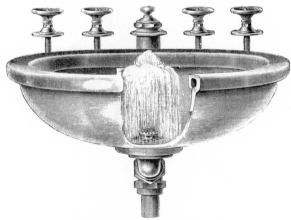

PLATE 407-G.

THE "OXFORD" OVAL FLUSHING-RIM DOUCHE BASIN WITH SUPPLY
FITTINGS AND "UNIQUE" WASTE.

One size, 19×15 inches outside the flange; marbleized or ivory-tinted.

Plate 407-G is the same as Plate 406-G, with the additional feature of the vertical spray. By turning the valves, lettered "hot spray" and "cold spray," a single stream or rose jet, as may be preferred, is thrown up in the centre of basin, as shown by the illustration. This gives a most delightful and refreshing spray bath for the face, and as a douche for weak or tender eyes is invaluable.

MOTT'S PATENT "NONPAREIL" BASIN.

PLATE 408-G.

THE "NONPAREIL" BASIN AND WASTE.

Two sizes: 19 × 15 inches and 17 × 14 inches, outside the flange.

Marbleized, White, Ivory-tinted or Decorated in any of the designs illustrated on subsequent pages.

THE illustration shows the Stand Pipe seated; to empty the Basin the Stand Pipe is raised and given a slight turn to the right or left; a still further turn will permit the Stand Pipe to be taken out and cleaned, without the use of any tool whatever.

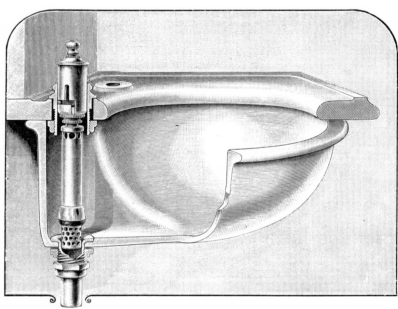

PLATE 409-G.

CROSS SECTION OF "NONPAREIL" BASIN.

Showing Stand Pipe raised as when water is being let out of Basin.

TO those who prefer a Standing Waste in the Basin we offer the above as in every way superior to anything of the kind yet brought out. It is simple, durable, cleanly and handsome to look at, in short, whatever is meritorious in this form of Wash Basin we claim for the "Nonpareil."

Decorated Wash Basins.

Design No. 707.

China Asters.

Design No. 363.

Oriental.

Design No. 616.

Chrysanthemums.

Design No. 684.

Orange.

Design No. 356.

Japanese.

Design No. 685.

Pomegranate.

SIZES:

Oval, 19 × 15 inches outside the flange, no overflow.   Oval, 17 × 14 inches outside the flange, no overflow.
"   19 × 15   "   "   "   "   common overflow.   "   17 × 14   "   "   "   "   common overflow.
Round, 14 inches, common overflow.

When ordering, size of Basin should be mentioned, also whether No Overflow or Common Overflow.

Reproduced in color on Plate B following page 26.

DECORATED WASH BASINS.

DESIGN NO. 285.
QUEEN ANNE

DESIGN NO. 284.
QUEEN ANNE

DESIGN NO. 699.
JAPANESE.

DESIGN NO. 592.
ORCHIDS.

DESIGN NO. 786.
LAUREL.

DESIGN NO. 774.
MORNING GLORIES.

SIZES:

Oval, 19 × 15 inches outside the flange, no overflow.   Oval, 17 × 14 inches outside the flange, no overflow.
"   19 × 15   "   "   "   "   common overflow.   "   17 × 14   "   "   "   "   common overflow.
Round, 14 inches, common overflow.

When ordering, size of Basin should be mentioned, also whether No Overflow or Common Overflow.

Reproduced in color on Plate C following page 26.

DECORATED WASH BASINS.

DESIGN NO. 480.

PEAR BLOSSOM.

DESIGN NO. 485.

JAPANESE QUINCE.

DESIGN NO. 479.

WILD ASTER.

DESIGN NO. 593.

ORCHID.

DESIGN NO. 544.

PRIMROSE.

DESIGN NO. 773.

CRAB APPLE.

SIZES:

Oval, 19 × 15 inches outside the flange, no overflow. Oval, 17 × 14 inches outside the flange, no overflow.
" 19 × 15 " " " " common overflow. " 17 × 14 " " " " common overflow.
Round, 14 inches, common overflow.

When ordering, size of Basin should be mentioned, also whether No Overflow or Common Overflow.

Reproduced in color on Plate D following page 26.

Decorated Wash Basins.

Design No. 698.
Field Daisy.

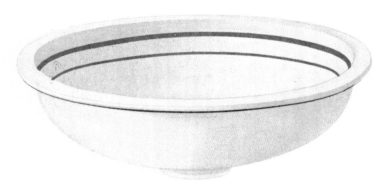

Design No. 1001.
Ivory and Gold.

Design No. 1000.
Plum.

Design No. 783.
Blackberry.

Design No. 66.
Floral.

Design No. 345.
Floral.

SIZES:

Oval, 19 × 15 inches outside the flange, no overflow. Oval, 17 × 14 inches outside the flange, no overflow.
" 19 × 15 " " " " common overflow. " 17 × 14 " " " " common overflow.
Round, 14 inches, common overflow.

When ordering, size of Basin should be mentioned, also whether No Overflow or Common Overflow.

Reproduced in color on Plate E following page 26.

Decorated Wash Basins.

DESIGN No. 652.

DESIGN No. 653.

DESIGN No. 726.

DESIGN No. 703.

DESIGN No. 731.

DESIGN No. 647.

SIZES:

Oval, 19 × 15 inches outside the flange, no overflow.
" 19 × 15 " " " " common overflow.

Oval, 17 × 14 inches outside the flange, no overflow.
" 17 × 14 " " " " common overflow.

Round, 14 inches, common overflow.

When ordering, size of Basin should be mentioned, also whether No Overflow or Common Overflow.

Reproduced in color on Plate F following page 26.

Decorated Wash Basins.

DESIGN NO. 677.

JAPANESE.

DESIGN NO. 493.

FORGET-ME-NOT.

DESIGN NO. 760.

DESIGN NO. 644.

DESIGN NO. 671.

DESIGN NO. 755.

SIZES:

Oval, 19 × 15 inches outside the flange, no overflow.   Oval, 17 × 14 inches outside the flange, no overflow.
" 19 × 15 " " " " common overflow.   " 17 × 14 " " " " common overflow.
Round, 14 inches, common overflow.

When ordering, size of Basin should be mentioned, also whether No Overflow or Common Overflow.

Reproduced in color on Plate G following page 26.

Mott's Open Lavatory.

PLATE 410-G.

Mott's Open Lavatory.

comprising

Marble Slab and Back with Cast Brass Brackets, Oval Wash Basin with "Unique" Waste and Cast Brass Trap, and Improved Faucets with Ebony Handles.   All the Brass Work furnished either Nickel or Silver-plated, or Polished.

THE Marble Slab shown is 33 × 22 inches and the Back 12 inches high, but can be furnished any size to order.   The Oval Basin is furnished in three sizes; it may be marbleized, ivory-tinted or white, or decorated in any of the designs illustrated on previous pages.   The "Unique" Waste is furnished with the Cast Brass Trap as shown, or with Coupling only.

For separate view and description of Basin and Waste, see pages 159, 160 and 161.

If so ordered, Brackets and Faucets as shown by Plate 412-G can be furnished; also Brass Supply and Waste Pipes as shown by Plate 417-G.

Mott's Open Lavatories are designed to meet the prevailing demand for fine plumbing appliances adapted to be fitted up without being encased; they are attractive and artistic in appearance, and fulfil all practical and sanitary requirements.

MOTT'S OPEN LAVATORY.

PLATE 411-G.

MOTT'S OPEN LAVATORY.

COMPRISING

Marble Slab and Back, Marble Front and Side Pieces with Brass Legs, Oval Wash Basin, "Unique" Waste and Cast Brass Trap, Mott's Low-down Faucets with Ivory-celluloid Handles.   All the Brass Work furnished either Nickel or Silver-plated, or Polished.

THE Marble Slab shown is 33 × 22 inches, with 12-inch Back, but any size of Slab or height of Back can be furnished to order ; depth of Front and Side Pieces, 5 inches.   The Oval Basin is furnished in three sizes ; it may be marbleized, ivory-tinted or white, or decorated in any of the designs illustrated on previous pages.   The "Unique" Waste is furnished with Cast Brass Trap as shown, or with Coupling only.

Low-down Faucets are preferred by many, as they are less in the way than the ordinary style of faucet, the discharge end of which projects more or less into the basin.   Our Low-down Faucets as shown above, are a thoroughly well made and durable article ; the handles may be ivory-celluloid or brass.

For separate view and description of Basin and Waste, see pages 159, 160 and 161.

Mott's Open Lavatories are designed to meet the prevailing demand for fine plumbing appliances adapted to be fitted up without being encased ; they are attractive and artistic in appearance, and fulfil all practical and sanitary requirements.

MOTT'S OPEN LAVATORY, THE "NONPAREIL."

PLATE 412-G.

MOTT'S OPEN LAVATORY.

COMPRISING

Marble Slab and Back with Cast Brass Brackets, the "Nonpareil" Oval Wash Basin with Cast Brass Trap, and Improved Faucets with Ebony Handles. All the Brass Work furnished either Nickel or Silver-plated, or Polished.

THE Marble Slab shown is 33 × 22 inches and the Back 12 inches high, but can be made any size to order. The "Nonpareil" Oval Basin is furnished in two sizes, 19 × 15 inches and 17 × 14 inches, outside the flange; it may be marbleized, ivory-tinted or white, or decorated in any of the designs of Oval Basins illustrated on previous pages. The "Nonpareil" Basin is furnished with the Cast Brass Trap as shown, or with Coupling only.

For separate view and description of "Nonpareil" Basin, see page 162.

If so ordered, Brackets and Faucets as shown by Plate 410-G can be furnished.

Mott's Open Lavatories are designed to meet the prevailing demand for fine plumbing appliances adapted to be fitted up without being encased; they are attractive and artistic in appearance, and fulfil all practical and sanitary requirements.

MOTT'S OPEN LAVATORY, "THE NONPAREIL."

PLATE 413-G.

MOTT'S OPEN LAVATORY.

COMPRISING

Marble Slab, Back and Side, with Brass Leg, "Nonpareil" Oval Wash Basin with Cast Brass Trap, Mott's Low-down Faucets with Ivory-celluloid Handles.   All the Brass Work furnished either Nickel or Silver-plated, or Polished.

THE Marble Slab shown is 33 × 22 inches, with 12-inch Back and Side, but any size of Slab or height of Back can be furnished to order. The "Nonpareil" Basin is furnished in two sizes, 19 × 15 and 17 × 14 inches outside the flange; it may be marbleized, ivory-tinted or white, or decorated in any of the designs illustrated on previous pages.   The "Nonpareil" Basin is furnished with Cast Brass Trap as shown, or with Coupling only.

Low-down Faucets are preferred by many, as they are less in the way than the ordinary style of faucet, the discharge end of which projects more or less into the basin.   Our Low-down Faucets as shown above, are a thoroughly well made and durable article; the handles may be ivory-celluloid or brass.

For separate view and description of "Nonpareil" Basin, see page 162.

Brass Waste Pipe as shown, or Supply and Waste Pipe as shown by Plate 417–G, can be furnished if ordered.

Mott's Open Lavatories are designed to meet the prevailing demand for fine plumbing appliances adapted to be fitted up without being encased; they are attractive and artistic in appearance, and fulfil all practical and sanitary requirements.

MOTT'S OPEN LAVATORY, THE "CAMBRIDGE."

PLATE 414-G.

MOTT'S OPEN LAVATORY.

COMPRISING

Marble Slab and Back with Cast Brass Brackets, the "Cambridge" Oval Flushing-rim Basin with Supply, and "Unique" Waste with Cast Brass Trap. All the Brass Work furnished either Nickel or Silver-plated, or Polished.

THE Marble Slab shown is 33 × 22 inches, and the Back is 12 inches high, but any size of Slab or height of Back can be made to order; The "Cambridge" Oval Flushing-rim Basin is 19 × 15 inches outside the flange; it may be marbleized or ivory-tinted, or decorated in any of the designs illustrated on previous pages. The "Unique" Waste is furnished with Cast Brass Trap as shown, or with Coupling only.

For separate view and description of the "Cambridge" Flushing-rim Basin and the "Unique" Waste, see pages 160 and 161.

If so ordered, Brackets as shown by Plate 412-G can be furnished; also Brass Supply and Waste Pipe as shown by Plate 417-G.

Mott's Open Lavatories are designed to meet the prevailing demand for fine plumbing appliances adapted to be fitted up without being encased; they are attractive and artistic in appearance, and fulfil all practical and sanitary requirements.

MOTT'S OPEN LAVATORY, THE "CAMBRIDGE."

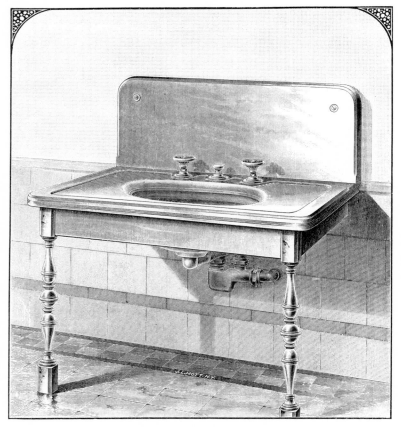

PLATE 415-G.

MOTT'S OPEN LAVATORY.

COMPRISING

Marble Slab and Back, Marble Front and Side Pieces with Brass Legs and the "Cambridge" Oval Flushing-rim Basin and Supply, "Unique" Waste and Cast Brass Trap. All the Brass Work furnished either Nickel or Silver-plated, or Polished.

THE Marble Slab shown is 33 × 22 inches with 12-inch Back, but any size of Slab or height of Back can be furnished to order ; depth of Front and Side Pieces, 5 inches. The "Cambridge" Oval Flushing-rim Basin is 19 × 15 inches outside the flange ; it may be marbleized or ivory-tinted, or decorated in any of the designs illustrated on previous pages. The "Unique" Waste is furnished with Cast Brass Trap as shown, or with Coupling only.

For separate view and description of the "Cambridge" Oval Flushing-rim Basin and the "Unique" Waste, see pages 160 and 161

Brass Supply and Waste Pipes, as shown by Plate 417-G, will be furnished if ordered.

Mott's Open Lavatories are designed to meet the prevailing demand for fine plumbing appliances adapted to be fitted up without being encased ; they are attractive and artistic in appearance, and fulfil all practical and sanitary requirements.

MOTT'S OPEN LAVATORY, THE "OXFORD."

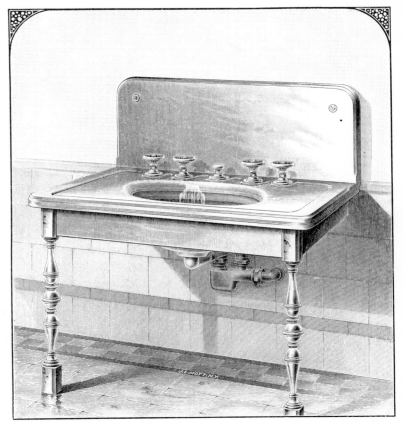

PLATE 416-G.

MOTT'S OPEN LAVATORY.

COMPRISING

Marble Slab and Back, Marble Front and Side Pieces with Brass Legs, and the "Oxford" Oval Flushing-rim Basin with Supply, "Unique" Waste and Cast Brass Trap.   All the Brass Work may be Nickel or Silver-plated, or Polished

THE Marble Slab shown is 33 × 22 inches, and the Back is 12 inches high, but any size of Slab and height of Back can be made to order; the depth of Front and Side Pieces is 5 inches.   The "Oxford" Oval Basin is 19 × 15 inches outside the flange; it may be marbleized or ivory-tinted, or decorated in any of the designs illustrated on previous pages.   The "Unique" Waste is furnished with Cast Brass Trap as shown, or with Coupling only.

The special feature of this Lavatory is the spray or douche; by turning the valves lettered "hot spray" and "cold spray," a douche, or rose jet (as may be preferred), is thrown up in the centre of basin, as shown by the illustration.

For separate view and description of the "Oxford" Flushing-rim Basin and the "Unique" Waste, see pages 160 and 161.

If so ordered, Brackets as shown by Plate 410-G can be furnished

Mott's Open Lavatories are designed to meet the prevailing demand for fine plumbing appliances adapted to be fitted up without being encased; they are attractive and artistic in appearance, and fulfil all practical and sanitary requirements.

MOTT'S OPEN RECESSED LAVATORY.

PLATE 417-G.

MOTT'S OPEN RECESSED LAVATORY.

COMPRISING

Marble Slab with Oval Wash Basin, "Unique" Waste with Cast Brass Trap, Improved Faucets, and Brass Supply and Waste Pipes to floor. All the Brass Work furnished either Nickel or Silver-plated, or Polished.

THE Marble Slab shown is 33 × 22 inches, but can be furnished any size to fit recess. Marble Back and Sides can be furnished when tile is not used. The Oval Wash Basin is furnished in three sizes; it may be marbleized, ivory-tinted or white, or decorated in any of the designs illustrated on previous pages. The "Unique" Waste is furnished with Cast Brass Trap and Pipe as shown, or with Coupling only. The beveled plate glass Mirror, with plate glass or marble shelf, can be furnished to order. The "Nonpareil" Basin, Plate 408-G, the "Cambridge," Plate 406-G, or the "Oxford," Plate 407-G, may be substituted for the Oval Basin shown.

For separate view and description of Basin and Waste, see pages 159, 160, 161 and 162.

Mott's Open Lavatories are designed to meet the prevailing demand for fine plumbing appliances adapted to be fitted up without being encased; they are attractive and artistic in appearance, and fulfil all practical and sanitary requirements.

Mott's Open Lavatory.

FOR USE IN BARBER SHOPS.

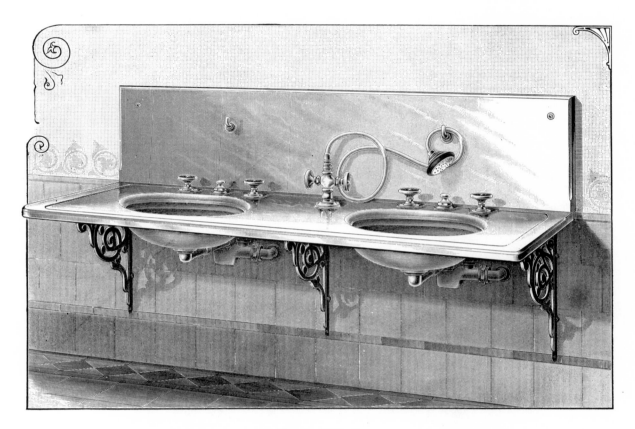

PLATE 418-G.

Mott's Open Lavatory.

COMPRISING

Marble Slab and Back, Cast Brass Brackets, the "Cambridge" Oval Flushing-rim Basin with Supply, Combination Wheel-handle Shampoo Faucet, and "Unique" Waste. All the Brass Work furnished either Nickel or Silver-plated, or Polished.

THE Marble Slab shown is 72 × 22 inches, and the Back is 20 inches high, but any size of Slab or height of Back can be made to order. The "Cambridge" Oval Flushing-rim Basin shown is 19 × 15 inches outside the flange, but extra large size, 21 × 16, can also be furnished; they may be marbleized or ivory-tinted, and the 19 × 15 can be furnished decorated in any of the designs illustrated on previous pages. Any of the Basins and methods of supply shown on previous pages may be used instead of the "Cambridge." The "Unique" Waste is furnished with Cast Brass Trap as shown, or with Coupling only.

For separate view and description of Basin and Waste, see pages 159, 160 and 161.

If so ordered, Brass Legs and Marble Front and Side Pieces, as shown by Plate 416-G can be furnished; also Brass Supply and Waste Pipes as shown by Plate 417-G.

Mott's Open Lavatories are designed to meet the prevailing demand for fine plumbing appliances adapted to be fitted up without being encased; they are attractive and artistic in appearance, and fulfil all practical and sanitary requirements.

Mott's Cabinet Lavatory.

PLATE 419-G.

Wash Stand, "Elizabethan" Design.

COMPRISING

Hand-carved Mahogany Stand and Back with Beveled Plate Glass Mirror. Marble Slab and Oval Wash Basin. "Unique" Waste and Improved Faucets.

No. 1: size, 36 × 22 inches.   No 2: size, 42 × 22 inches.

The "Nonpareil" Oval Basin, Plate 408–G, the "Cambridge" Oval Basin, Plate 406–G, or the "Oxford" Oval Basin, Plate 407–G, may be used instead of the regular Oval as shown.

For separate view and description of Basins and Wastes, see pages 159, 160, 161 and 162.

MOTT'S CABINET LAVATORIES.

PLATE 420-G.

WASH STAND, "EASTLAKE" DESIGN.

COMPRISING

Mahogany, Cherry, Black Walnut or **Ash** Stand with Marble Slab and Back, Oval Wash Basin, "Unique" Waste and Improved Faucets.
Size of Stand, 36 × 22 inches; Back, 15 inches high.

PLATE 421-G.

WASH STAND, "EASTLAKE" DESIGN.

COMPRISING

Black Walnut, Ash, Cherry or **Ebonized Cherry** Stand with Marble Slab and Back, Round or Oval Wash Basin, "Unique" Waste and
Compression Faucets
Size, 36 × 22 inches. Back, 12 inches high.
The **"Nonpareil"** Oval Basin, Plate 408-G, the "Cambridge" Oval Basin, Plate 406-G, or the "Oxford" Oval Basin, Plate 407-G, may be used
instead of those shown above
For separate view and description of Basins and Wastes, see pages 159, 160, 161 and 162.

MOTT'S CABINET LAVATORIES.

PLATE 422-G.
WASH STAND.
COMPRISING

Black Walnut, Cherry or Ash Stand, with Marble Slab and Back, Round or Oval Wash Basin, Nickel-plated Brass Plug with Rubber Stopper, Chain and Stay, and Swing Faucets.
No. 1: size, 30 × 22 inches.   No. 2: size, 33 × 22 inches.   Back, 12 inches high.

PLATE 423-G.
WASH STAND.
COMPRISING

Black Walnut, Cherry or Ash Stand, with Marble Slab and Back, Round or Oval Wash Basin, Nickel-plated Brass Plug with Rubber Stopper, Chain and Stay, and Swing Faucets.
No. 1: size, 33 × 22 inches.   No. 2: size, 36 × 22 inches.   Back, 12 inches high.
The "Nonpareil" Oval Basin, Plate 408-G, the "Cambridge" Oval Basin, Plate 406-G, or the "Oxford" Oval Basin, Plate 407-G, may be used instead of the regular round or oval basin; also "Unique" Waste instead of plug and stopper.

Mott's Cabinet Lavatories

Plate 424-G.

Wash Stand.

COMPRISING

Black Walnut, Cherry or Ash Stand, with Marble Slab and Back, Round or Oval Wash Basin, Nickel-plated Brass Plug with Rubber Stopper, Chain and Stay, and Compression Faucets.

No. 1: size, 30 × 22 inches.   No. 2: size, 33 × 22 inches.   Back, 12 inches high.

Plate 425-G.

Corner Wash Stand.

COMPRISING

Black Walnut, Cherry or Ash Stand, with Marble Slab and Back, Round Wash Basin, Nickel-plated Brass Plug with Rubber Stopper, Chain and Stay, and Compression Faucets.

No. 1: size, 22 inches on side.   No. 2: size, 24 inches on side.   Back, 12 inches high.

MOTT'S PORCELAIN CABINET LAVATORIES.

PLATE 426-G.

PORCELAIN LAVATORY, MARBLEIZED OR IVORY-TINTED.

With Straight-front Oval Basin, "Unique" Waste, and Mott's
Low-down Faucets.

Size 1 : Slab, 27×20 inches ; Basin, 16½×12 inches : Back, 4 inches high.
" 2 :   "   30×22   "   "   19¼×13½ "   "   4   "   "

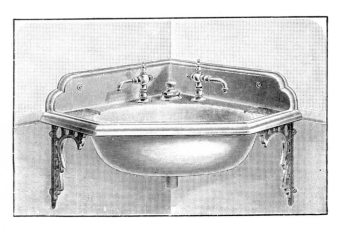

PLATE 427-G.

PORCELAIN CORNER LAVATORY, MARBLEIZED OR IVORY-TINTED.

With Straight-front Oval Basin, Polished or Nickel-plated Cast
Brass Brackets, the " Unique " Waste and Swing Faucets.

Length of Slab across front, 27 inches ; length of side, 20 inches ;
Basin, 17½ × 11 inches ; Back, 4 inches high.

PLATE 428-G.

CABINET LAVATORY.

With Straight-front Oval Basin, the "Unique" Waste, Mott's
Low-down Faucets, and Cherry, Black Walnut, Ash
or Mahogany Stand.

For sizes, see Plate 426-G.

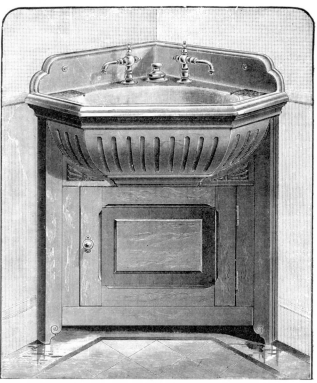

PLATE 429-G.

CABINET LAVATORY FOR CORNER.

With Straight-front Oval Basin, the "Unique" Waste, Swing
Faucets, and Cherry, Black Walnut, Ash
or Mahogany Stand.

For size, see Plate 427-G.

THE illustrations represent a style of Wash Stand that will commend itself to many. In appearance they are neat and attractive, the glazed porcelain Lavatory giving a bright and cleanly effect. The Basin is semi-oval, having a straight front and a dip toward the back where the Waste is located. The Lavatory has a Soap and Tooth Brush Tray, which drain into the Basin.

IMPORTED PORCELAIN LAVATORIES.

PLATE 430-G.

Lavatory with Patent Overflow and one Faucet Hole.

Length of Back, 12 inches; diameter of Basin, 10 inches.

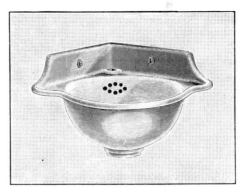

PLATE 431-G.

Corner Lavatory with Patent Overflow and one Faucet Hole.

Length of Side, 12 inches; diameter of Basin, 10 inches.

PLATE 432-G.

Lavatory with Patent Overflow and two Faucet Holes.

Length of Back, 14 inches; diameter of Basin, 11 inches.

PLATE 433-G.

Corner Lavatory with Patent Overflow and two Faucet Holes.

Length of Side, 15 inches; diameter of Basin, 13 inches.

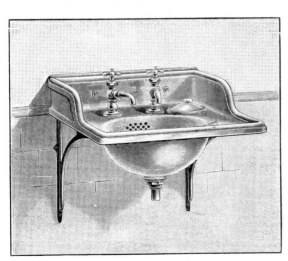

PLATE 434-G.

Lavatory with Patent Overflow, Soap Dish, Bronzed or Galvanized Iron Brackets and Nickel-plated Compression Faucets.

Size of Slab, 18 × 18 inches; diameter of Basin, 11 inches.

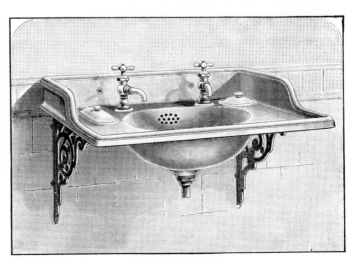

PLATE 435-G.

Lavatory with Patent Overflow, Soap and Tooth Brush Dish, Bronzed or Galvanized Iron Brackets, and Nickel-plated Compression Faucets.

Size of Slab, 24 × 18 inches; size of Oval Basin, 14 × 11 inches.

Imported Porcelain Lavatories.

Plate 436-G.

Lavatory with Patent Overflow, Soap Dish, Black Walnut, Cherry or Ash Stand, Nickel-plated Brass Plug with Rubber Stopper and Nickel-plated Swing Faucets.

Length on side, 19 inches; diameter of Basin, 11 inches.

Plate 437-G.

Lavatory with Patent Overflow, Soap Dish, Black Walnut, Cherry or Ash Stand, Nickel-plated Brass Plug with Rubber Stopper, and Nickel-plated Compression Faucets.

Size, 18 × 18 inches; diameter of Basin, 11 inches.

Plate 438-G.

Lavatory with Patent Overflow Soap Dish, Tooth-brush Dish, Black Walnut, Cherry or Ash Stand, Nickel-plated Brass Plug with Rubber Stopper, and Nickel-plated Compression Faucets.

Size, 24 × 18 inches; Oval Basin, 14 × 11 inches.

MOTT'S WASH STANDS.

ALL DESIGNS PATENTED.

PLATE 439-G.
CORNER WASH STAND.

With Patent Overflow, Nickel-plated Brass Plug and Coupling, and Rubber Stopper: Plain, Painted, Galvanized or Enameled Slab and Bowl, with Plain, Painted, Galvanized or Marbleized Frame.

Dimensions : height to slab, 28 inches ; height to top of back, 34½ inches · width of front, 26 inches ; length of side, 18 inches ; diameter of bowl, 12 inches.

PLATE 440-G.
HALF-CIRCLE WASH STAND.

With Patent Overflow, Nickel-plated Brass Plug and Coupling, and Rubber Stopper ; Plain, Painted, Galvanized or Enameled Slab and Bowl, with Plain, Painted, Galvanized or Marbleized Frame.

Dimensions : height to slab, 28 inches ; height to top of back, 35 inches ; length of back, 30 inches ; diameter of bowl, 12 inches.

NOTE. — Unless otherwise ordered, the above Wash Stands are furnished with two faucet holes.

MOTT'S ENAMELED WASH STANDS.

PLATE 441-G.

HALF-CIRCLE WASH STAND.

Same as Plate 442-G, with
nickel and tile
ornament.

PLATE 442-G.

HALF-CIRCLE WASH STAND.

With Patent Overflow, Nickel-plated Brass Plug and Coupling, and
Rubber Stopper; Standard Bronzed.

Dimensions : height to front of slab, 31½ inches ; height to top of back,
39 inches ; length of back, 24 inches ; diameter of bowl, 12 inches.

PLATE 443-G.

CORNER WASH STAND.

With Patent Overflow, Nickel-plated Brass Plug and Coupling, and
Rubber Stopper; Standard Bronzed.

Dimensions : height to front of slab, 31½ inches ; height to top of back,
39 inches; length of side, 17 inches; diameter of bowl, 12 inches.

NOTE. — Unless otherwise ordered, the above Wash Stands are furnished with two faucet holes.

MOTT'S ENAMELED WASH STANDS.

PLATE 444-G.

HALF-CIRCLE WASH STAND.

Same as Plate 445-G, with
nickel and tile
ornament.

PLATE 445-G.

HALF-CIRCLE WASH STAND.

With Patent Overflow, Nickel-plated Brass Plug and Coupling, and
Rubber Stopper; Standard Bronzed.

Dimensions : height to front of slab, 31 inches ; height to top of back,
39 inches ; length of back, 22½ inches ; diameter of bowl, 12 inches.

PLATE 446-G.

CORNER WASH STAND.

With Patent Overflow, Nickel-plated Brass Plug and Coupling, and
Rubber Stopper; Standard Bronzed.

Dimensions : height to front of slab, 31 inches ; height to top of back,
39 inches ; length of side, 16 inches ; diameter of bowl, 12 inches.

NOTE. — Unless otherwise ordered, the above Wash Stands are furnished with two faucet holes.

MOTT'S WASH STANDS.

PLAIN, PAINTED, GALVANIZED AND ENAMELED.

PLATE 447-G.   PLATE 448-G.

With Patent Overflow, Nickel-plated Brass Plug and Coupling, and Rubber Stopper.

Dimensions: height to front of slab, 29½ inches; height to top of back, 40 inches; length of back, 26½ inches; diameter of bowl, 12 inches.

PLATE 449-G.   PLATE 450-G.

With Patent Overflow, Nickel-plated Brass Plug and Coupling, and Rubber Stopper.

Dimensions: height, 28½ inches; length of back, 24 inches;   Dimensions: height, 31½ inches; length of back, 24½ inches;
diameter of bowl, 12 inches   diameter of bowl, 12 inches.

NOTE.—Unless otherwise ordered, the above Wash Stands are furnished with two faucet holes.

Mott's Wash Stands.

Plain, Painted, Galvanized and Enameled.

PLATE 451-G.

HALF-CIRCLE WASH STAND.

PLATE 452-G.

CORNER WASH STAND.

With Patent Overflow, Nickel-plated Brass Plug and Coupling, and Rubber Stopper.

Dimensions : height to front of slab, 27½ inches ; height to top of back, 32½ inches ; length of back, 19 inches ; diameter of bowl 12 inches.

Dimensions : height to front of slab, 27½ inches ; height to top of back, 32½ inches; length of side, 13½ inches; diameter of bowl, 12 inches.

PLATE 453-G.

HALF-CIRCLE WASH STAND.

PLATE 454-G.

CORNER WASH STAND.

With Patent Overflow, Nickel-plated Brass Plug and Coupling, and Rubber Stopper.

Dimensions : height to front of slab, 29 inches ; height to top of back, 32½ inches; length of back, 22 inches; diameter of bowl, 12 inches.

Dimensions : height to front of slab, 29 inches ; height to top of back, 32½ inches ; length of side 15 inches ; diameter of bowl, 12 inches.

Note. — Unless otherwise ordered, the above Wash Stands are furnished with two faucet holes

MOTT'S DOUBLE WASH STANDS.

PLAIN, PAINTED, GALVANIZED AND ENAMELED.

PLATE 455-G.

On Standards, with Patent Overflow, Nickel-plated Brass Plug and Coupling, and Rubber Stopper.

Dimensions : height, 28½ inches ; length of back, 46 inches ; diameter of bowls, 12 inches.

PLATE 456-G.

On Frame, with Patent Overflow, Nickel-plated Brass Plug and Coupling, and Rubber Stopper.

Dimensions : height, 31½ inches ; length of slab, 46 inches ; diameter of bowls, 12 inches.

NOTE.— Unless otherwise ordered, the above are furnished with two faucet holes for each bowl.

SECTIONAL WASH STANDS.

PLAIN, PAINTED, GALVANIZED AND ENAMELED.

PLATE 457-G.

With Patent Overflow, Nickel-plated Brass Plug and Coupling, and Rubber Stopper.

PLATE 458-G.

Draped, with Patent Overflow, Nickel-plated Brass Plug and Coupling, and Rubber Stopper.

DIMENSIONS of Plates 457-G and 458-G: length of each slab, 24 inches (can be made 18 or 21 inches if desired); width of slab, 20 inches; height to front of slab, 29 inches; height of back, 10½ inches; diameter of bowls, 12 inches.

Any number can be placed together. Also furnished with right or left end piece (or both), as shown by Plates 463-G and 464-G; also furnished with Sink, as shown by Plates 465-G and 466-G.

When ordering, it is advisable to send us a rough sketch indicating how the slabs are to finish.

Sectional Slabs and Bowls on Brackets.

Plain, Painted, Galvanized and Enameled.

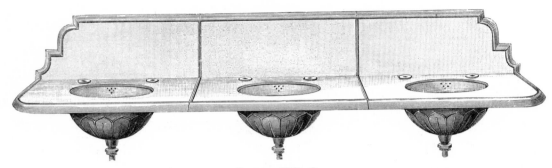

PLATE 459-G.

Sectional Slabs and Bowls.

With Patent Overflow, Nickel-plated Brass Plug and Coupling, and Rubber Stopper.

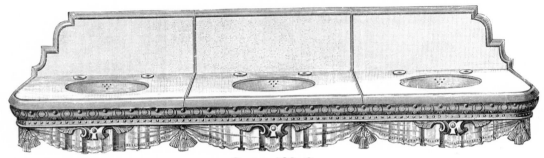

PLATE 460-G.

Sectional Slabs and Bowls, Draped.

With Patent Overflow, Nickel-plated Brass Plug and Coupling, and Rubber Stopper.

Dimensions of Plates 459–G and 460–G: length of each slab, 24 inches (can be made 18 and 21 inches if desired); width of slab, 20 inches; height of back, 10½ inches; diameter of bowl, 12 inches.

ANY number of the above may be used together. If end of slab finishes against a wall, a right or left end piece, as shown by Plates 463–G and 464–G, is required; if both ends finish against a wall, both right and left end pieces are required. Brackets as shown by Plate 461–G will be sent, unless those as shown by 462–G are ordered. When ordering it is advisable to send us a rough sketch indicating how the slabs are to finish.

The above Slabs are particularly adapted for and have been largely used in Asylums, Hospitals, etc.

PLATE 461-G.

Bracket for Sectional Slabs and Bowls, Plain, Bronzed and Galvanized.

This Bracket is always sent with Sectional Slabs and Bowls, unless Plate 462–G is specially ordered.

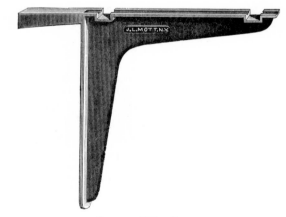

PLATE 462-G.

Bracket for Sectional Slabs and Bowls, Plain, Bronzed and Galvanized.

Bracket to build into Brick Wall.

The J. L. Mott Iron Works. New York.

193

Sectional Slabs and Bowls and Sinks,

PLAIN, PAINTED, GALVANIZED AND ENAMELED.

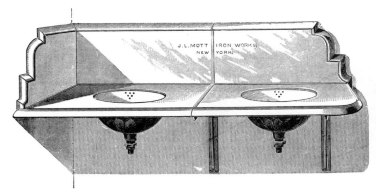

Plate 463-G.

SECTIONAL SLABS AND BOWL.

With Left End Piece, Patent Overflow, Nickel-plated Brass Plug
and Coupling, and Rubber Stopper.

Plate 464-G.

SECTIONAL SLABS AND BOWLS, DRAPED,

With Left End Piece, Patent Overflow, Nickel-plated Brass Plug
and Coupling, and Rubber Stopper.

Plates 463-G and 464-G will be furnished with Right End Piece instead of Left, or with both Left and Right End Pieces, if so ordered.

Dimensions : Length of each Slab, 24 inches, (can be made 21 inches or 18 inches if desired); Width of Slab, 20 inches ; Height of Back, 10½ inches ;
Diameter of Bowl, 12 inches.

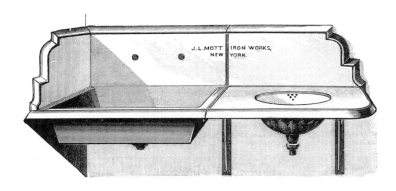

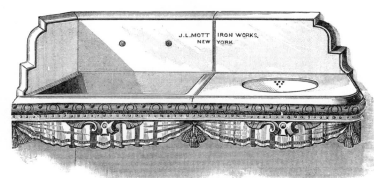

Plate 465-G.

SECTIONAL SLAB AND BOWL AND SINK,

With Left End Piece, Patent Overflow, Nickel-plated Brass Plug
and Coupling, and Rubber Stopper.

Plate 466-G.

SECTIONAL SLAB AND BOWL AND SINK, DRAPED,

With Left End Piece, Patent Overflow, Nickel-plated Brass Plug
and Coupling, and Rubber Stopper.

Plates 465-G and 466-G will be furnished with Right End Piece instead of Left, or with both Left and Right End Pieces, if so ordered. The
Sink may be placed in any part of a line of Sectional Slabs and Bowls instead of at the end as shown.

Dimensions : Length of Slab, 24 inches ; Width of Slab, 20 inches ; Height of Back, 10½ inches; Sink, 24 × 20 × 6 inches deep ; Diameter of Bowl,
12 inches.

Brackets as shown by Plate 461–G will be sent unless Plate 462–G are specially ordered.

When ordering it is advisable to send a rough sketch indicating how the Slabs are to finish.

SLABS AND BOWLS.

PLAIN, PAINTED, GALVANIZED AND ENAMELED.

PLATE 467-G.

HALF CIRCLE SLAB AND BOWL,

Dimensions : Length of Back, 19 inches ; Height of Back, 5 inches ;
Diameter of Bowl, 12 inches.

PLATE 468-G.

CORNER SLAB AND BOWL,

Dimensions : Length of Side, 13½ inches ; Height of Back,
5 inches ; Diameter of Bowl, 12 inches.

PLATE 469-G.

HALF CIRCLE SLAB AND BOWL,

Dimensions : Length of Back, 22 inches ; Height of Back, 6 inches ;
Diameter of Bowl, 12 inches.

PLATE 470-G.

CORNER SLAB AND BOWL,

Dimensions : Length of Side, 15 inches ; Height of Back, 6 inches ;
Diameter of Bowl, 12 inches.

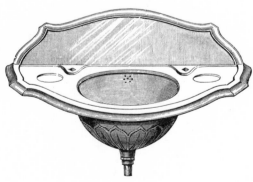

PLATE 471-G.

HALF CIRCLE SLAB AND BOWL,

Dimensions : Length of Back, 30 inches ; Height of Back, 7 inches ;
Diameter of Bowl, 12 inches.

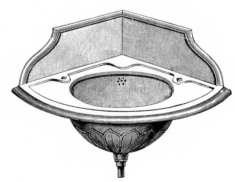

PLATE 472-G.

CORNER SLAB AND BOWL,

Dimensions : Length of Side, 18 inches ; Height of Back, 7 inches ;
Diameter of Bowl, 12 inches.

All of above have Patent Overflow, Nickel-plated Brass Plug and Coupling and Rubber Stopper. They will be furnished with 2 Faucet holes
as shown, unless otherwise ordered.

COMBINED SLABS AND BOWLS

PLAIN, PAINTED, GALVANIZED AND ENAMELED.

PLATE 473-G.

COMBINED SLAB AND BOWL,

Length of Back, 13 inches.

PLATE 474-G.

COMBINED CORNER SLAB AND BOWL,

Length of Side, 12 inches.

PLATE 475-G.

COMBINED SLAB AND BOWL,

Length of Back, 13 inches.

All of the above have Common Overflow. The diameter of Bowl is 11 inches.

PLATE 476-G.

WASH BASIN,

With Patent Overflow, Brass Coupling and Rubber Stopper.

Three Sizes: 10½ in., 11¾ in. and 14 in. inside diameter.

PLATE 477-G.

WASH BASIN,

With Common Overflow.

Three Sizes: 11 in., 12½ in. and 13½ in. inside diameter.

MOTT'S PATENT FOLDING WASH STAND.

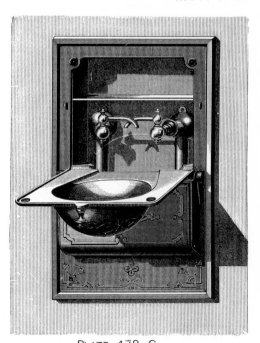

PLATE 478-G.

FOLDING WASH STAND, OPEN.

PLATE 479-G

FOLDING WASH STAND, CLOSED.

THE Receiver is Porcelain lined: the outside is Bronzed, Marbleized, or Painted one coat, so that it may be painted same style as wood work in room if desired. Size of Frame of Folding Wash Stand is 29½ × 17½ inches. Depth let into the wall, 3 inches. Bowl projects into the room when open 13½ inches. Bowl projects into the room when closed, 4 inches. Diameter of Bowl, 10 inches. Made with one or two faucets; also made without faucets. It can be built in the wall, as shown by cut, or fitted in a frame outside the wall. The Slab and Bowl are cast in one piece, and can be removed so that any part of receiving sink can be got at and cleaned. It is furnished with Brass Couplings for Supply and Waste; in short, the whole apparatus is complete in itself, requiring no plumbing work further than connecting the pipes.

PATENT FOLDING WASH STANDS.

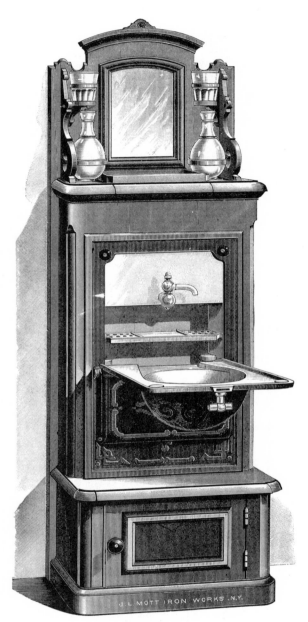

PLATE 480-G.   PLATE 481-G.

FOLDING WASH STAND,   FOLDING WASH STAND,

With Black Walnut, Cherry or Ash Case.

With Copper Reservoir, Nickel-plated Faucet, and Black Walnut Cherry or Ash Case.

The above cut shows Wash Stand closed, fitted up in wood work, suitable for Office or Steamship use; when fitted up in private residences or offices, wood work would not project at the bottom, as no slop pail would be used, connection being made with waste pipe.

The illustration shows more particularly Wash Stand fitted up for ship use, with Galvanized Receiver at bottom for waste, although some have been put up and connected directly with Bilge Pipe.

The above cut shows Wash Stand fitted up in wood work with Copper Water Reservoir. This style is very desirable for country use where there is no direct supply of water, also for ship use, as the Reservoir would carry more than a day's supply, and do away with the trouble of replenishing Water Bottles. The Top of Wood Work is so arranged that Reservoir can be readily filled up, and also cleaned out if necessary.

MOTT'S CAST IRON SECTIONAL WASH SINK.

FOR FACTORIES, GOVERNMENT BARRACKS, PUBLIC INSTITUTIONS, ETC.

PLAIN, GALVANIZED, ENAMELED AND "RUSTLESS."

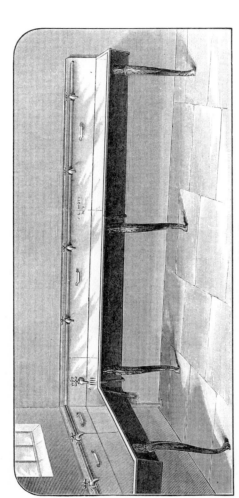

PLATE 482-G.

WASH SINK ON LEGS, WITH CORNER SECTION, BACK, FAUCETS, SOAP CUPS, PATENT OVERFLOW AND PLUG.

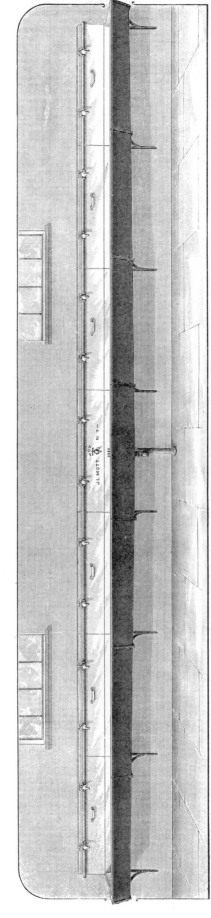

PLATE 483-G.

WASH SINK ON BRACKETS WITH BACK, FAUCETS, SOAP CUPS, PATENT OVERFLOW AND PLUG.

THE illustrations represent a Sink in which a greater or less number of men can wash together. The extreme length that we can furnish the Wash Sink is 55 feet consisting of 11 sections, each 5 feet long, the section with Waste being in the centre with 5 sections to the right and left all having a drain toward the centre. The depth of centre section is 8 inches; the depth of the extreme end sections is 5 inches. Plate 483-G shows only 3 sections on each side of Waste Section. Any number of sections from 1 to 11 will be furnished as may be ordered. Where the Sink turns a corner, it is made as shown by Plate 482-G. The Back is 10 inches high.

Various methods of supply can be used to suit local requirements. The one shown consists of 2 Compression Faucets for cold water for each section, and one Hot Water Faucet, which may be placed in center as shown, or any other convenient part of the Sink; the supply is preferably through Wrought Iron Pipe. For the first wash (to remove dirt and soot) hot water is desirable; this can be obtained by filling the Sink with water of a desired temperature through the hot and cold Faucets; after this first wash all the men can use the cold water Faucets individually for cleansing and rinsing. Standing Overflow to insert in Waste Plug will be furnished instead of Stopper, if so ordered.

MOTT'S PATENT PORCELAIN FLUSHING-RIM SLOP SINK, THE "HYGEIA."

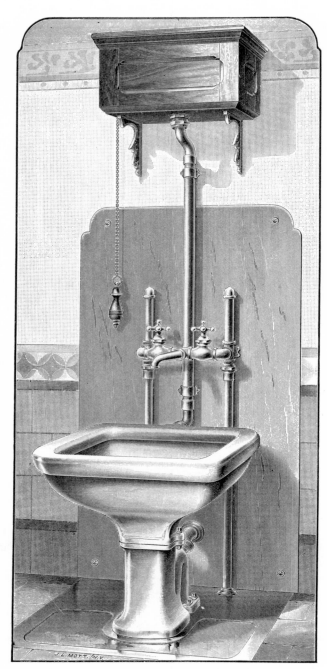

PLATE 484-G.

PORCELAIN FLUSHING RIM SLOP SINK, THE "HYGEIA,"

With No. 4 Cabinet-finish Design B Cistern, Brass Combination
Supply Faucet, Brass Flush Pipe, Brass Cistern Brackets,
Chain and Ivory-celluloid Pull.

The Brass work may be Polished or Nickel-plated. The Cistern may be Cherry, Black Walnut or Ash, or Painted or Porcelain-lined Iron, or Plain Wood. Size of Cistern, 18×9×10 in. deep.

PLATE 485-G.

PORCELAIN FLUSHING-RIM SLOP SINK, THE "HYGEIA,"

With Polished or Nickel-plated Brass Combination Supply and
Flush Faucet.

When a Cistern cannot be conveniently used, the Sink can be flushed by the Combination Flush and Supply Faucet as shown by the above illustration.

Size of the "Hygeia" Slop Sink : 21 inches × 21 inches on top ; height, 22 inches ; Outlet, 3 inches.

IN the "Hygeia" Slop Sink are combined all the requisites of a first-class article of its kind ; it is absolutely perfect from a sanitary standpoint ; the entire interior of the Sink is thoroughly flushed and cleansed by drawing down the pull and releasing it at once ; it stands open, a beautiful piece of white porcelain without any wood work whatever ; the Combination Faucets as shown are well adapted for the purpose and are very neat and attractive in appearance. Each Sink is furnished with a removable Brass Strainer, Brass Inlet and Vent Couplings, and Brass Floor Flange with Bolts. The Countersunk Italian Marble Floor Slab adds greatly to the fine appearance of the Sink.

If so ordered, we will furnish Brass Supply Pipe for Faucet and Cistern.

"Imperial" Porcelain Slop Sinks.

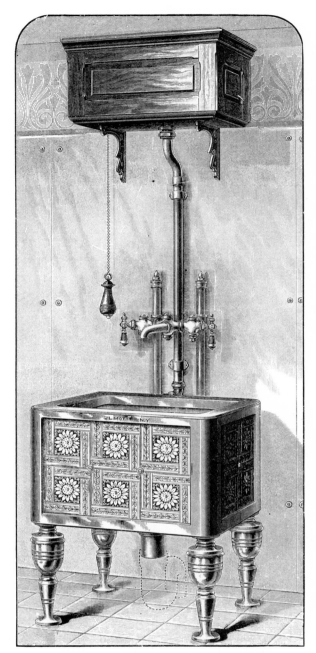

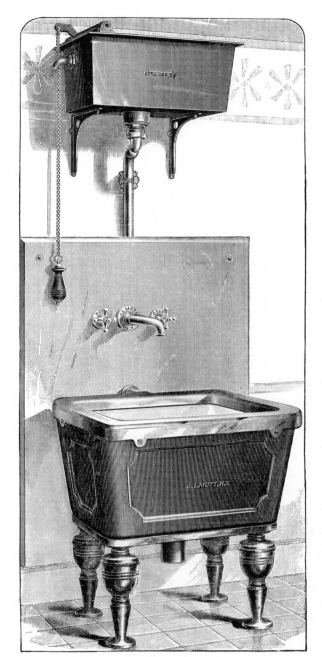

PLATE 486-G.

The "Newport" Slop Sink,

COMPRISING

"Imperial" Porcelain Sink with Cast Brass Flushing-rim combined with Brass Frame and Legs, and inlaid with English Tile ; Improved Combination Supply Faucet, No. 4 Cabinet-finish Cistern, Design B, Brass Flush Pipe, Brass Brackets, Chain and Ivory-celluloid Pull.

Dimensions : Sink, 23 inches × 20 inches on top ; height on legs, 27 inches ; Outlet, 3 inches.

PLATE 487-G.

"Imperial" Porcelain Slop Sink,

With Polished or Nickel-plated Cast Brass Flushing-rim, Bronzed or Galvanized Iron Standard, Combination Supply Faucet, No. 4 Syphon Cistern, Brackets, Chain and Pull.

The Cistern is furnished Painted or Porcelain-lined, or Wood Copper-lined.

Dimensions : No. 1, 20 × 16 × 12 inches deep ; No. 2, 22 × 18 × 12 inches deep ; No. 3, 24 × 20 × 12 inches deep.

Plates 486-G and 487-G can be furnished with Faucet as shown by Plate 484-G or 485-G, if so ordered.

Plate 486-G represents the handsomest and most elaborate combination ever devised in the way of a Slop Sink, and one that fulfils every practical and sanitary requirement ; it should be seen to be appreciated as no adequate idea of it can be formed from the illustration.

Plate 487-G represents an excellent form of Slop Sink for use in Hotels and Public Buildings where it is desirable that all the plumbing appliances be strong, durable and easily kept clean.

THE "Imperial" Porcelain Slop Sink is in material and finish the same as our celebrated "Imperial" Porcelain Baths ; they are non-absorbent ; have a perfectly smooth surface and are not liable to break or crack with usage.

"IMPERIAL" PORCELAIN SLOP SINKS.

PLATE 488-G.

"IMPERIAL" PORCELAIN SLOP SINK.

With Bronzed or Galvanized Iron Standard, Ash, Cherry, Black Walnut or Marble Rim, Marble Back, Combination Supply Faucet and 3 inch Brass Plug and Coupling with Nickel-plated Strainer.

PLATE 489-G.

"IMPERIAL" PORCELAIN SLOP SINK,

With Bronzed or Galvanized Iron Standard, and 3 inch Brass Plug and Coupling with Nickel-plated Strainer.

PLATE 490-G.

"IMPERIAL" PORCELAIN SLOP SINK,

With 3 inch Brass Plug and Coupling with Nickel plated Strainer.

Sizes: No. 1, 20 × 16 × 12 inches deep; No. 2, 22 × 18 × 12 inches deep; No. 3, 24 × 20 × 12 inches deep.

THE "Imperial" Porcelain Slop Sink is in material and finish the same as our celebrated "Imperial" Porcelain Baths; they are non-absorbent and durable, the glaze being a beautiful ivory or cream color.

The "Imperial" Porcelain Slop Sinks have been extensively used during the past six years in private residences, hotels and public buildings, and have given entire satisfaction.

NOTE.—Our "Yorkshire" Brown Glazed Earthenware Sinks can be furnished in same sizes as the "Imperial" Porcelain. The "Yorkshire" is made of Earthenware having a rich, dark brown glaze on the inside and outside; they are non-absorbent, strong and durable.

DEMAREST'S PORCELAIN-LINED SLOP SINK WITH BRASS FLUSHING-RIM.

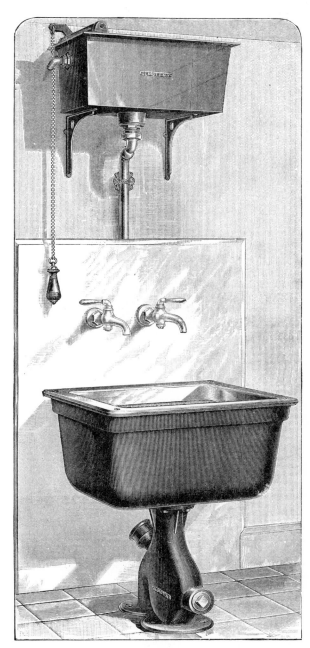

PLATE 491-G.

PORCELAIN-LINED SLOP SINK WITH BRASS FLUSHING-RIM, ON
COMBINATION TRAP STANDARD,

With Mott's Nickel-plated Faucets, No. 4 Syphon Cistern, Brackets,
Nickel-plated Chain and Pull.

Also furnished with Faucets and Brass Flush Pipe, as shown by
Plate 484-G, 485-G or 487-G if so ordered.

PLATE 491-G represents a most complete combination, designed for use in the very best work. The Flushing-Rim, which is of polished or nickel-plated cast brass, distributes the water equally over the entire surface of the Sink, thereby washing it out thoroughly every time the Cistern is operated. The Trap, which also serves as a stand, is furnished with a 2½ inch brass screw so that it can be readily cleaned out; it also has a 2-inch connection for ventilation pipe.

Three Sizes : No 1, 20 × 16 × 12 inches deep.   No. 2, 22 × 18 × 12 inches deep.   No. 3, 24 × 20 × 12 inches deep.

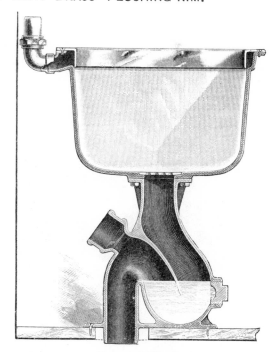

PLATE 492-G.

SECTIONAL VIEW OF PLATE 491-G.
Sink can also be furnished with S Trap, having spigot for Iron
Waste Pipe connection.

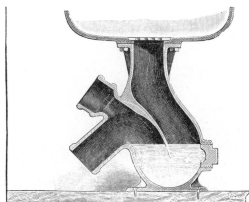

PLATE 493-G.

SHOWING ¾ S TRAP FOR FLUSHING-RIM SLOP SINK.

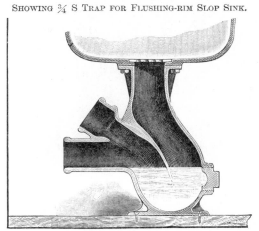

PLATE 494-G.

SHOWING ½ S TRAP FOR FLUSHING RIM SLOP SINK.

DEMAREST'S SLOP SINKS.

PLAIN, GALVANIZED AND PORCELAIN-LINED.

PLATE 495-G.

DEMAREST SLOP SINK ON COMBINATION TRAP STANDARD,

With 3 inch Brass Plug and Nickel-plated Strainer.

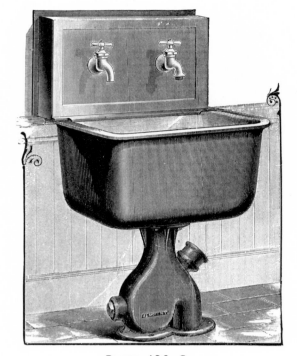

PLATE 496-G

DEMAREST SLOP SINK ON COMBINATION TRAP STANDARD,

With 3 inch Brass Plug and Nickel-plated Strainer, Box or Projecting Back and Nickel-plated Compression Faucets.

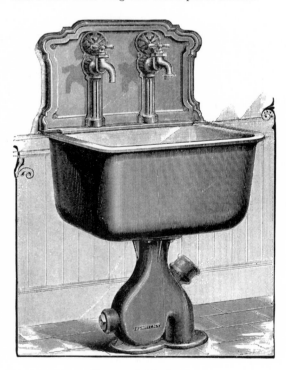
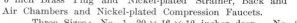

PLATE 497-G.

DEMAREST SLOP SINK ON COMBINATION TRAP STANDARD,

With 3 inch Brass Plug and Nickel-plated Strainer, Back and Air Chambers and Nickel-plated Compression Faucets.

Three Sizes : No. 1, 20 × 16 × 12 inches deep. No. 2, 22 × 18 × 12 inches deep. No. 3, 24 × 20 × 12 inches deep.

PLATE 498-G.

DEMAREST SLOP SINK ON COMBINATION TRAP STANDARD,

With 3 inch Brass Plug and Nickel-plated Strainer, Marble Back and Mott's Nickel-plated Faucets. The Back is 18 in. high

The above Sinks can be furnished with Frame and Legs similar to Plate 489–G, and Brass Coupling, instead of with Trap Standard, if so ordered

IRON SLOP SINKS.

PLAIN, GALVANIZED AND PORCELAIN-LINED.

PLATE 499-G.

SLOP SINK,

With Coupling and Strainer.

Sizes: 16 × 16 × 10 inches deep.   20 × 14 × 12 inches deep.   20 × 16 × 12 inches deep.   24 × 20 × 12 inches deep.

30 × 20 × 12 inches deep.   36 × 18 × 12 inches deep.   36 × 21 × 12 inches deep.   23 × 15 × 15 inches deep.   36 × 21 × 16 inches deep.

48 × 20 × 12 inches deep.   48 × 20 × 17 inches deep.   60 × 20 × 12 inches deep.   72 × 20 × 12 inches deep.

Can be furnished with Patent Overflow, or with Patent Overflow and Plug Strainer, or with Brass Strainer, if so ordered.

PLATE 500-G.

SLOP SINK,

With Coupling and Strainer and Legs.

PLATE 501-G.

CORNER SLOP SINK,

With Coupling and Strainer.

Size: Length of side 18½, depth 12 inches.

Can be furnished with Patent Overflow, or with Patent Overflow
and Plug Strainer, or with Brass Strainer, if so ordered.

PLATE 502-G.

SQUARE SLOP SINK WITH ROUND CORNERS ON BOTTOM,

With Coupling and Strainer.

Size: 22 × 20 × 12 inches deep.

Can be furnished with Goose Neck Overflow, and with
Brass Strainer, if so ordered.

SLOP HOPPER SINKS.

PLAIN, GALVANIZED AND PORCELAIN LINED.

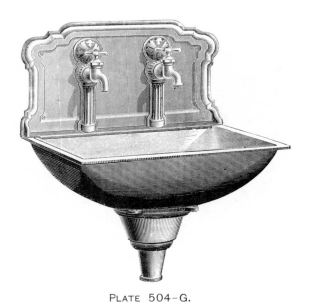

PLATE 503-G.

MERRY'S SLOP HOPPER SINK.

PLATE 504-G.

MERRY'S SLOP HOPPER SINK,
With Back, Air Chambers and Nickel-plated Compression Faucets.

Sizes: No. 1—22 × 17 × 9 inches deep to Strainer.   No. 2—28 × 20 × 9 inches deep to Strainer.

Diameter of Strainer, 8 inches.   Depth of Hopper, 9 inches.

Outlet, 3 inches   4-inch Outlet to order.

PLATE 505-G.

HOSPITAL SLOP HOPPER SINK.

Sizes: 24 × 20 × 12 inches deep. 30 × 20 × 12 inches deep.

36 × 21 × 12 inches deep.

Depth of Hopper, 18 inches. Outlet, 4 inches.

PLATE 506-G.

HOSPITAL SLOP HOPPER SINK.

Sizes: 24 × 20 × 12 inches deep. 30 × 20 × 12 inches deep.

36 × 21 × 12 inches deep.

Depth of Hopper, 9 inches. Outlet, 4 inches.

SLOP HOPPERS AND SINKS.

PLAIN, GALVANIZED AND PORCELAIN-LINED.

PLATE 507-G.

HOSPITAL SLOP HOPPER SINK WITH TRAP ATTACHED.

Sizes : 24 × 20 × 12 inches deep.   30 × 20 × 12 inches deep.   36 × 21 × 12 inches deep.

Depth of Hopper and Trap, 17 inches.   Outlet, 4 inches.

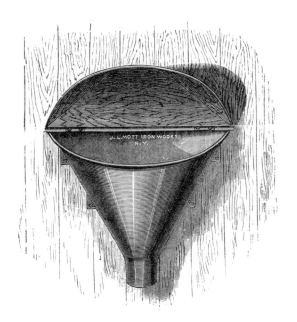

PLATE 508-G.

HALF CIRCLE SLOP HOPPER WITH WOODEN COVER.

Size : Length on Back, 21 inches.   Width, 12½ inches.   Depth, 18 inches.
Outlet, 3 inches.
Furnished with or without Wooden Cover.

PLATE 509-G.

FLUSHING RIM SLOP HOPPER.

Size : Width on Top, including Flange, 18 inches.   Width of Top Opening, 13 inches.   Depth of Hopper, 19 inches.   Outlet, 4 inches.
Depth to Strainer, 8 inches.   Diameter of Strainer, 9 inches.

"IMPERIAL" PORCELAIN KITCHEN SINKS.

PLATE 510-G.

"IMPERIAL" PORCELAIN KITCHEN SINK,

With Polished or Nickel plated Cast Brass Legs and Frame, Patent Enamel Decorated Metal Tiles for Front and Ends, Cherry, Ash, Mahogany or Marble Rim, Marble Back 18 inches high, Mott's Polished or Nickel-plated Brass Faucets, and 2 inch Brass Plug and Coupling with Nickel plated Strainer.

Dimensions of Sinks.   Four Sizes: 30 × 20 × 7 inches deep.   36 × 23 × 7 inches deep.   42 × 24 × 7 inches deep.   48 × 24 × 7 inches deep.

Dimensions given are outside, except depth which is inside.

Either of the Traps shown on page 210 may be used with the above Sink.

The "Imperial" Porcelain Kitchen Sinks are in material and finish the same as our celebrated "Imperial" Porcelain Baths.

PLATE 510-G represents a most elegant and complete Sink, especially adapted for use in Kitchens that are finished in Tile or Marble.   The Cast Brass Legs are finished and chased in the best manner, and contribute to the fine appearance of the combination.   The Enameled Decorated Metal Tiles for the front and ends of the Sink give the same effect as real Tile and are much more durable; the metal is wrought iron, enameled on both sides, and is rustless.   The design shown is furnished in two colors, brown and blue.   Three pieces constitute a set of Tiles; they rest upon the Brass Legs and are held in place by the wood or marble rim.

"IMPERIAL" PORCELAIN KITCHEN SINKS.

PLATE 511-G.

'IMPERIAL" PORCELAIN KITCHEN SINK,

With Polished or Nickel-plated Heavy Brass Tube Legs with Spun Brass Ornaments and Cast Brass Frame, Patent Enamel Decorated Metal Tiles for Front and Ends, Cherry, Ash, Black Walnut, Mahogany or Marble Rim, Marble Back 18 inches high, Polished or Nickel-plated Brass Faucets, and 2 inch Brass Plug and Coupling with Nickel-plated Strainer.

Dimensions of Sinks.　Four Sizes:　$30 \times 20 \times 7$ inches deep.　$36 \times 23 \times 7$ inches deep.　$42 \times 24 \times 7$ inches deep.　$48 \times 24 \times 7$ inches deep.

Dimensions given are outside, except depth which is inside.

Either of the Traps shown on page 210 may be used with the above Sink.

Plate 511-G is the same as Plate 510-G except that the legs are Heavy Brass Tube with Spun Brass Ornaments, instead of Cast Brass.

"IMPERIAL" PORCELAIN KITCHEN SINKS.

PLATE 512-G.

"IMPERIAL" PORCELAIN KITCHEN SINK,

With Bronzed or Galvanized Iron Legs and Frame, Patent Enamel Decorated Metal Tile for Front and Ends, Cherry, Black

Walnut, Ash, Mahogany or Marble Rim, Marble Back 18 inches high, Mott's Polished or Nickel-plated

Brass Faucets, and 2 inch Brass Plug and Coupling with Nickel-plated Strainer.

Four Sizes: 30 × 20 × 7; 36 × 23 × 7; 42 × 24 × 7; 48 × 24 × 7.   The dimensions are outside except depth which is inside.

Either of the Traps shown on page 210 may be used with the above Sink.

THE "YORKSHIRE" BROWN GLAZED EARTHENWARE KITCHEN SINKS.

PLATE 513-G.

THE "YORKSHIRE" BROWN GLAZED EARTHENWARE SINK.

With Bronzed Iron Legs and Frame, Black Walnut, Cherry or Ash Rim, Marble Back 18 inches high, and Polished or Nickel-plated Brass Faucets.

Four Sizes: 30 × 20 × 7 inches deep.   36 × 23 × 7 inches deep.   42 × 24 × 7 inches deep.   48 × 24 × 7 inches deep.

Dimensions given are outside, except depth which is inside.

The "Yorkshire" is made of earthenware, 1½ inches thick, having a dark brown glaze on the inside and outside. They are non-absorbent, strong and durable.

TRAPS FOR KITCHEN SINKS.

The outside Cylinder of Mott's Patent Grease Trap is of cast iron, porcelain-lined, the inside Portable Cylinder being of tinned Copper, with Brass Tubes, &c. The Brass Strainer and Knob which show in sink are nickel-plated. The outer Cylinder, with its brass pipe connections, forms the Trap, while the inside Cylinder, which can be lifted out, affords an easy means of removing the accumulated grease.

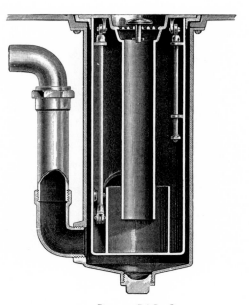

PLATE 514-G.

MOTT'S PATENT GREASE TRAP, FOR "IMPERIAL" PORCELAIN SINKS.

PLATE 515-G.

SECTIONAL VIEW OF GREASE TRAP, ATTACHED TO A CAST IRON SINK.

PLATE 516-G.

MOTT'S GREASE TRAP, TO REST ON FLOOR. (Patent applied for.)

The Body of Trap is Iron, Porcelain-lined : the connections are all of 2 inch Cast Brass and are furnished Polished or Nickel-plated.

Dimensions : Body of Trap, 8½ inches high, and 14 inches diameter on Top. The Trap can be cleaned out at any time by simply raising the Cover on Top. The Local Vent (connected with hot Flue) will carry off any odor that may be generated in Trap. Where a Grease Trap is found to be a necessity, we think this is the very best and simplest form.

PLATE 517-G.

MOTT'S BRASS TRAP, TO REST ON FLOOR.

Polished or Nickel-plated.

Dimensions : Body of Trap, 10 inches high, and 5 inch diameter.

Inlet and Outlet Couplings, 2 inch ; Vent Coupling, 2 inch.

The Brass Screw on Top can be removed when it is desired to clean interior of Trap.

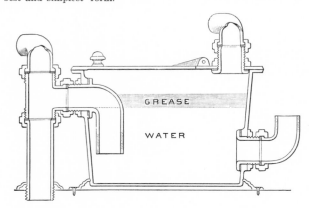

SECTIONAL VIEW OF MOTT'S GREASE TRAP, PLATE 516-G.

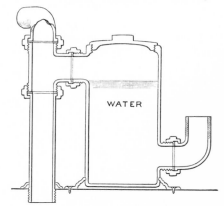

SECTIONAL VIEW OF MOTT'S BRASS TRAP, PLATE 517-G.

"IMPERIAL" PORCELAIN SINKS.

PLATE 518-G.

"IMPERIAL" PORCELAIN CORNER KITCHEN SINK.

With 2 inch Brass Plug and Coupling, and Nickel-plated Strainer.

One Size : Length on side, 20½ inches ; length across front 28½ inches ; inside depth, 5 inches.

PLATE 519-G.

"IMPERIAL" PORCELAIN KITCHEN SINK.

With 2 inch Brass Plug and Coupling and Nickel-plated Strainer.

Four sizes : 30 × 20 × 7 inches deep.   36 × 23 × 7 inches deep.   42 × 24 × 7 inches deep.   48 × 24 × 7 inches deep.   Thickness, 1½ inches.

Dimensions given are outside, except depth, which is inside.

NOTE.—The "Imperial" Sinks are furnished in two qualities, namely, "Firsts" and "Seconds."
We also furnish the same sizes in our Brown "Yorkshire" ware.

"Imperial" Porcelain Sinks.

PLATE 520-G.

'Imperial" Porcelain Housemaid (or Deep Pantry) Sink.

With 1½ inch Brass Plug and Coupling with Rubber Stopper, Brass Overflow with Nickel plated Strainer and Chain.
Two Sizes : 28 × 18 × 10 inches deep and 30 × 20 × 10 inches deep.

Either of the Traps shown on page 210 may be used with the above.

PLATE 521-G.

"Imperial" Porcelain Pantry Sink,

With 1¼ inch Brass Plug and Coupling with Rubber
Stopper, Brass Overflow with Nickel-plated
Strainer and Chain.

PLATE 522-G.

"Imperial" Porcelain Pantry Sink,

With 1¼ inch Polished or Nickel-plated Brass Standing Overflow.

The Standing Overflow does away with the Brass or Rubber Stopper and Chain.

Five Sizes : 20 × 14 × 5. 23 × 16 × 6. 24 × 17 × 6. 28 × 17 × 6. 30 × 20 × 7.
Measurements are outside, except depth which is inside.

With the 28 inch and 30 inch Pantry Sinks, Mott's Grease Trap, Plate 514–G can be used. Traps as shown by Plates 516 and 517–G, can be used with all sizes.

The "Imperial" Porcelain Pantry Sinks are in material and finish the same as our celebrated Imperial Porcelain Baths.

WHITE EARTHENWARE PANTRY SINKS.

PLATE 523-G.

IMPORTED WHITE EARTHENWARE PANTRY SINK WITH PATENT OVERFLOW.

Five Sizes : 20 × 12 × 4½ inches deep.   20 × 14 × 4½ inches deep.   23 × 16 × 5½ inches deep.   24 × 17 × 5½ inches deep.   25 × 17 × 5½ inches deep.

Dimensions are outside, except depth which is inside.

COPPER PANTRY SINKS.

PLATE 524-G.

PLATE 525-G.

OVAL COPPER PANTRY SINK.

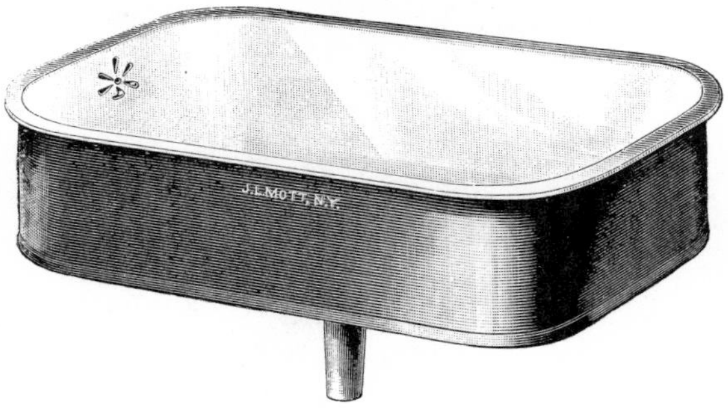

SQUARE COPPER PANTRY SINK.

Sizes : 12 × 18.   12 × 20.   14 × 16.   14 × 20.   14 × 24.   16 × 24.   16 × 30.   18 × 30.

MOTT'S "EASTLAKE" KITCHEN SINKS.

PLAIN, BRONZED, GALVANIZED AND ENAMELED.

PLATE 526-G.

"EASTLAKE" KITCHEN SINK, ON BRACKETS,

With Back, Air Chambers and Faucets.

Sizes: 30 × 23 × 9 inches deep.   36 × 23 × 9 inches deep.   42 × 23 × 9 inches deep.   48 × 23 × 9 inches deep.

PLATE 527-G.

"EASTLAKE" KITCHEN SINK, ON LEGS,

With Back, Air Chambers and Faucets.

Sizes: 30 × 23 × 9 inches deep.   36 × 23 × 9 inches deep.   42 × 23 × 9 inches deep.   48 × 23 × 9 inches deep.

Traps as shown on page 210 can be used with the "Eastlake" Sink.

THE "Eastlake" is not only beautiful in design, but is large and roomy, being wider and deeper than any Kitchen Sink made hitherto. The Strainer is always in the centre of the bottom at the back, the bottom of Sink being made with considerable dip towards Strainer, so that all the water is readily drained off.

MOTT'S "EASTLAKE" KITCHEN SINKS.

PLAIN, BRONZED, GALVANIZED AND ENAMELED.

PLATE 528-G.

"EASTLAKE" KITCHEN SINK, ON BRACKETS,

With Marble Back 18 inches high and Nickel-plated Faucets.

Sizes : 30 × 23 × 9 inches deep.   36 × 23 × 9 inches deep.   42 × 23 × 9 inches deep.   48 × 23 × 9 inches deep.

PLATE 529-G.

"EASTLAKE" KITCHEN SINK ON LEGS,

With Marble Back 18 inches high and Nickel-plated Faucets.

Sizes : 30 × 23 × 9 inches deep.   36 × 23 × 9 inches deep.   42 × 23 × 9 inches deep.   48 × 23 × 9 inches deep.

Either of the Traps shown on page 210 can be used with the Eastlake Sink.

DEMAREST KITCHEN SINKS.

PLAIN, BRONZED, GALVANIZED AND PORCELAIN-LINED.

PLATE 530-G.

DEMAREST KITCHEN SINK,

With Brackets, Back, Air Chambers, and Faucets.

Four Sizes : 30 × 22 × 7 inches deep.   36 × 22 × 7 inches deep.   42 × 22 × 7 inches deep.   48 × 22 × 7 inches deep.
Strainer in Centre of Bottom at Back.

PLATE 531-G.

DEMAREST KITCHEN SINK.

With Legs, Back, Air Chambers, and Faucets.

Four Sizes : 30 × 22 × 7 inches deep.   36 × 22 × 7 inches deep.   42 × 22 × 7 inches deep.   48 × 22 × 7 inches deep.

Strainer in Centre of Bottom at Back.   If so ordered, Sink can be furnished to waste through Right or Left Leg.

DEMAREST KITCHEN SINKS.

PLAIN, BRONZED, GALVANIZED AND ENAMELED.

PLATE 532-G.

DEMAREST KITCHEN SINK,

With Brackets and Back.

Four Sizes: 30 × 22 × 7 inches deep.   36 × 22 × 7 inches deep.   42 × 22 × 7 inches deep.   48 × 22 × 7 inches deep.

Strainer in Centre of Bottom at Back.

PLATE 533-G.

DEMAREST KITCHEN SINK,

With Legs and Back.

Four Sizes: 30 × 22 × 7 inches deep.   36 × 22 × 7 inches deep.   42 × 22 × 7 inches deep.   48 × 22 × 7 inches deep.

Strainer in Centre of Bottom at Back.

If so ordered, Sink can be furnished to waste through Right or Left Leg.

SINKS.

PLAIN, GALVANIZED AND ENAMELED.

PLATE 534-G.

SINKS WITH OPEN STRAINER.

Sizes.	Sizes.	Sizes.	Sizes.
16½ × 12½ × 5 inches deep.	24 × 18 × 6 inches deep.	32½ × 21 × 6 inches deep.	24 × 14 × 8 inches deep.
18 × 12 × 6 "	25½ × 17½ × 6 "	36 × 18 × 6 "	30 × 24 × 8 "
16 × 16 × 6 "	27 × 15 × 6 "	36 × 21½ × 6 "	62 × 22 × 8 "
22 × 14 × 6 "	24 × 20 × 6 "	38 × 20 × 6 "	56 × 32 × 9 "
23 × 15 × 6 "	28 × 17 × 6 "	42 × 22 × 6 "	60 × 28 × 10 "
25½ × 15½ × 6 "	28 × 20 × 6 "	48 × 20 × 6 "	62 × 20 × 12 "
20 × 12½ × 6 "	30 × 16 × 6 "	48 × 23 × 6 "	72 × 20 × 12 "
20 × 14 × 6 "	30 × 18 × 6 "	50 × 24 × 6¼ "	78 × 28 × 10 "
20 × 20 × 6 "	30 × 20 × 6 "	50 × 26 × 6½ "	94 × 24 × 10 "
24 × 14 × 6 "	32½ × 18 × 6 "	76 × 22 × 7 "	120 × 22 × 6 "
24½ × 16 × 6 "			

PLATE 535-G.

SINK WITH PATENT OVERFLOW AND OPEN STRAINER.

Made all sizes same as Plate 534-G.

PLATE 536-G.

SINK WITH PATENT OVERFLOW AND PLUG STRAINER.

Made all sizes same as Plate 534-G.

Sinks furnished with Brass Strainers to order.

SINKS.

PLAIN, GALVANIZED AND ENAMELED.

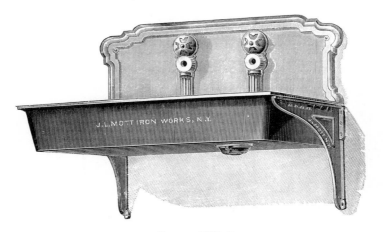

PLATE 537-G.

SINK WITH BRACKETS, BACK AND AIR CHAMBERS.

Also furnished with Back less Air Chambers, as shown by Plate 540-G, or with Box Back, Plate 539-G.

PLATE 538-G.

SINK WITH LEGS, BACK AND AIR CHAMBERS.

PLATE 539-G.

SINK WITH LEGS, AND BOX, OR PROJECTING BACK.

For Sizes of Sinks, see Plate 534-G. Backs as shown are furnished with any size Sink, up to 48 inches long.

Larger Backs made to order in sections.

NOTE.—When ordering Sinks with Back and Air Chambers, it is necesary to state whether waste of Sink is to be right or left.

SINKS.

PLATE 540-G.

SINK WITH LEGS AND BACK.

For Sizes of Sinks, see Plate 534–G.   Backs as shown are furnished up to 48 inches long ; larger sizes made to order in sections.

PLATE 541-G.

HALF CIRCLE SINK.

No.	Length of Back.	Width.	Depth.
1	24 inches.	14 inches.	6 inches.
2	27 "	14 "	6 "
3	28 "	16 "	8 "
4	31½ "	17 "	6 "

Sizes.

Can be furnished with Patent Overflow, same as Plate 535–G.
Or with Patent Overflow and Plug Strainer, same as Plate 536–G.

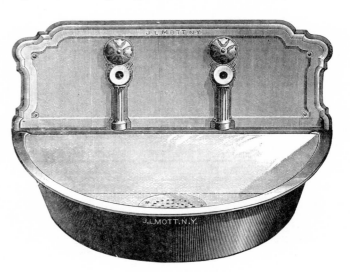

PLATE 542-G.

HALF CIRCLE SINK,

With Back and Air Chambers,

Also furnished with Back less Air Chambers.

No.	Length of Back.	Width.	Depth.
1	24 inches.	14 inches.	6 inches
2	27 "	14 "	6 "
3	28 "	16 "	8 "
4	31½ "	17 "	6 "

Sizes.

Can be furnished with Patent Overflow, same as Plate 535–G.
Or with Patent Overflow and Plug Strainer, same as Plate 536–G.

CORNER SINKS.

PLAIN, GALVANIZED AND ENAMELED.

PLATE 543-G.

CORNER SINK,

With Open Strainer.

PLATE 544-G.

CORNER SINK,

With Open Strainer, Back and Air Chambers,
Also furnished with Back, less Air Chambers.

Three Sizes : No. 1, 17 inches on side × 4½ inches deep.   No. 2, 20 inches on side × 6 inches deep.   No. 3, 22 inches on side × 6½ inches deep.

Can be furnished with Patent Overflow, same as Plate 535-G, or with Patent Overflow and Plug Strainer, same as Plate 536-G.

SINK BACKS.

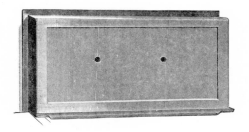

PLATE 545-G.

BOX OR PROJECTING BACK FOR SINK.
Made all sizes up to 48 inches long.

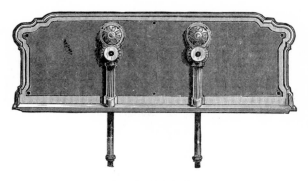

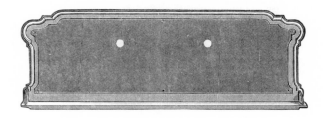

PLATE 546-G.

SINK BACK WITH AIR CHAMBERS, PIPES AND COUPLINGS.

Made as shown up to 48 inches in length ; larger sizes made to order
in sections.   Can be furnished with 1 Air Chamber, if so ordered.

PLATE 547-G

SINK BACK,

Made as shown up to 48 inches in length ; larger sizes made to order
in sections.   Can be furnished with 1 hole, if so ordered.

SINK LEGS AND BRACKETS.

PLAIN AND GALVANIZED.

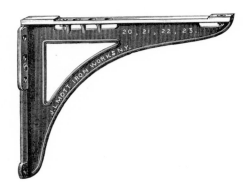

PLATE 548-G.

SINK LEG.

For all sizes of Sinks.

PLATE 549-G.

PATENT SINK BRACKETS.

Sizes : No. 1, takes Sink up to 18 inches wide.
" 2, " " " 23 "
" 3, " " " 32 "

SINK FITTINGS.

PLATE 550-G.
OPEN SINK STRAINER.
Plain, Galvanized, Enameled Iron or Brass.

PLATE 551-G.
SINK BOLTS.
Plain and Nickeled.
Length 2¼ in.

PLATE 552-G.
PLUG SINK STRAINER.
Plain, Galvanized or Enameled Iron or Brass.

PLATE 553-G.
SINK COUPLING.
Plain and Galvanized.

PLATE 554-G.
SINK COUPLING.
Extra Heavy, Tapped for Iron Pipe.
Plain and Galvanized.

PLATE 555-G.
SOAP CUP.
Plain Galvanized and Enameled.
SIZE : 5¼ × 3¼ in.

PLATE 556-G.
S TRAP,
For Lead Waste
Pipe Connection.

PLATE 557-G.
S TRAP,
For Iron Waste
Pipe Connection.

PLATE 558-G.
½ S TRAP,
For Lead Waste Pipe
Connection. Also made for
Iron Pipe Connection.

PLATE 559-G.
¾ S TRAP,
For Lead Waste Pipe
Connection. Also made for
Iron Pipe Connection.

PLATE 560-G.
STRAIGHT CONNECTION,
For Iron Pipe.

The above Traps can be furnished for wrought iron pipe connection if so ordered.

"IMPERIAL" PORCELAIN WASH TUBS.

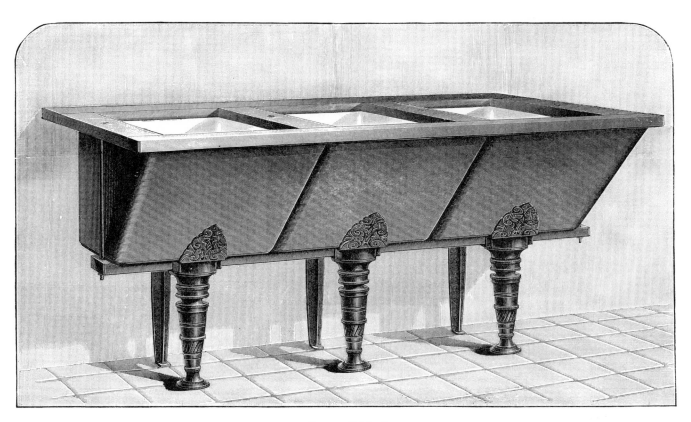

PLATE 561-G.

Set of Three "Imperial" Porcelain Wash Tubs with Patent Galvanized Iron Standards and Heavy Ash Top.

Two Sizes : Size A, length from right to left, 29½ inches ; width from front to back, 24 inches ; depth inside, 16½ inches ; thickness, 1½ inches.

Size B,   "   "   26½ "   "   "   24 "   "   16½ "   "   1½ "

NOTE —When ordering it will be necessary to state if the Tubs are desired with or without Faucet Holes in Back.

Size A Tubs will be furnished unless Size B are ordered.

THE "Imperial" Porcelain Wash Tubs are in material and finish the same as our celebrated "Imperial" Porcelain Baths. There is no limit to their durability ; they are perfectly modeled ; the glaze is of a beautiful cream tint, delicate and uniform in color and unapproached by anything of the kind yet made. Special attention is called to the neat and complete manner in which they are set up by means of our Patent Standards and Ash Top.

In the manufacture of large pieces of Porcelain, such as Wash Tubs, a greater or less number when taken out of the kiln are found to have slight defects which in no way detract from the practical value or fine appearance of the article ; in fact our "Seconds" as we term them, are equal to the best ware of any other make we have yet seen, and are only classed as such in view of the very high standard we have set up for our "Firsts." These "Seconds" are well adapted for use not only in private residences, but especially in hospitals, asylums, apartment houses and public buildings, where cost is a consideration.

"Imperial" Porcelain Wash Tubs.

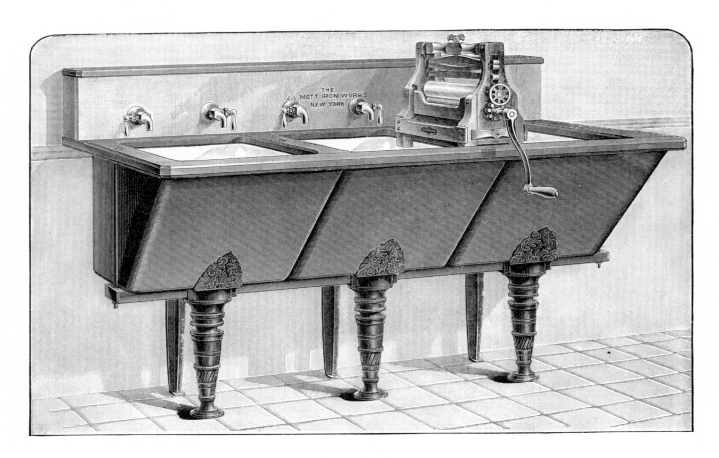

Plate 562-G.

Set of three "Imperial" Porcelain Wash Tubs with Patent Galvanized Iron Standards, Heavy Ash Top rabbeted, fitted and finished with Back, the

"Excelsior" Wringer, and Improved Flange and Thimble Faucets.

Two Sizes : A and B.

For dimensions see page 223.

T HE above illustration shows the "Imperial" Porcelain Wash Tubs set up without covers, and with Faucets over Top, which is now considered the most approved style of fitting up these Tubs, as it not only gives more room inside, but admits of a much better arrangement of the Supply Pipes, getting them, instead of behind, over the Tubs, where they can be readily got at in case of leak or necessary repairs ; furthermore the Tubs can be placed close to the wall if so desired.

Note.—Size A Tubs will be furnished unless Size B are ordered.

"Imperial" Porcelain Wash Tubs.

PLATE 563-G.

Set of three "Imperial" Porcelain Wash Tubs, with Patent Galvanized Iron Standards, Heavy Ash Top rabbetted, fitted and finished Covers, and Improved Flange and Thimble Faucets.

Two Sizes: A and B.

For dimensions see page 223.

Size A Tubs will be furnished unless Size B are ordered.

The "Excelsior" Wringer as shown by Plate 562-G, can be furnished with above, if so ordered.

"YORKSHIRE" BROWN GLAZED EARTHEN WASH TUBS.

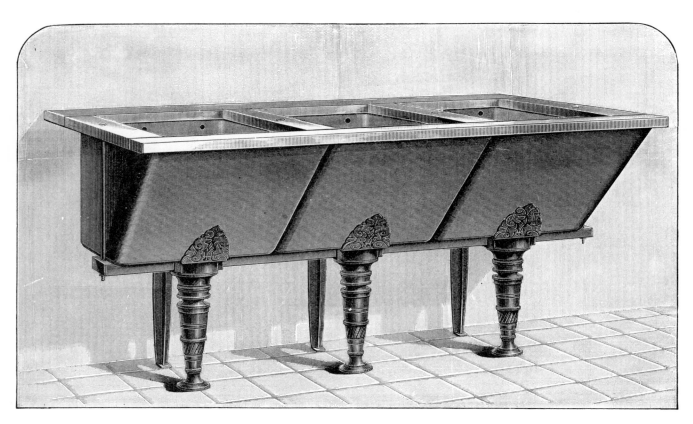

PLATE 564-G.

SET OF THREE "YORKSHIRE" BROWN GLAZED EARTHEN WASH TUBS.

With Patent Bronzed Iron Standards and Heavy Ash Top.

Dimensions: Length from right to left, 29½ inches; width from front to back, 24 inches;

depth inside, 16½ inches; thickness 1½ inches.

NOTE.—Tubs with Faucet Holes as shown, will be furnished unless ordered without holes.

THE "Yorkshire" Wash Tubs are covered on the inside and outside with a rich, dark brown glaze which renders them absolutely non-absorbent. Being made in one piece of Earthenware 1½ inches thick, they are necessarily durable and will not leak. The Tubs after being set up require no finishing or decorating on the outside—in short the "Yorkshire" possess all the advantages of a first class Wash Tub at an extremely moderate price, and their superiority to Wooden Tubs, or Tubs made of Concrete or other Compositions which are entirely without glaze, or Soapstone or Slate Tubs made of several pieces, must be obvious.

PORCELAIN-LINED AND GALVANIZED IRON WASH TUBS.

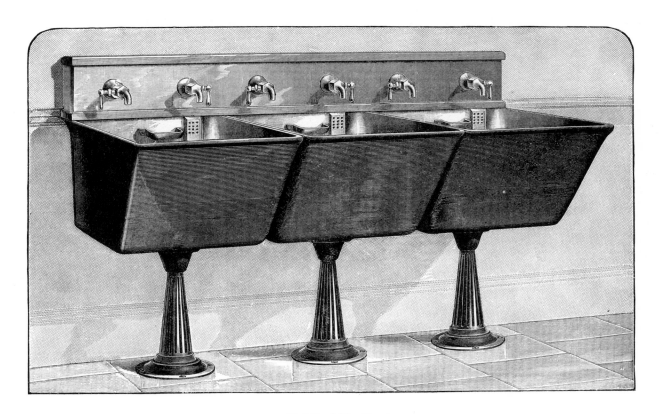

PLATE 565-G.

SET OF THREE PORCELAIN-LINED OR GALVANIZED IRON WASH TUBS.

Each Tub having Patent Overflow, Nickel plated Plug w th Rubber Stopper and Chain, and Soap Cup;
with Ash or Black Walnut Back, and Faucets.

Dimensions : Height, including Standard, 32 inches.   Length of each Tub, from right to left, 24 inches.

Width, from front to back, 24 inches.   Inside depth, 14 inches.

NOTE.—In ordering Tubs as above, please say "without faucet holes in back."

O UR Porcelain-lined and Galvanized Iron Wash Tubs are cleanly, durable, non-absorbent and neat in appearance.   They are made in one piece, and, in consequence, are free from the objections to which all tubs made up of several pieces are open; the joints in the latter, usually of cement, soon become defective, causing the Tub to leak.

The quality of our Porcelain-lined goods is so well known that they require no comment from us.

PORCELAIN-LINED AND GALVANIZED IRON WASH TUBS.

PLATE 566-G.

SET OF THREE PORCELAIN-LINED OR GALVANIZED IRON WASH TUBS.

Each Tub having Patent Overflow, Nickel-plated Plug with Rubber Stopper and Chain and Soap Cup;

with Ash or Black Walnut Covers, and Faucets.

For dimensions see page 227.

NOTE.—In ordering Tubs as above, please say "with faucet holes in back."

DECORATED PORCELAIN FOLDING URINALS.

Design No. 1389.

GOLD LINES.

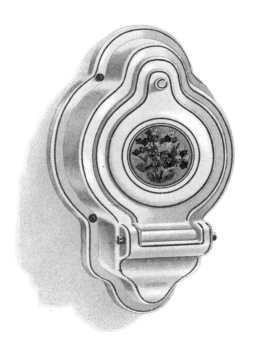

Design No. 1392.

"HELIOTROPE."

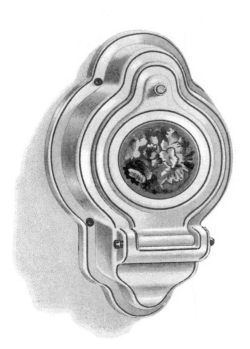

Design No. 1393.

"CHINESE PEONY."

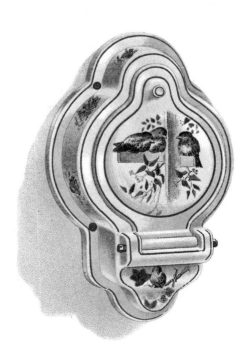

Design No. 1355.

"BIRDS AND FLOWERS."

Major Knapp & Co., 56 & 58 Park Place, N.Y.

PATENT FOLDING URINALS.
ALL-PORCELAIN AND PORCELAIN-LINED IRON.

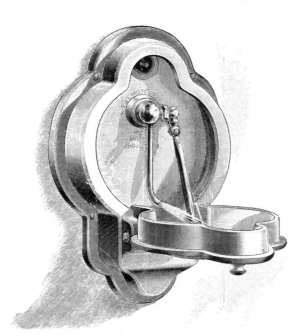

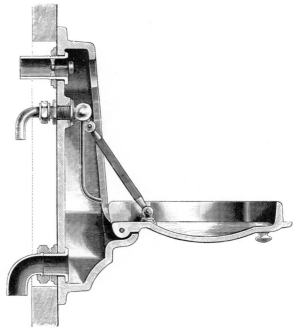

PLATE 567-G.
ALL-PORCELAIN FOLDING URINAL.

Illustration shows Urinal open as when in use   It is simply two pieces of the finest imported Porcelain, with nickel-plated Brass Mountings.

PLATE 568-G
SECTION.

Illustration shows Urinal cut through the centre.

The Couplings for supply and waste, also for air vent, are of Brass.

IT has been our desire for many years to get a Urinal at once sightly, cleanly, and one that would be adapted for private use in all rooms set aside for gentlemen's use, such as Billiard and Smoking Rooms, Private Offices, &c. This Urinal is not only a novel but a handsome fixture and being entirely of Porcelain, of course there is no rusting or corroding. It cannot be used without turning on the water, consequently it is thoroughly washed every time it is used; furthermore, as shown by Section, it can be perfectly ventilated.

These Urinals are of the finest English ware, either in pure white or in the handsome hand-painted decorations shown on previous page.

PLATE 569-G.
PORCELAIN-LINED IRON URINAL.
Shows Urinal Open.

PLATE 570-G.
PORCELAIN-LINED IRON URINAL.
Shows Urinal Closed.

THE above is, in most respects, the same as the Patent All-Porcelain Urinal, and is also particularly adapted for use in private Bath Rooms, Billiard Rooms, Offices, &c., meeting a want very long felt; the ordinary styles of Urinals not being adapted for use in such places, from the fact that it is impossible to keep them clean and free from offensive odor. They are, besides, offensive to the eye and take up a great deal of room. A great many of these Urinals have been sold during the past few years, and every one without a single exception, has given the most unqualified satisfaction.

They are Porcelain-lined and Painted One Coat Outside, or they can be furnished Bronzed or Marbleized.

URINALS WITH DEMAREST'S PATENT AUTOMATIC FLUSHING CISTERN.

PLATE 571-G.

PORCELAIN FLAT BACK LIPPED URINALS,

With Demarest's Automatic Flushing Cistern, and Marble or Slate Stalls.

The illustration shows the Demarest Patent Flushing Cistern set up over Urinals. Any number of Urinals may be placed in a row, and flushed from one or more of the Automatic Flushing Cisterns, the quantity of water for each Urinal being governed by local conditions, more especially by the available water supply.

No. 1, Automatic Cistern, with Single Coupling, is suitable for 1 Urinal.	No. 4 Automatic Cistern, with Triple Coupling, is suitable for 5 to 8 Urinals.
" 1, " " " Double " " " " 2 "	" 5 " " " " Double " " " " 8 " 10 "
" 2, " " " " " " " 2 to 4 "	" 5 " " " " " Triple " " " " 9
" 3, " " " " " " " 4 "	" 8 " " " " " " " " " 9 " 15 "
" 3, " " " " Triple " " " 5 or 6 "	" 10 " " " " " " " " " 12 " 18 "
" 4, " " " " Double " " " 6 to 8 "	

For separate view and description of Urinals and Flushing Cisterns, see subsequent pages.

URINALS WITH DEMAREST'S PATENT SYPHON CISTERN.

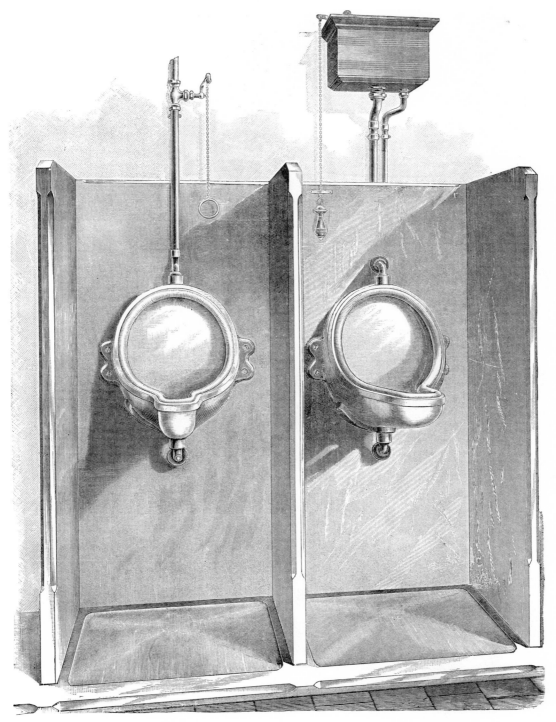

PLATE 572-G.

PORCELAIN FLAT BACK LIPPED URINAL,

With Self-closing Cock, Chain and Pull.

PLATE 572 ½-G.

PORCELAIN FLAT BACK LIPPED URINAL,

With Demarest Patent Syphon Cistern, Pull and Chain.

WHERE a non-automatic Urinal is desired, we know of no better arrangement than that shown by Plate 572½-G. A touch and let go of the Pull starts the Syphon and contents of Cistern (1 gallon) descend to the Urinal, thoroughly flushing and cleansing it. The Pull we furnish of Ebonized Wood or Ivory-Celluloid, and being neat and clean in appearance, and hanging at a convenient height, the chances are that every person using the Urinal will flush it; whereas with the ordinary compression or self-closing cock (which is usually placed very near the Urinal) very few stop to flush the Urinal. The Cistern is furnished Cabinet-finish as shown by Plate 572½-G, or of Iron or Wood Copper-lined.
With Plate 572-G, water passes to Urinal only while Pull is held down.

COMPARTMENT URINAL.

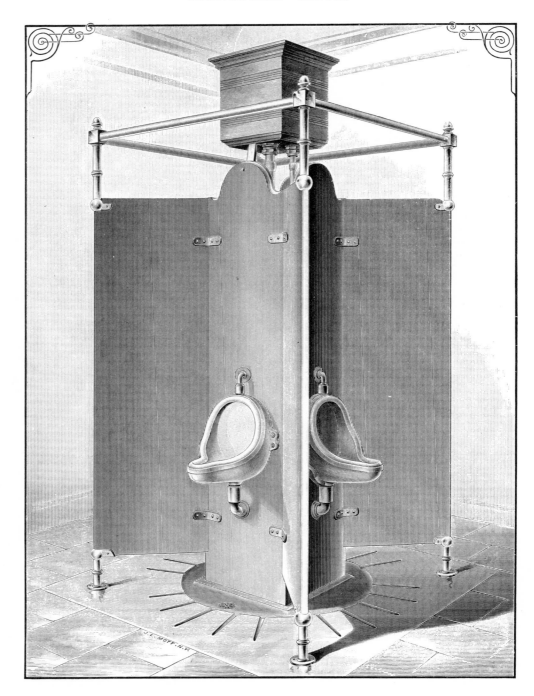

PLATE 573-G.

SQUARE FOUR STALL MARBLE OR SLATE URINAL,

With Polished or Nickel-plated Brass Fittings, Porcelain Lipped Urinals and Black Walnut, Cherry
or Ash Copper lined Demarest Automatic Flushing Cistern.

PLATE 573-G represents an arrangement of Urinals for use in Hotels and Public Buildings, in cases where it is preferable to place them in
the centre of an apartment instead of at the side against the wall as usual.   The Base is grooved and counter-sunk to drain into two outlet
pipes connected with a single waste.   The four Backs form a central hollow space about 18 inches square, within which all the pipes are located.   In
putting up the Urinals, three of the Stalls are completed; the Back Slab and Urinal of the remaining Stall are then placed in position.   In case of repairs
or leakage, access to all the pipes is obtained by removing one Urinal and Back Piece   We furnish the Stalls with or without the ornamental Brass
Top Rail.

For flushing the Urinals we recommend the Demarest Automatic Cistern; it may be Cherry, Black Walnut or Ash, as shown, or Iron or Cast
Brass polished.   The size shown is two gallon, which is sufficient for four Urinals.

URINAL WITH DEMAREST'S TREADLE URINAL PLATFORM.

PLATE 574-G.

PORCELAIN LIPPED URINAL,

With Adjustable Supply and Waste Couplings, and Demarest's Treadle.

PLATE 575-G.

DEMAREST'S TREADLE URINAL PLATFORM,

With Single Acting Valve.

Size of Top, $18\frac{1}{2} \times 14\frac{1}{2}$ inches: height, $4\frac{1}{2}$ inches.

Iron part galvanized with brass fittings.

WHEN the treadle is stepped upon it actuates the Valve which is connected by a pipe with the Urinal; the Valve continues to run as long as Treadle is depressed, and washes the interior of Urinal and Treadle every time operated. The cover of Treadle can be readily removed for cleaning.

MOTT'S SECTIONAL URINAL TROUGHS:

WITH FLUSHING-PIPE AND DEMAREST PATENT AUTOMATIC FLUSHING CISTERN.

PLATE 576-G.

IRON SECTIONAL URINAL TROUGH, PAINTED, GALVANIZED OR PORCELAIN-LINED,

With Perforated Galvanized Wrought Iron or Brass Flushing-pipe and Demarest Patent Automatic Cistern,

Dimensions of Urinal Trough: Depth, 10½ inches; Width, 10 inches; Back, 6 inches high but can be furnished 16 inches high to order.

The Trough is made in 5 foot Sections and can be furnished any length to order.

For further description of Urinal Troughs, see page 239.

P LATE 576-G represents a Urinal Trough adapted for use in Factories, Schools and Public Buildings. The Automatic Cistern discharges its contents at desired intervals, thoroughly flushing the interior of the Urinal Trough.

For description of Demarest Patent Flushing Cistern, see page 243.

STEVENS' PATENT VENTILATING URINALS.

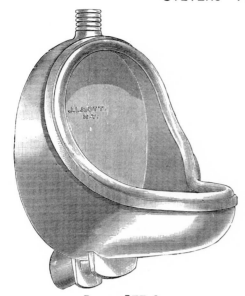

PLATE 577-G.

STEVENS' URINAL WITH TOP INLET.

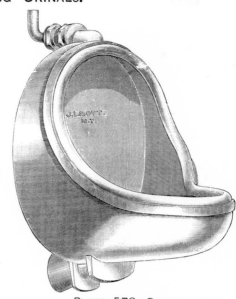

PLATE 578-G.

STEVENS' URINAL WITH BRASS BACK INLET COUPLING.

Size of Urinal 14 × 18 inches.

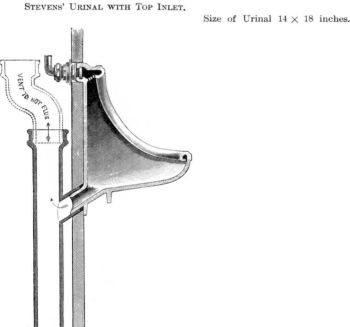

PLATE 579-G.

STEVENS' URINAL WITH FITTINGS.

Back Inlet and ½ S Trap.

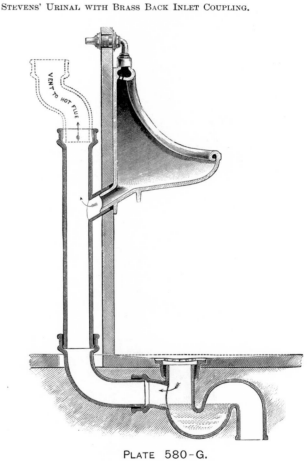

PLATE 580-G.

STEVENS' URINAL WITH FITTINGS.

Top Inlet and S Trap.

The Fittings are Porcelain-lined Iron, 3 or 4 inch, with Porcelain or Brass Grating.

PLATES 579-G and 580–G show the Steven's Urinal set up with Enameled Iron Fittings. The advantages of this system of drainage and ventilation must be at once apparent to all those who have given any attention whatever to the subject of Urinals. It is a well known fact that nothing in the whole line of plumbing is so difficult to handle as this matter of Urinals, as no amount of water, no matter how applied, will keep a line of Urinals in any public building sweet and clean, unless they are properly ventilated, and no more perfect or simpler system than Mr. Stevens' can well be imagined; i. e. where a Hot Flue can be had in which to run the Vent, otherwise the principal feature of the system is lost; this is very readily found as a general thing in all large buildings, and there is no trouble carrying out the system when the plans are arranged for it. As shown, the Urinal has a 2½ inch open outlet, i. e. no strainer, thus allowing all matter (which is usually dropped into Urinals to lay there until taken out by hand), to pass through and be carried off same as matter from a Water Closet.

IMPORTED PORCELAIN URINALS.

PLATE 581-G.

IMPORTED PORCELAIN FLAT BACK URINAL, LIPPED,

Patent Overflow.

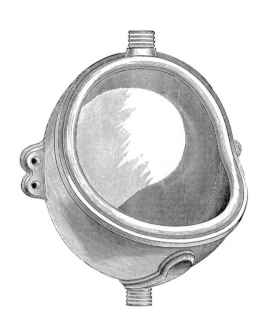

PLATE 582-G.

IMPORTED PORCELAIN FLAT BACK URINAL,

Patent Overflow.

Sizes: No. 1, 11 × 14½ inches;   No. 2, 12½ × 16½ inches;   No. 3, 15½ × 18½ inches.

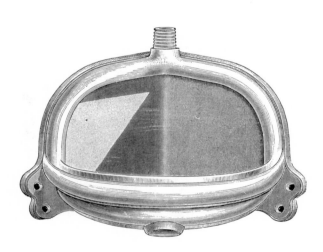

PLATE 583-G

IMPORTED PORCELAIN CORNER URINAL,

Patent Overflow.

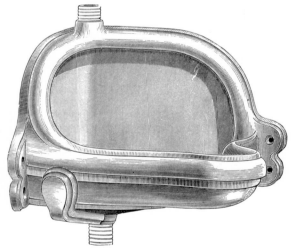

PLATE 584-G.

IMPORTED PORCELAIN CORNER URINAL, LIPPED,

Patent Overflow.

Sizes: No. 1, 8½ × 11 inches;   No. 2, 10 × 14 inches;   No. 3, 12½ × 16½ inches.

MOTT'S URINAL FITTINGS.

NICKEL-PLATED OR POLISHED BRASS.

PLATE 585-G.

DEMAREST'S ADJUSTABLE INLET CONNECTION.

PLATE 586-G.

INLET CONNECTION,

For Pipe to run in Front of Marble.

PLATE 587-G.

DEMAREST'S ADJUSTABLE OUTLET CONNECTION.

PLATE 588-G.

TOP URINAL SHIELD.

PLATE 589-G.

BOTTOM URINAL SHIELD FOR LIPPED URINALS.

PLATE 590-G.

BOTTOM URINAL SHIELD FOR URINALS WITHOUT LIP.

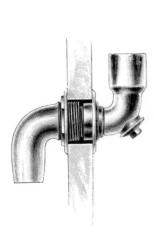

PLATE 591-G.

OUTLET CONNECTION,

With Clean out and Bent Coupling.

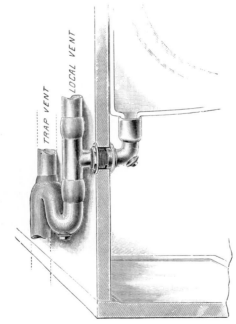

PLATE 592-G.

SHOWING PORCELAIN URINAL,

With Outlet Connection Plate 593–G connected with
Lead Trap and Pipe leading to Hot Flue.

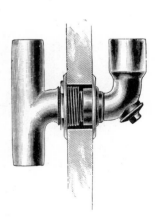

PLATE 593-G.

OUTLET CONNECTION,

With Clean-out and T for connection with
Trap and Local Vent,
as shown by Plate 592–G.

MOTT'S SECTIONAL URINAL TROUGHS.

PLAIN, GALVANIZED AND PORCELAIN-LINED.

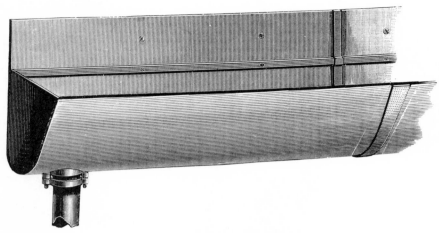

PLATE 594-G.

SECTIONAL URINAL TROUGH.

The Trough is made in 5 foot sections, and can be furnished any length to order.

Dimensions : Depth of Trough, 10½ inches ; Width, 10 inches ; Back, 6 inches high.

Extra high Back (16 inch) furnished to order.

NOTE.—The illustration shows the Trough with Outlet on left hand but it can be furnished with Outlet on right hand if so ordered.

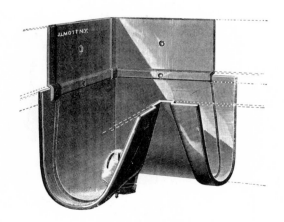

PLATE 595-G.

CORNER PIECE.

The above is to connect Urinal Trough so as to make it continuous on two or more sides of the room.

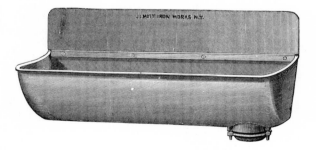

PLATE 596-G.

URINAL TROUGH.

Sizes : Length, 36 inches ; Width, 13 inches ; Depth, 12 inches.
"   42   "   "   13   "   "   12   "
"   48   "   "   13   "   "   12   "

Mott's Iron Urinals.

PLAIN, GALVANIZED AND ENAMELED.

PLATE 597-G.

FLAT BACK LIPPED URINAL,

With Brass Fan, Supply and Waste Couplings.

Dimensions: Width of Back, 17 inches. Length of Back, 18 inches.
Lip projects 11 inches.

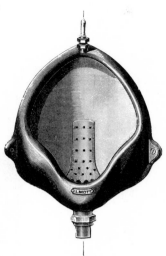

PLATE 598-G.

CORNER LIPPED URINAL,

With Brass Fan, Supply and Waste Couplings.

Dimensions: Length on Side, 9 inches. Length of Back, 14 inches.
Lip projects 12 inches.

Plates 597-G, and 598-G, can be furnished with Ventilating Hood having Brass Coupling, if so ordered.

PLATE 599-G.
HALF CIRCLE URINAL.

PLATE 600-G.
HALF CIRCLE URINAL WITH HOOD.

PLATE 601-G.
CORNER URINAL.

With opening behind for lead pipe.
12 inches on Side.

Sizes: No. 1, Length of Back, 12 inches; No. 2, Length of Back, 15 inches.

PLATE 602-G.
CORNER URINAL.

PLATE 603-G.
CORNER URINAL,
With opening behind for lead pipe.

PLATE 604-G.
CORNER URINAL,
With Ventilating Hood
and opening behind for lead pipe.

Sizes: No. 1, 8 inches on Side. No. 2, 10 inches on Side. No. 3, 12 inches on Side.

MOTT'S SECTIONAL STREET OR PARK URINALS,

WITH OR WITHOUT LAMP, PAINTED.

PLATE 605-G.

ONE PERSON URINAL

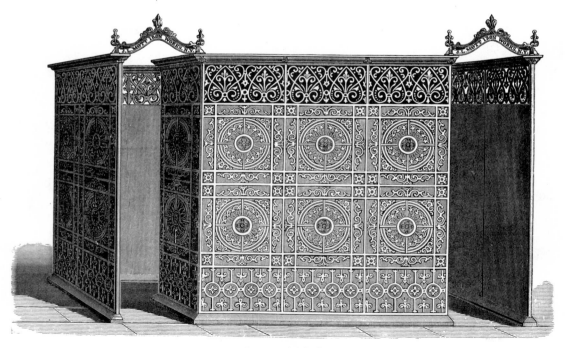

PLATE 606-G.

THREE PERSON URINAL WITH TWO ENTRANCES.

THESE Urinals are made entirely of Cast Iron, including the Floors, rendering each Urinal complete in itself, and requiring only a couple of Brick Piers as a foundation on which to place them. Each division is furnished with one of our large Enameled Urinals. They are perfectly fitted and thoroughly painted with our metallic paint, each plate and piece being marked, same as plan sent with each Urinal, so there can be no difficulty in their erection. As shown by ground plans on next page, these Urinals can be extended to any length required.

ONE PERSON.

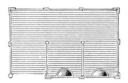

TWO PERSON.

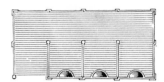

THREE PERSON.

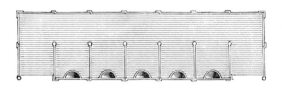

FIVE PERSON, TWO ENTRANCES.

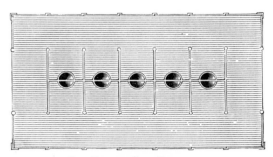

TEN PERSON, TWO ENTRANCES.

Ground Plans of Sectional Urinals.

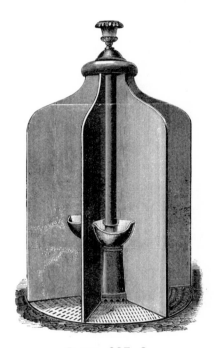

PLATE 607-G.

SIX PERSON ROUND URINAL.

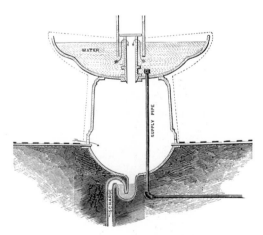

PLATE 608-G.

SECTIONAL VIEW OF SIX PERSON ROUND URINAL.

Porcelain-lined Bowl, with Slate or Iron Partitions.

The above Urinal is particularly adapted for use inside Railroad Depots, Hotels and other public Buildings. This Urinal is furnished with one large Bowl, which has six projecting Lips; said Bowl is kept perfectly odorless by a constant supply of water. The Stand Pipe or Plug, as shown in Section, Plate 608-G, is carried inside the pipe which hangs from the top, thereby forming a perfect trap. It is also furnished with a basin which is placed under Iron Floor of Urinal, so as to catch any drippings from the floor. The Stand Pipe or Plug is arranged so it can be raised at any time to flush Pipes and clean out the Bowl.

DEMAREST'S PATENT FLUSHING CISTERNS FOR URINALS AND HOPPERS.

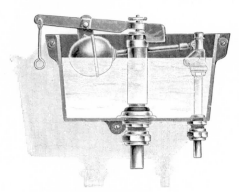

PLATE 609-G.

DEMAREST SYPHON CISTERN FOR URINAL.

Painted or Porcelain lined Iron, or Wood Copper-lined.

Capacity, 1 gallon; Dimensions : 13 × 6 × 6½ inches deep.

This Cistern is operated by the Pull as indicated by Plate 572½-G. Page 232. When the Pull is drawn down (it may be released immediately or held in the hand) the contents of Cistern (1 gallon) descend and flush the Urinal.

PLATE 610-G.

DEMAREST COPPER-LINED CABINET FINISH SYPHON CISTERN FOR URINAL.

Cherry, Black Walnut, Ash or Oak.

Capacity, 1 gallon; Dimensions : 14 × 7 × 6½ inches deep.

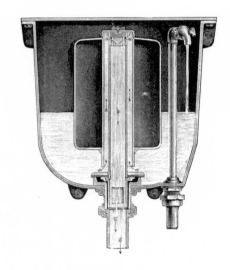

PLATE 611-G.

DEMAREST PATENT AUTOMATIC FLUSHING CISTERN.

Painted or Porcelain-lined Iron.

Plate 611-G, shows Cistern after Float has raised and Syphon started, that is, the Cistern in the act of discharging.

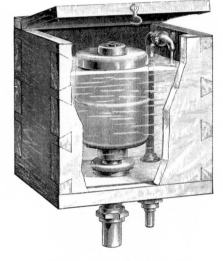

PLATE 612-G.

DEMAREST PATENT AUTOMATIC FLUSHING CISTERN.

Wood, Copper-lined.

Plate 612-G shows Copper Float at rest and Cistern gradually filling up to point where Float will be raised and Syphon started.

Seven Sizes : Nos. 1, 2, 3, 4, 5, 8 and 10, the number indicating the capacity in gallons.

PLATE 613-G.

DOUBLE COUPLING.

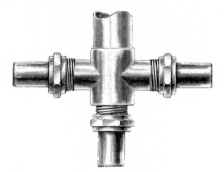

PLATE 614-G.

TRIPLE COUPLING.

THE Demarest Automatic Flushing Cistern is exceedingly simple and reliable in operation and has no delicate moving parts liable to wear and get out of order. The action is as follows : The water from the Supply Cock gradually fills the Cistern until it comes to about 1 inch from the top of the Copper Float ; the buoyancy of the Float is then sufficient to raise the Valve from its seat (to which however it at once returns) when the water entering the discharge pipe starts the Syphon, which continues to run until the water in Cistern descends below the lower end of the Syphon ; the Cistern then gradually fills as before. The arrangement of couplings is made with a view to meet all circumstances under which the Cistern may be used, i. e where it is desired to use more or less water. The interval of flushing is regulated by the faucet in the Cistern, the operation being just as certain with a small supply as with a full stream.

PATENT AUTOMATIC TILTING FLUSHING CISTERN FOR URINALS AND HOPPERS.

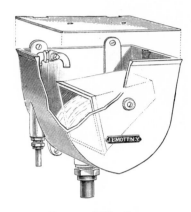

PLATE 615-G.

SECTION SHOWING BUCKET IN ACT OF TILTING.

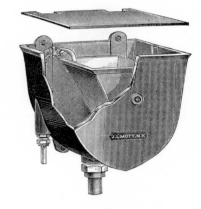

PLATE 616-G.

AUTOMATIC TILTING FLUSHING CISTERN.

No. 1 with Single Coupling. Discharges 1 gallon of water and is suitable for 1 Urinal or Hopper.

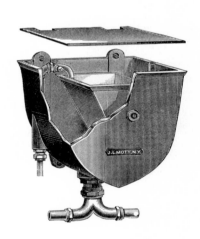

PLATE 617-G.

AUTOMATIC TILTING FLUSHING CISTERN.

No 1 with Double Coupling.
Discharges 1 gallon and is suitable for 2 Urinals.

PLATE 618-G.

AUTOMATIC TILTING FLUSHING CISTERN.

Nos. 3 and 5 with Double Coupling; also furnished with Triple
Coupling if so ordered.
The No. 3 discharges 3 gallons of water, and is suitable
for 2 Hoppers, or 4, 5, or 6 Urinals.
The No. 5 discharges 5 gallons of water, and is suitable
for 4 Hoppers, or from 7 to 10 Urinals.

THE Tilting Cistern is an excellent form of Automatic Flushing Apparatus for Urinals and Hoppers where no larger size than 5 gallons is desired. As indicated by the illustrations, it is simply a Bucket hung in a Cistern, working in Brass Journals. The filling of this Tilting Bucket is regulated by a faucet inside of Cistern as shown, and when full tips over, emptying the entire contents at once, thereby charging the pipes and giving a thorough wash to the Closets or Urinals. The interval of Flushing is regulated by the faucet, which can be turned on to let the water in slowly or quickly so as to flush the closets or Urinals every few seconds or even every hour or two, in short at any interval desired.

MOTT'S SECTIONAL CAST IRON WATER TANKS.

PAINTED, GALVANIZED AND "RUSTLESS."

PLATE 619-G.

SQUARE SECTIONAL TANK.

These Tanks are made in plates 18 × 18 inches and 18 × 9 inches, and are perfectly fitted together at our works. They can be made any length and width, and any depth up to 6 feet, that the size of the plates will admit of. They are shipped in plates, with the necessary Bolts, Braces and Cement, each plate being numbered to correspond with the Plan which we send with the Tanks, thus avoiding any trouble in fitting up.

Holes for connection put in any part of the Tank desired.

PLATE 620-G.

CIRCULAR SECTIONAL TANK.

SIZES.

Diameter.	Depth.	Capacity.	Diameter.	Depth.	Capacity.	Diameter.	Depth.	Capacity.
5 feet.	2 feet.	300 gallons.	6 feet 9 inches.	2 feet.	500 gallons.	10 feet.	2 feet.	1175 gallons.
5 "	4 "	600 "	6 " 9 "	4 "	1000 "	10 "	4 "	2350 "
5 "	6 "	900 "	6 " 9 "	6 "	1500 "	10 "	6 "	3525 "
5 "	8 "	1200 "	6 " 9 "	8 "	2000 "	10 "	8 "	4700 "

The Circular Tanks are made and shipped in plates, same as the Square Tank, Plate 619-G.

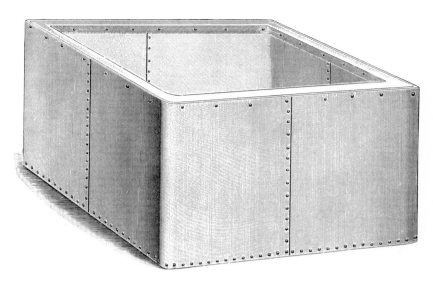

PLATE 621-G.

WROUGHT IRON WATER TANK.

These Tanks can be made any shape or size to order.   Up to 1,000 gallons capacity they are shipped mounted as shown, over 1,000 gallons they are shipped in sections with the necessary Bolts and Braces

In estimating on large Tanks we can give prices including putting together at destination, if so desired.

DEMAREST'S GREASE INTERCEPTORS.

PLATE 622-G.

DEMAREST'S GREASE INTERCEPTOR.

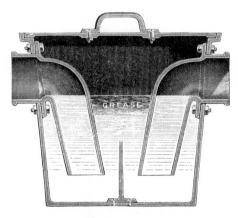

PLATE 623-G.

SECTIONAL VIEW OF DEMAREST'S GREASE INTERCEPTOR.

Sizes : No. 1, $21\frac{1}{2} \times 18 \times 18\frac{1}{2}$ inches deep   Inlet and Outlet, 4 inches ; can be made 2 inches· to order.

" 2, $25\frac{1}{2} \times 21\frac{1}{2} \times 18\frac{1}{2}$ "   "   Inlet   "   4   "   "   "   2   "   "

" 3, $31\frac{1}{2} \times 21\frac{1}{2} \times 18\frac{1}{2}$ "   "   Inlet   "   4   "   "   "   2   "   "

THE above is designed for Hotels and large Private establishments where there is a large amount of Grease passing through the pipes from Kitchen, Butler's Pantry or Scullery Sinks ; it is intended to be placed in some convenient place where the Main Pipe from all the Sinks can be connected.   By reference to sectional cut it can readily be seen how the fatty matter can be disintegrated and intercepted, first by dropping into a large body of cold water, then by being driven against the centre partition before an outlet can be gained.   The specific gravity of the fat naturally carries it to the surface in a chilled condition, where it collects, to be removed as often as may be necessary   The Inlet and Outlet are placed at one end of the Box in order to leave a large space comparatively undisturbed for the accumulation of fat or grease.

DEMAREST'S PATENT PRESSURE REDUCING VALVE AND HOUSE FILTER.

PLATE 624-G.

DEMAREST'S PATENT PRESSURE REDUCING VALVE.
The Valve is made of Brass.

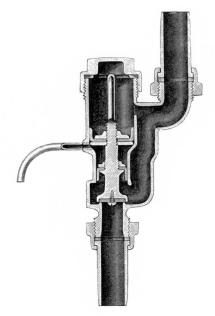

PLATE 625-G.

SECTION OF DEMAREST'S PATENT PRESSURE REDUCING VALVE.
Size: ¾ inch.

This Valve is designed for use in localities where the water pressure is very heavy, and consequently very trying on the Pipes, Valves, Faucets and other plumbing fixtures throughout a building, and should be located in the pipe from which all water is supplied to the house. It reduces the pressure just about one-half, that is to say, where the original pressure is 100 pounds it will reduce it to 50 pounds. To insure the proper working of the Valve, care must be taken to clean the pipes out well before turning on the water, so that the Valve Seat will be perfectly clean.

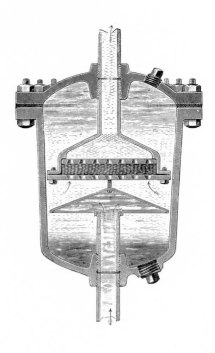

PLATE 626-G.

SECTION OF PLATE 627-G.

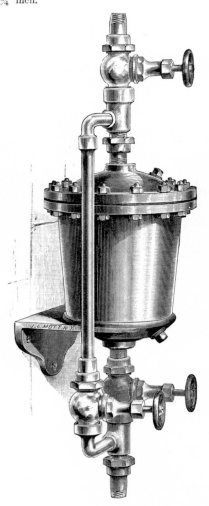

PLATE 627-G.

DEMAREST'S PATENT HOUSE FILTER.

THIS Filter is designed for use in localities where the water is charged with either floating or heavy matter or both. Inside of vessel or Iron part is Enameled, all the inside Brass parts are extra Silver Plated, the Strainer consisting of eight ply of Silver Gauze. The water is let in at the bottom and is deflected towards the sides, this breaking of the current gives the sediment a chance to separate, the light matter ascending and floating on the top while the heavier particles fall and settle in the lower part of the vessel, this deflection and consequent separation prevents all but the finest particles from coming in contact with the fine Strainer and lessens the chance of its getting clogged up, and if Filter be washed out regularly (just how often would depend on the state of the water), the Strainer will continue in good working order for a long time; if it should get choked up it can readily be taken out and cleaned or a new one inserted at small cost. To wash out Filter, shut Valves at bottom and top, then screw out bottom plug and open the Side Valve, this will allow the water from the main to pass into Filter at top and wash it out.

RANGE BOILERS, BOILER STANDS AND PIPE HANGERS.

ROUND HEAD COPPER BOILERS.

Sizes: 30, 35, 40, 45, 50, 60, 70, 80, 90 and 100 gallons.

GALVANIZED IRON BOILERS.

CAPACITY.	DIMENSIONS.		
18 gallons.	3	feet × 12	inches.
21 "	3½ "	× 12	"
24 "	4 "	× 12	"
24 "	3 "	× 14	"
27 "	4½ "	× 12	"
28 "	3½ "	× 14	"
30 "	5 "	× 12	"
32 "	4 "	× 14	"
35 "	5 "	× 13	"
36 "	6 "	× 12	"
36 "	4½ "	× 14	"
40 "	5 "	× 14	"
42 "	4 "	× 16	"
47 "	4½ "	× 16	"

GALVANIZED IRON BOILERS.

CAPACITY.	DIMENSIONS.		
48 gallons.	6	feet × 14	inches.
52 "	5 "	× 16	"
53 "	4 "	× 18	"
63 "	6 "	× 16	"
66 "	5 "	× 18	"
79 "	6 "	× 18	"
82 "	5 "	× 20	"
98 "	6 "	× 20	"
100 "	5 "	× 22	"
120 "	6 "	× 22	"
120 "	5 "	× 24	"
144 "	6 "	× 24	"
168 "	7 "	× 24	"
192 "	8 "	× 24	"

PLATE 628-G.

COPPER OR GALVANIZED IRON BOILER.

PLATE 630-G.

CAST IRON OR BRASS PIPE HANGER,

For 1 Pipe.

PLATE 631-G.

CAST IRON OR BRASS PIPE HANGER,

Can be furnished for 2, 3 or 4 Pipes.

For ½, ¾, 1 or 1¼ inch pipe.

PLATE 629-G.

MOTT'S IMPROVED LOCKWOOD BOILER STAND.

Plain, Galvanized and Bronzed.

Sizes: 12, 13, 14, 15, 16, 17, 18, 20, 22 and 24 inch Ring. Height, 21 inches.

Extension piece to raise Standard to 30 inches, furnished to order.

PLATE 632-G.

PORTABLE BASKET SLOP HOPPER.

PLATE 633-G.

SECTION.

Diameter across Top, 14 inches. Depth of Basket, 10 inches. Total depth, 16 inches. Outlet, 4 inches The Basket Slop Hopper is intended for use in Yards. As shown by sectional cut, it is trapped so that no smell can come from the sewer. The Basket or Receiver is portable.

PLATE 634-G.

CHARCOAL FURNACE.

Sizes: No. 1, 10 inches diameter on Top.
  " 2, 12   "   "   "
  " 3, 13   "   "   "
  " 4, 14   "   "   "
  " 5, 15   "   "   "

PLATE 635-G.

SOLDER POT.

No. 1, 5 inches diameter on Top.
  " 2, 6   "   "   "
  " 3, 6½ "   "   "
  " 4, 8   "   "   "
  " 5, 9   "   "   "
  " 6, 10½ "   "   "
  " 7, 13½ "   "   "

PLATE 636-G.

FURNACE AND CALDRON FOR MELTING LEAD

Capacity of Caldron, 8 gallons.

Height of Furnace. 30 inches. Diameter, 20 inches.
The grate or fire surface being extra large, the metal placed
in Caldron can be melted very quickly. The
Furnace is of heavy Sheet Iron.

PLATE 637-G.

FURNACE AND CALDRON FOR MELTING LEAD.

Capacity of Caldron, 8 gallons.

The Cast Iron Top is made with a Slide Cover, to open
when taking out the melted metal.
The small pipe attached to the conical top conveys the offensive
smoke from scrap lead into the smoke pipe.

BACK WATER VALVE, BELL TRAP, AND FRESH AIR INLET.

PLATE 638-G.

DEMAREST'S BACK WATER VALVE.

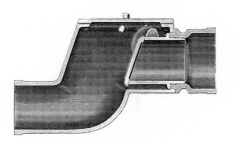

PLATE 639-G.

SECTION OF BACK WATER VALVE.

Sizes: 4, 5 and 6 inch.

The above is a simple and thoroughly well made Valve, the inside pipe and gate being of Cast Brass; the Cast Iron part can either be Plain or Porcelain-lined.

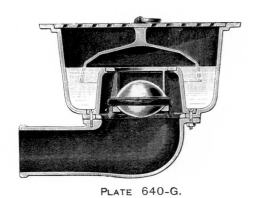

PLATE 640-G.

DEMAREST'S PATENT BACK WATER BELL TRAP.

Section showing Trap open to Sewer.

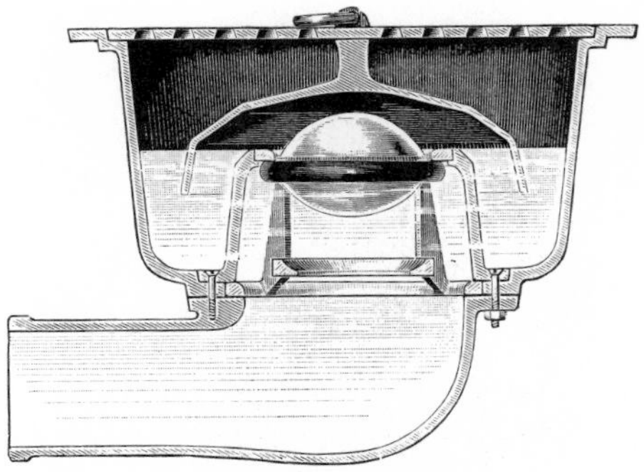

PLATE 641-G.

DEMAREST'S PATENT BACK WATER BELL TRAP.

Section showing water backed up from Sewer and Trap closed.

Dimensions: Top, 16 × 16 inches.   Height, 12¾ inches.   Outlet, 4 inches.

The above Bell Trap Cesspool is for use in Basements or Cellars where there is a chance of water backing up from Sewer.

PLATE 642-G.

SQUARE SIDEWALK GRATING FOR FRESH AIR INLET.

Size: Frame, 13¾ × 4¾ inches.   Grating, 11¾ × 3 inches.

PLATE 643-G.

OVAL SIDEWALK GRATING FOR FRESH AIR INLET.

Size: Frame, 13¾ × 6 inches.   Grating, 11½ × 3¾ inches.

PLATE 645-G.

STREET WASHER KEY.

PLATE 647-G.

STOP COCK BOX.

Plumber's address cast on Cover to order.

PLATE 648-G.

STREET WASHER BOX.

Plumber's address cast on Cover to order.

PLATE 644-G.

LONG STOP COCK BOX.

Length 3 feet 10 inches.

PLATE 646-G.

STREET WASHER ROD.

PLATE 649-G.

SOLDER MOULD.

Two and Four Bars.

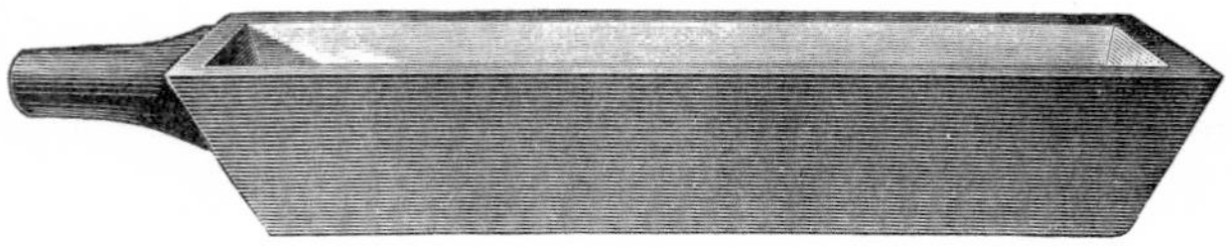

PLATE 650-G.

PIG LEAD MOULD.

PLATE 651-G.

STRAP SOLDER MOULD.

Square Bar.

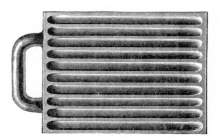

PLATE 652-G.

STRAP SOLDER MOULD.

Half Round Bar.

CESSPOOLS.

PLATE 653-G.

HYDRANT CESSPOOL.

PLATE 654-G.

HYDRANT CESSPOOL, WITH BELL TRAP.

SIZES : 12 × 12 × 6 inches deep.   14 × 14 × 6 inches deep.
16 × 16 × 6 inches deep.   18 × 18 × 6 inches deep.

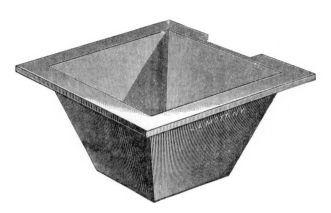

PLATE 655-G.

HEAVY HYDRANT CESSPOOL,

With Flange cut out for Hydrant.

SIZE : Top, 20 inches square.   Bottom, 10 inches square.   Depth, 11 inches.

PLATE 656-G.

CESSPOOL WITH BELL TRAP AND GRATING.

SIZE : Top, 16 inches square.   Depth, 10 inches.   Outlet, 4 inches.   Grating 13½ inches square.

Suitable for Yards and Stables.

PLATE 657-G.

SECTION OF PLATE 656-G.

CESSPOOLS.

PLATE 658-G.

OPEN TOP CESSPOOL.

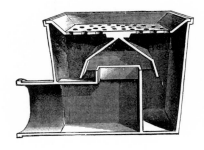

PLATE 659-G.

SECTION OF PLATE 658-G.

With Bell Trap. Top, 13 inches square. Depth, 10 inches. Specially adapted for Drain Connections.

PLATE 660-G.

LARGE HEAVY CESSPOOL.

With Bell Trap.

Size: Top, 24 inches square. Depth, 10 inches.

Outlet, 4 or 6 inches.

Suitable for Markets, Breweries, &c.

PLATE 661-G.

LARGE HEAVY CESSPOOL,

With Portable Bell Trap.

Size: Length, 27 inches. Width 19½ inches. Depth, 14 inches.

Outlet, 4 or 6 inches.

Suitable for Markets, Breweries, &c.

CESSPOOLS.

PLATE 662-G.

CESSPOOL WITH BELL TRAP.

Also furnished without Bell Trap, to order.

SIZES : No. 1, Top 9 inches square. Outlet 3 inches.
No. 2, Top 13 inches square. Outlet 4 inches.

PLATE 663-G.

SECTION OF PLATE 662-G.

PLATE 664-G.

ROUND CESSPOOL,

Without Bell Trap.

Diameter on Top 13 inches. Outlet 4 inches.

PLATE 665-G.

CESSPOOL WITH BELL TRAP.

SIZE: 8 inches square. Outlet 3 inches.

PLATE 666-G.

CESSPOOL WITH BELL TRAP.

SIZE : 6 inches square. Outlet 2 inches.

PLATE 667-G.

CURVED CESSPOOL PLATE.

SIZES : 8 × 10 ; 10 × 10, and 12 × 12 inches.
Special sizes made to order.

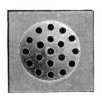

PLATE 668-G.
CESSPOOL PLATE.

SIZES : 4 × 4 ; 5 × 5 ; 6 × 6 ; 7 × 7 ; 7½ × 7½ ;
8 × 8 ; 9 × 9 ; 10 × 10 ; 12 × 12 ;
18 × 18 ; 20 × 20 inches.

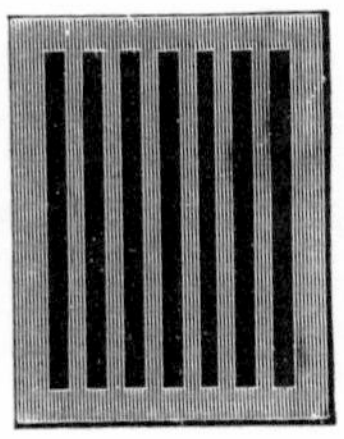

PLATE 669-G.
CESSPOOL PLATE.

SIZE : 6 × 6 inches.
8 × 6 "

PLATE 670-G.
CESSPOOL PLATE.

SIZES : 5, 6 and 12 inches diameter.

PLATE 671-G.
CESSPOOL PLATE.

SIZE : 8 × 6 inches.

MOTT'S CAST IRON SOIL PIPE AND FITTINGS.

"STANDARD" AND "EXTRA HEAVY."

<table>
<tr><td>

PLATE 672-G.

CAST IRON SOIL PIPE.

Single Hub.

SIZES: 2, 3, 4, 5, 6, 7, 8, 10, 12 and 15 inches inside diameter.
</td><td>

PLATE 673-G.

CAST IRON SOIL PIPE.

Double Hub.

SIZES: 2, 3, 4, 5, 6 and 8 inches inside diameter.
</td></tr>
</table>

All sizes made in 5 feet lengths, excepting the 12 inch, which is 6 feet   The length does not include the Hub, consequently the Pipe measures 5 or 6 feet full, when laid down.

———————

THE superiority of Cast Iron Soil Pipe over all other kinds is so thoroughly demonstrated and so well known to all Sanitarians, Engineers, Architects and Plumbers, that anything we might say on the subject would simply be a reiteration of established facts; hence the only point to which we would call special attention, and we consider it one of the utmost importance from a sanitary point of view, is, *that all Cast Iron Soil Pipe should be the very best quality, thoroughly sound, uniform in casting, of smooth finish and so that it can be readily cut without splitting*, qualities which we claim in a pre-eminent degree for our Soil Pipe and Fittings, in the manufacture of which only the very best No. 1 X Iron is used, our special patented machinery insuring a uniform thickness, and a perfectly smooth surface inside and out.

We are now prepared to furnish all sizes of Pipe and Fittings *Porcelain-lined*, which undoubtedly makes a Soil Pipe simply perfect, both as regards cleanliness and durability.   At the very moderate price at which we supply it, we hope to see it very generally used in all fine work.

Would also call special notice to our *Extra Heavy Soil Pipe and Fittings*, which are now being generally used in all large Public and Private Buildings.   We are prepared to furnish all sizes from 2 to 12 inches, and Fittings of all kinds   The *average* weights of the Extra Heavy Pipe, per foot, are as follows:

2 inch.	3 inch.	4 inch	5 inch.	6 inch.	7 inch.	8 inch.	10 inch.	12 inch.
5½ lbs.	9½ lbs.	13 lbs.	17 lbs.	20 lbs.	27 lbs.	33½ lbs.	45 lbs.	54 lbs.

SPECIAL NOTE —Architects desiring to use our Soil Pipe should be careful to observe the following when writing specifications: when it is desired to use our "Standard" Soil Pipe, write, "*Motts 'Standard' Soil Pipe and Fittings;*" when the Extra Heavy is wanted, write, "*Mott's Extra Heavy Soil Pipe and Fittings,*" also inserting the weights as given above.   All our Extra Heavy Pipe and Fittings have cast on in raised letters, "*Mott's X Heavy.*"   We give these hints as we find very often where our "Standard" Soil Pipe is called for, that inferior and cheaper grades are put in. Also in cases where our X Heavy Pipe and Fittings have been called for, Pipe X Heavy so called, weighing but little more per foot than our "Standard" Pipe, has been used.

CAST IRON SOIL PIPE FITTINGS.

PLATE 674-G.

QUARTER BEND.

SIZES: 2, 3, 4, 5, 6, 7, 8, 10, 12 and 15 inch.

PLATE 675-G.

QUARTER BEND,

with Inlet on Right or Left Side.

SIZES: 2 × 2; 3 × 2; 4 × 2; 5 × 2; 5 × 3; 6 × 2; 6 × 3; 6 × 4; 8 × 4 and 10 × 4 inches.

PLATE 676-G.

QUARTER BEND,

with Inlet on Heel.

PLATE 677-G.

QUARTER BEND,

with Double Hub.

SIZES: 2, 3. 4, 5 and 6 inch.

PLATE 678-G.

SHORT QUARTER BEND.

SIZE: 4 inch.

PLATE 679-G.

SIXTH BEND

SIZES: 2, 3, 4, 5, 6 and 8 inch.

PLATE 680-G.

EIGHTH BEND.

SIZES: 2, 3, 4, 5, 6, 8, 10, 12 and 15 inch.

PLATE 681-G.

EIGHTH BEND.
Double Hub.

SIZE: 4 inch.

PLATE 682-G.

SIXTEENTH BEND.

SIZES: 2, 3, 4, 5, 6, 7, 8, 10, 12 and 15 inch.

PLATE 683-G.

RETURN BEND.

SIZES: 2, 3, 4, 5 and 6 inch.

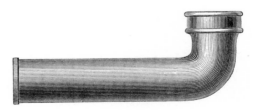

PLATE 684-G.

LONG BEND.

18 inches in the clear

SIZES: 4, 5 and 6 inch.

CAST IRON SOIL PIPE FITTINGS.

PLATE 685-G.

T BRANCH.

PLATE 686-G.

T WITH SIDE INLET, RIGHT OR LEFT.

PLATE 687-G.

CROSSHEAD BRANCH.

PLATE 688-G.

T-Y BRANCH.

PLATE 689-G.

T-Y, WITH SIDE INLET, RIGHT OR LEFT.

PLATE 690-G.

DOUBLE T-Y.

Sizes of Plates 685, 686, 687, 688, 689 and 690-G.

2 × 2 inches.	5 × 2 inches.	7 × 4 inches.	8 × 2 inches.	12 × 12 inches.
3 × 3 "	6 × 6 "	7 × 3 "	10 × 10 "	12 × 10 "
3 × 2 "	6 × 5 "	7 × 2 "	10 × 8 "	12 × 8 "
4 × 4 "	6 × 4 "	8 × 8 "	10 × 7 "	12 × 6 "
4 × 3 "	6 × 3 "	8 × 7 "	10 × 6 "	12 × 5 "
4 × 2 "	6 × 2 "	8 × 6 "	10 × 5 "	12 × 4 "
5 × 5 "	7 × 7 "	8 × 5 "	10 × 4 "	12 × 3 "
5 × 4 "	7 × 6 "	8 × 4 "	10 × 3 "	12 × 2 "
5 × 3 "	7 × 5 "	8 × 3 "	10 × 2 "	15 × 15 "

PLATE 691-G.

T WITH HAND HOLE FOR CLEAN OUT.

SIZES : 2, 3, 4, 5, 6, 8 and 10 inches

PLATE 692-G.

LONG T BRANCH.

SIZES : 4 × 4, 5 × 4 and 6 × 4; 24, 27, 30, 33 and 36 inches long.

The above is specially made for use where a line of Hoppers is put in 2 feet or more apart.

Long T-Y branch furnished same sizes to order.

CAST IRON SOIL PIPE FITTINGS.

PLATE 693-G.

HALF Y BRANCH.

SIZES	2 × 2 inch.	4 × 2 inch.	6 × 6 inch.	8 × 8 inch.
	3 × 3 "	5 × 5 "	6 × 5 "	8 × 6 "
	3 × 2 "	5 × 4 "	6 × 4 "	8 × 5 "
	4 × 4 "	5 × 3 "	6 × 3 "	8 × 4 "
	4 × 3 "	5 × 2 "	6 × 2 "	8 × 3 "
				8 × 2 "

PLATE 694-G.

DOUBLE HALF Y BRANCH.

PLATE 695-G.

ANGLE Y BRANCH.

SIZES: 4 × 4 inch. 5 × 4 inch.
6 × 4 inch.

PLATE 696-G.

Y BRANCH.

SIZES	2 × 2 inch.	5 × 5 inch.	6 × 4 inch.	7 × 4 inch.	8 × 3 inch.	10 × 3 inch.
	3 × 3 "	5 × 4 "	6 × 3 "	7 × 2 "	8 × 2 "	10 × 2 "
	3 × 2 "	5 × 3 "	6 × 2 "	8 × 8 "	8 × 7 "	12 × 12 "
	4 × 4 "	5 × 2 "	7 × 7 "	7 × 6 "	10 × 8 "	12 × 8 "
	4 × 3 "	6 × 6 "	7 × 6 "	8 × 6 "	10 × 6 "	12 × 6 "
	4 × 2 "	6 × 5 "	7 × 5 "	8 × 5 "	10 × 5 "	12 × 4 "
				8 × 4 "	10 × 4 "	15 × 15 "

PLATE 697-G.

Y WITH SIDE INLET. RIGHT OR LEFT.

PLATE 698-G.

DOUBLE Y BRANCH.

SIZES	2 × 2 inch.	6 × 6 inch.	8 × 4 inch.
	3 × 3 "	6 × 5 "	8 × 3 "
	3 × 2 "	6 × 4 "	8 × 2 "
	4 × 4 "	6 × 3 "	10 × 10 "
	4 × 3 "	6 × 2 "	10 × 8 "
	4 × 2 "	7 × 7 "	10 × 6 "
	5 × 5 "	7 × 4 "	10 × 5 "
	5 × 4 "	8 × 8 "	10 × 4 "
	5 × 3 "	8 × 6 "	10 × 3 "
	5 × 2 "	8 × 5 "	10 × 2 "

PLATE 699-G.

MONITOR BRANCH.

SIZES. 6 × 4 and 5 × 4 inch.

PLATE 700-G.

LONG Y BRANCH.

SIZES : 4 × 4, 24 inches in the clear.	5 × 4, 36 inches in the clear.
4 × 4, 30 " "	6 × 4, 24 " "
4 × 4, 36 " "	6 × 4, 30 " "
5 × 4, 24 " "	6 × 4. 36 " "
5 × 4, 30 " "	

PLATE 701-G.

ANTI-SYPHONING Y BRANCH.

SIZES : 2 × 2; 3 × 2; 4 × 4; 4 × 2;
5 × 4; 6 × 5; 6 × 4 inch.

The above is specially adapted for use in prison construction. *i. e.* to take Four Water Closets where upright Pipe is placed in wall in center of four cells

The above is made 24, 30 and 36 inches in the clear, and is specially designed for use where a line of Hoppers or Water Closets are put in, 2 feet, 30 or 36 inches apart ; they can be made any special length to order.

The Anti-syphoning Y Branch is designed for connecting Water Closets, Bath or Basin Traps to main Pipe, *i. e.* where Traps are not vented into air or soil Pipe running to roof.

Cast Iron Soil Pipe Fittings.

PLATE 702-G.
ASYLUM HOPPER CONNECTION.

SIZES : 4 × 4 inch.
6 × 6 "

PLATE 703-G.
OFFSET.

2 inch to offset 2 inch.		4 inch to offset 2 inch.		5 inch to offset 4 inch.	
2 "	" 4 "	4 "	" 4 "	5 "	" 6 "
2 "	" 6 "	4 "	" 6 "	5 "	" 8 "
2 "	" 8 "	4 "	" 8 "	5 "	" 10 "
2 "	" 10 "	4 "	" 10 "	5 "	" 12 "
2 "	" 12 "	4 "	" 12 "	5 "	" 14 "
2 "	" 14 "	4 "	" 14 "	5 "	" 16 "
2 "	" 16 "	4 "	" 16 "	6 "	" 4 "
2 "	" 18 "	4 "	" 18 "	6 "	" 6 "
3 "	" 4 "	4 "	" 20 "	6 "	" 8 "
3 "	" 6 "			6 "	" 10 "
3 "	" 8 "			6 "	" 12 "
3 "	" 10 "				
3 "	" 12 "				
3 "	" 14 "				
3 "	" 16 "				
3 "	" 18 "				

PLATE 704-G.
OFFSET WITH 2 INCH INLET.

SIZES : 4 inch to offset 4 inch.

4 "	" 6 "
4 "	" 8 "
4 "	" 10 "
4 "	" 12 "
4 "	" 14 "
4 "	" 16 "
4 "	" 18 "
4 "	" 20 "

PLATE 705-G.
VENT BRANCH FOR BACK AIR PIPE.

SIZES : 2 × 2 ; 3 × 2 ; 4 × 2 ; 4 × 3 ; 4 × 4 ; 5 × 2 ; 5 × 3 ; 5 × 4 ;
6 × 2 ; 6 × 3 ; 6 × 4 ; 8 × 4 and 8 × 5 inch.

PLATE 706-G.
INVERTED Y BRANCH

SIZE : 4 × 2 inch.

PLATE 707-G.
INCREASER.

SIZES : 2 to 3 ; 2 to 4 ; 2 to 5 ; 3 to 4 ; 3 to 5 ;
4 to 5 ; 4 to 6 ; 5 to 7 and 6 to 8 inch.

PLATE 708-G.
REDUCER.

4 inch to 2 inch.		8 inch to 3 inch.	
5 "	2	8 "	4 "
5 "	3	8 "	5 "
5 "	4	8 "	6 "
6 "	2	10 "	6 "
6 "	3	10 "	7 "
6 "	4	10 "	8 "
7 "	3	12 "	6 "
7 "	4	12 "	8 "
7 "	5	12 "	10 "

PLATE 709-G.
DOUBLE HUB.

PLATE 710-G.
SINGLE HUB.

PLATE 711-G.
STRAIGHT SLEEVE.

SIZES of Plates 709-G, 710-G and 711-G.
2, 3. 4, 5, 6, 7, 8, 10 and 12 inch.

PLATE 712-G.
T SADDLE HUBS.

PLATE 713-G.
HALF Y SADDLE HUBS.

PLATE 714-G.
Y SADDLE HUBS.

2 × 2 inch.	4 × 2 inch.	6 × 6 inch.	8 × 8 inch.	8 × 2 inch.	12 × 12 inch.
3 × 3 "	5 × 5	6 × 5 "	8 × 6 "	10 × 10 "	12 × 10 "
3 × 2 "	5 × 4	6 × 4 "	8 × 5 "	10 × 8 "	12 × 8 "
4 × 4 "	5 × 3	6 × 3 "	8 × 4 "	10 × 6 "	12 × 6 "
4 × 3 "	5 × 2	6 × 2 "	8 × 3 "	10 × 5 "	12 × 5 "
				10 × 4 "	12 × 4 "

NOTE.—The Y and ½ Y Saddles are not made over 6 inches.

CAST IRON SOIL PIPE FITTINGS.

PLATE 715-G.

S TRAP.

SIZES: 2, 3, 4, 5 and 6 inch.

PLATE 716-G.

THREE-QUARTER S TRAP.

SIZES: 2, 3, 4, 5 and 6 inch.

PLATE 717-G.

HALF S TRAP.

SIZES: 2, 3, 4, 5 and 6 inch.

PLATE 718-G.

S TRAP, WITH 2 INCH VENT.

PLATE 719-G.

¾ S TRAP, WITH 2 INCH VENT.

SIZES: 2, 3, 4, 5 and 6 inch.

PLATE 720-G.

½ S TRAP WITH 2 INCH VENT.

Any of the above furnished with Inlet as shown by Plate 722-G, or 723-G, to order.

PLATE 721-G.

HALF S TRAP,

without Hand Hole.

SIZE: 4 inch.

PLATE 722-G.

S TRAP,

Inlet in Heel.

SIZE: 4 inch, with 2 inch Inlet.

PLATE 723-G.

HALF S TRAP,

Inlet on Right or Left side.

SIZE: 4 inch, with 2 inch Inlet.

CAST IRON SOIL PIPE FITTINGS.

PLATE 724-G.

S TRAP WITH TWO INCH VENT,

and Brass Screw,

PLATE 725-G.

¾ S TRAP WITH TWO INCH VENT,

and Brass Screw.

SIZES: 2, 3, 4, 5 and 6 inch.

PLATE 726-G.

½ S TRAP WITH TWO INCH VENT,

and Brass Screw.

PLATE 727-G.

S TRAP WITH FLANGE AND VENT.

SIZE: 4 inch.

Also furnished ¾ or ½ S and with Hand Hole instead of Vent.

PLATE 728-G.

RUNNING TRAP.

SIZES: 2, 3, 4, 5, 6, 7, 8, 10 and 12 inch.

PLATE 729-G.

RUNNING TRAP,

with Hub for Vent Pipe.

SIZES: 4 inch with 4 inch Vent.   5 inch with 4 inch Vent.
6 inch with 4 inch Vent.   8 inch with 6 inch Vent.

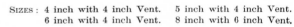

PLATE 730-G.

RUNNING TRAP,
with Hubs for Double Vent.

SIZES: 4 inch with 4 inch Vent.   5 inch with 4 inch Vent.
6 inch with 4 inch Vent.   8 inch with 6 inch Vent.

PLATE 731-G.

Y BRANCH RUNNING TRAP.

SIZES: 4 × 4 inch.
5 × 4 and 6 × 4 inch.

The above is a most desirable fitting to make
fresh air Inlet connection.

PLATE 732-G.

RUNNING TRAP,
with Inlet on Dip.

SIZES: 4 × 4 inch and 6 × 6 inch.

Also furnished with Vent and Hand Hole, or
two Vents or two Hand Holes, as may be ordered.

CAST IRON SOIL PIPE FITTINGS.

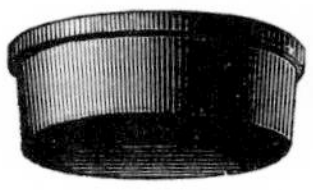

PLATE 733-G.

PIPE PLUG.

SIZES : 2, 3, 4, 5, 6, 7,
8, 10 and 12 inch.

PLATE 734-G.

PIPE BAND,

with Outlet.

SIZES : 2 × 2 ; 3 × 3 ; 3 × 2 ; 4 × 4 ; 4 × 3 ;
4 × 2 ; 5 × 5 ; 5 × 4 ; 5 × 3 ; 5 × 2 ; 6 × 6 ;
6 × 5 ; 6 × 4 ; 6 × 3 and 6 × 2 inch.

PLATE 735-G.

PIPE BAND.

SIZES : 2, 3, 4, 5 and 6 inch.

PLATE 736-G.

THIMBLE,

with Cover.

SIZES : 4, 5, 6 and 8 inch.

PLATE 737-G.

THIMBLE.

SIZES : 2, 3, 4, 5
and 6 inch.

PLATE 738-G.

BRASS FERRULE.

PLATE 739-G.

BRASS FERRULE, WITH TRAP SCREW.

SIZES : 2, 3, 4, 5 and 6 inch.

PLATE 740-G.

VENTILATING CAP.

SIZES : 2, 3, 4, 5,
and 6 inch.

PLATE 741-G.

ROOF IRON.

SIZES : 2, 3, 4, 5,
and 6 inch.

PLATE 742-G.

BATH TUB CONNECTION.

SIZE : 2 inch.

PLATE 743-G.

NO. 1 PIPE EAR.

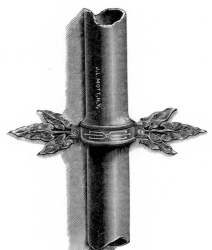

PLATE 745-G.

NO. 5 PIPE EAR.

Showing Section of Pipe, with No 5 Ornamental Pipe Ear.

SIZES : For 2, 3, 4, 5 and 6 inch Pipe.

The above Ears are made to take the place of the ordinary Pipe Hook.

Being very ornamental, they are quite a pleasing feature
in the architecture.

PLATE 744-G.

NO. 3 PIPE EAR.

PLATE 746-G.

NO. 2 PIPE EAR.

PLATE 747-G.

NO. 4 PIPE EAR.

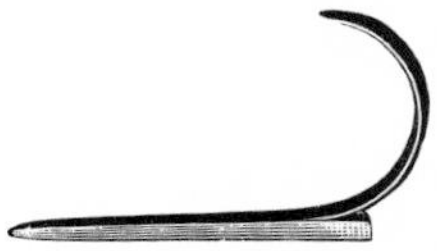

PLATE 748-G.

PIPE HOOK.

SIZES : 2, 3, 4, 5, 6 and 8 inch.

PLATE 749-G.

PIPE REST.

SIZES : 2, 3, 4, 5, 6, 7, 8, and 10 inch.

LEADER PIPES.

PLATE 750-G.

LEADER PIPE WITHOUT LUGS.

SIZES: 3, 4, 5 and 6 inch.   Length, 4 feet 6 inches.

PLATE 751-G.

LEADER PIPE WITH LUGS.

SIZES: 3, 4, 5 and 6 inch.   Length, 4 feet 6 inches.

PLATE 752-G.

LEADER PIPE, BOSTON PATTERN.

SIZES: 3, 4 and 5 inch.   Length, 7 feet.

MOTT'S PIPE TESTING PLUGS.

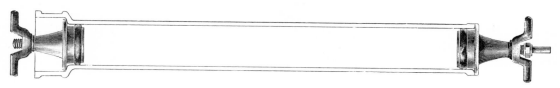

PLATE 753-G.   PLATE 754-G.

The above illustration shows both kinds of Pipe Testing Plugs, i e. the ordinary plug to stop end of pipe, also plug
with coupling to be attached to pump.

Cast Iron Fittings for Greenhouse.

Plate 756-G.	Plate 757-G.	Plate 758-G.	Plate 759-G.	Plate 760-G.	Plate 761-G.
No. 1–A, 32 × 10.	No. 1–B, 32 × 10.	No. 1–C, 32 × 10.	No. 1–D, 32 × 10.	No. 1–E, 32 × 10.	No. 1–F, 32 × 10.
No. 2–A, 48 × 10.	No. 2–B, 48 × 10.	No. 2–C, 48 × 10.	No. 2–D, 48 × 10.	No. 2–E, 48 × 10.	No. 2–F, 48 × 10.

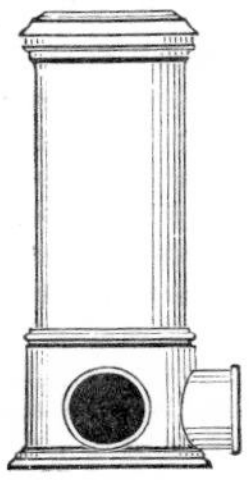

Plate 755-G.

Expansion Tank.

Sizes : No. 1, 32 inches high. 10 inches diameter.
" 2, 48 " " 10 " "

Plate 762-G.

Evaporating Pan.

Length, 48 inches. Width, 7 inches. Depth, 6 inches.

Plate 763-G.

Stop Valve, without Hubs.

2½ inch Valve Passage.

Plate 764-G.

Stop Valve, with Hubs.

2½ inch Valve Passage.

Plate 765-G.

Demarest Return Valve.

Above is placed either vertically or horizontally at the
divisions in the House, to open a way between the Flow and
Return, when the water is shut off from the rooms beyond.

Plate 766-G.

Demarest Stop Valve.

4 inch Valve Passage.

CAST IRON FITTINGS FOR GREENHOUSE.

FOUR INCH INSIDE DIAMETER.

PLATE 767-G.

SHORT QUARTER BEND.

Single Hub.

PLATE 768-G.

LONG ELBOW.

Single Hub.

PLATE 769-G.

LONG ELBOW.

No Hub.

PLATE 770-G.

EIGHTH BEND.

Double Hub.

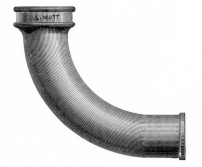

PLATE 771-G.

LARGE QUARTER BEND.

Single Hub.

PLATE 772-G.

QUARTER BEND.

Double Hub.

PLATE 773-G.

EIGHTH BEND.

Single Hub.

PLATE 774-G.

OFFSET.

PLATE 775-G.

DOUBLE ELBOW.

PLATE 776-G.

TRIPLE ELBOW.

PLATE 777-G.

THREE WAY BRANCH.

CAST IRON FITTINGS FOR GREENHOUSE.

FOUR INCH INSIDE DIAMETER.

PLATE 778-G.

RETURN BEND.

Double Hub.

PLATE 779-G.

RETURN BEND.

Hub Back Outlet.

PLATE 780-G.

RETURN BEND.

Spigot Back Outlet.

PLATE 781-G.

H BRANCH.

PLATE 782-G.

CROSS HEAD.

PLATE 783-G.

T BRANCH.

PLATE 784-G.

SLEEVE.

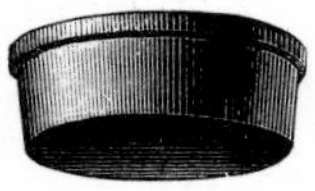

PLATE 785-G.

PLUG.

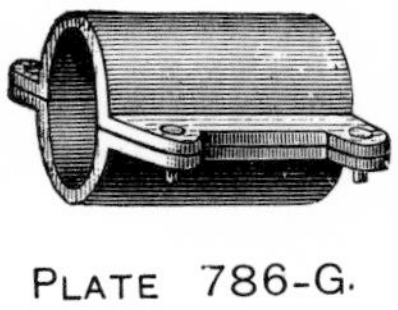

PLATE 786-G.

BAND.

For repairing cracks or leaks in pipe.

PLATE 787-G.

PIPE CHAIR.

Two Pipes.

PLATE 788-G.

PIPE CHAIR.

Three Pipes.

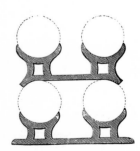

PLATE 789-G.

PIPE CHAIR.

Four Pipes.

GRATE BARS, DOORS AND FRAMES.

PLATE 790-G.

GRATE BAR.

SIZES : 18 22, 24, 30, 36, 42 and 48 inches.

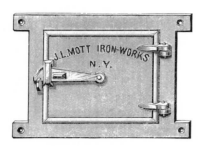

PLATE 791-G.

HEAVY SINGLE DOOR AND FRAME,

For Brick Furnace.

DIMENSIONS : Door Opening, 12 inches wide $\times$ 10 inches high.
                   12   " $\times$ 16   "
                   14   " $\times$ 20   "
                   16   " $\times$ 22   "

PLATE 792-G.

LIGHT DOOR AND FRAME,

For Brick Furnace.

DIMENSIONS : Door Opening, 8 inches wide $\times$ 6 inches high.
                   8   " $\times$ 10   "
                  10   " $\times$ 12   "
                  12   " $\times$ 12   "
                  15   " $\times$ 12   "
                  20   " $\times$ 15   "

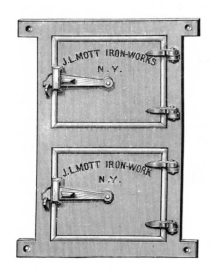

PLATE 793-G.

HEAVY DOUBLE DOOR AND FRAME,

For Brick Furnace.

DIMENSIONS : Frame 26 $\times$ 20 inches   Doors, 10 $\times$ 12 inches.

PLATE 794-G.

SLIDING DAMPER AND FRAME.

SIZES : Openings, 8 $\times$ 8.   8 $\times$ 12.   12 $\times$ 12 inches.

MOTT'S STEAM KETTLES WITH MOVABLE LEGS.

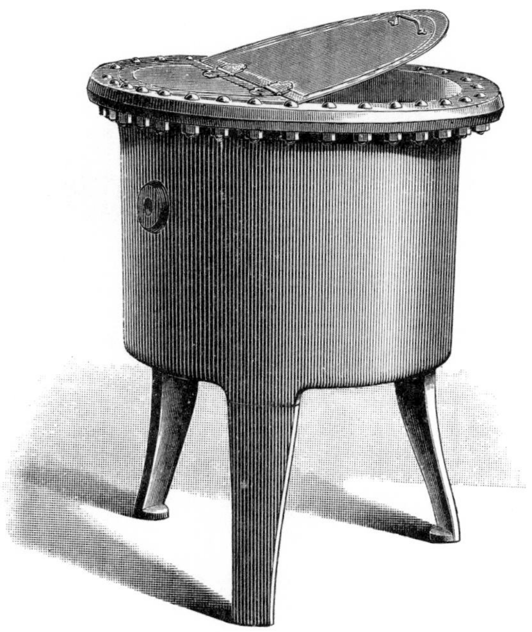

PLATE 795-G.

STEAM KETTLE WITH HEAVY WROUGHT IRON COVER.

Sizes as given below.

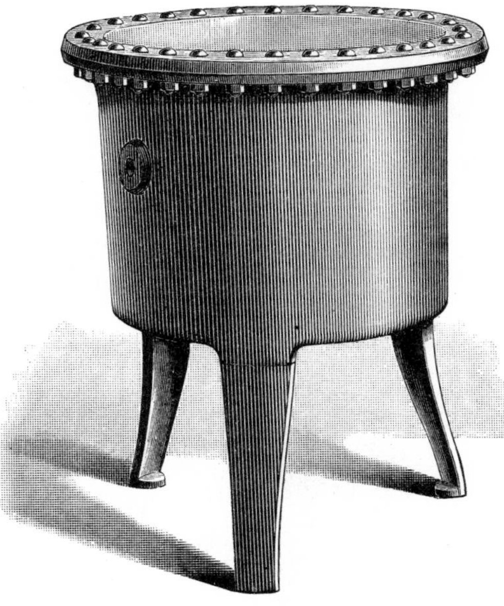

PLATE 796-G.

STEAM KETTLE.

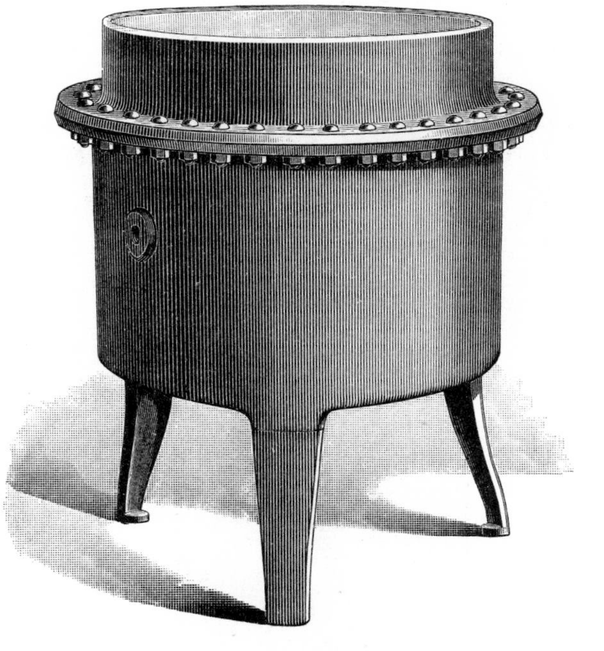

PLATE 797-G.

STEAM KETTLE, WITH CURB.

Actual Capacity.	Outside Diameter.	Inside Diameter.	Inside Depth.	Extreme Height.
5 gallons.	19½ inches.	12⅛ inches.	12 inches.	29 inches.
8 "	21½ "	14¼ "	14 "	31½ "
11 "	23 "	15½ "	15⅛ "	33½ "
18 "	26 "	18¾ "	17¼ "	33¾ "
28 "	29½ "	23¾ "	19⅝ "	36½ "
47 "	34½ "	26¾ "	21¾ "	38 "
76 "	40 "	31¾ "	24½ "	39½ "
130 "	46¼ "	38 "	30¼ "	40½ "
180 "	52¼ "	44¼ "	30 "	43¾ "

Actual Capacity.			Extreme Height.
37 gallons,	same as 28 gallons,	with 5½ inch curb,	36 inches.
60 "	47 "	6 "	38 "
100 "	76 "	7 "	40½ "
150 "	130 "	5 "	39½ "
208 "	180 "	5 "	42¾ "
230 "	180 "	10 "	47¾ "
250 "	180 "	15 "	52¾ "
268 "	180 "	20 "	57¾ "
286 "	180 "	25 "	62¾ "
300 "	180 "	30 "	67¾ "

Inside Caldron made of Copper, to order.

DEMAREST'S PATENT SYPHON WATER CLOSETS, THE "MONARCH" AND "WARWICK."

THE "MONARCH" AND "WARWICK" belong to that form of Water Closet known as Syphon or Pneumatic, which has two Traps, with means for creating a rarefaction of the air between said Traps when the atmospheric pressure upon the water in the Bowl causes Syphonic action to take place. Water Closets of this description, as heretofore made, have been more or less complicated in construction: realizing this, it has been our aim to produce one that, while quick, efficient and thorough in operation, would be simple and economical in construction.

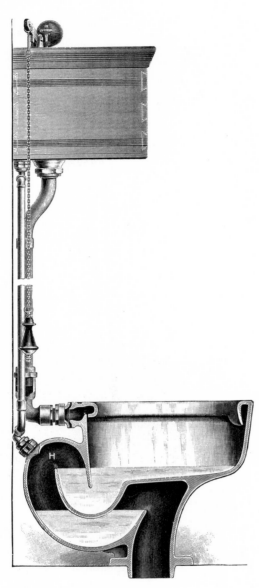

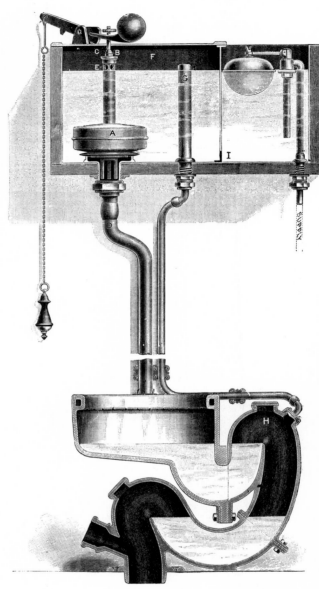

PLATE 798-G.

Sectional view of No. 1 "Monarch" Back-outlet Syphon Water
Closet and Cistern.

The "Monarch" has Brass Inlet, Air Pipe and Vent
Couplings, and Brass Floor Bolts.

PLATE 799-G.

Sectional view of No. 1 "Warwick" Side-outlet Syphon Water
Closet and Cistern.

The Bowl of the "Warwick" is of Porcelain and the Traps are
Iron Porcelain-lined throughout. The Inlet and Air
Pipe Couplings are Brass.

The illustrations show the Closets ready for use. The Pull is drawn down and immediately released; this raises the Float A, which is then buoyed up by the increased depth of water below it, and closes the Valve C, thus making it air-tight. As the water passes from the Cistern into Pipe D it creates a rarefaction of the air in Outlet Section H; the atmospheric pressure upon the water in the Bowl then causes Syphonic action to take place, when the contents of the Bowl are precipitated into the Lower Trap and thence to Soil Pipe; the Syphonic action continues until the depth of water in Compartment F is reduced and Float A begins to descend, when the admission of air breaks the Syphon. The remaining water in Compartment F then re-fills the Bowl, and Compartment F re-fills through Opening I, and the Water Closet is again ready for use.

From the foregoing it will be observed that there are few working or moving parts to get out of order or to require repairs; that the operation is so simple that a child can use the Closets; that they are waste-preventing, as only contents of Compartment F can be used at each operation.

The "Monarch" Closet and Bowl of "Warwick" are of the best English ware, warranted not to craze or discolor. Each has a Flushing-rim which washes all parts of the Bowl.

BACK-OUTLET FLUSHING-RIM SYPHON WATER CLOSET, THE "MONARCH."

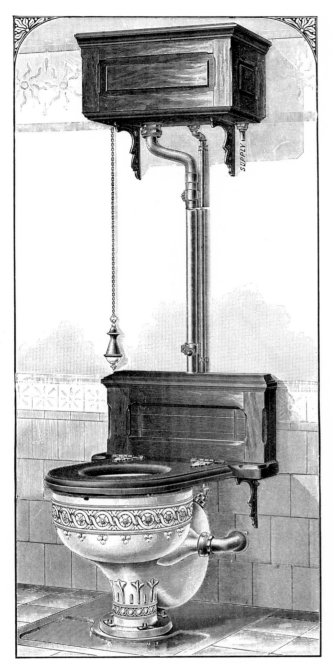

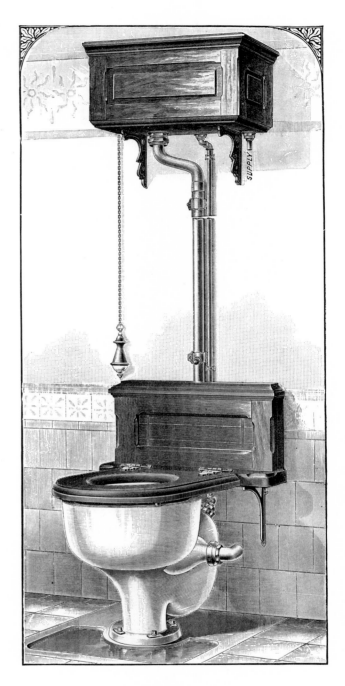

PLATE 800-G.

THE "MONARCH" EMBOSSED, IVORY-TINTED OR WHITE PORCELAIN,

With Cabinet-finish Copper-lined Cistern (Design B), Open Seat
and Back, Polished or Nickel plated Brass Flush and Air
Pipes, Polished or Nickel plated Brass Vent Pipe
and Brackets for Seat and Cistern, Ivory-
celluloid Pull and Chain.

PLATE 801-G.

THE "MONARCH" No. 1, IVORY-TINTED OR WHITE PORCELAIN,

With Cabinet-finish Copper-lined Cistern (Design B), Open Seat
and Back, Polished or Nickel plated Brass Flush and Air
Pipes, Polished or Nickel plated Brass Brackets
for Seat and Cistern, Ivory-celluloid
Pull and Chain.

The above Closets must not have a Trap below the Floor.   Directions for setting are sent with each Closet and must
be observed to insure its proper working.

BACK-OUTLET FLUSHING-RIM SYPHON WATER CLOSET, THE "MONARCH."

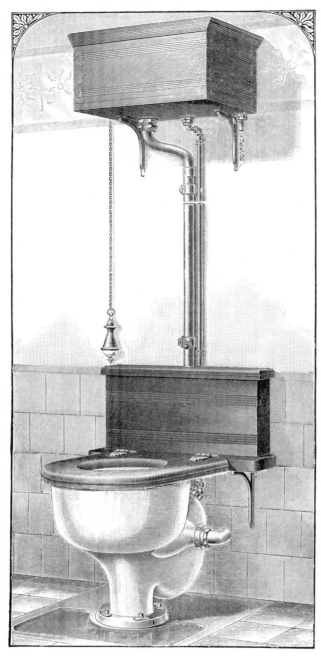

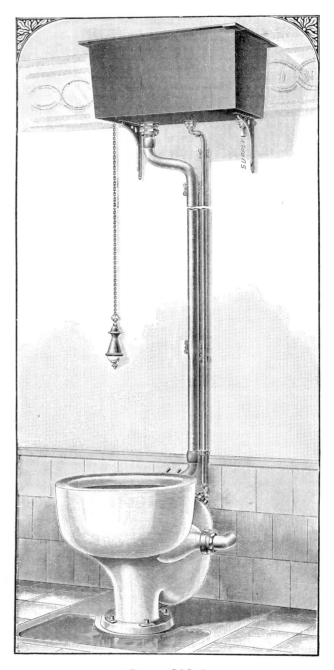

PLATE 802-G.

THE "MONARCH" NO. 1, IVORY-TINTED OR WHITE PORCELAIN,

With Copper-lined Stained Wood Cistern, Cherry or Black Walnut
Seat and Back, Japanned Seat and Cistern Brackets
Nickel-plated Chain Pull.

PLATE 803-G.

THE "MONARCH" NO. 1, IVORY-TINTED OR WHITE PORCELAIN,

With Iron Cistern, Brackets, Chain and Pull.

For sectional view and description of the "Monarch," see page 269.

Our Stained Cisterns are made of seasoned Whitewood stained to represent Cherry or Black Walnut.

The No. 1 "Monarch" must not have a Trap below the Floor. Directions for setting are sent with each Closet and must be observed
to insure its proper working.

BACK-OUTLET FLUSHING-RIM SYPHON WATER CLOSET, THE "MONARCH."

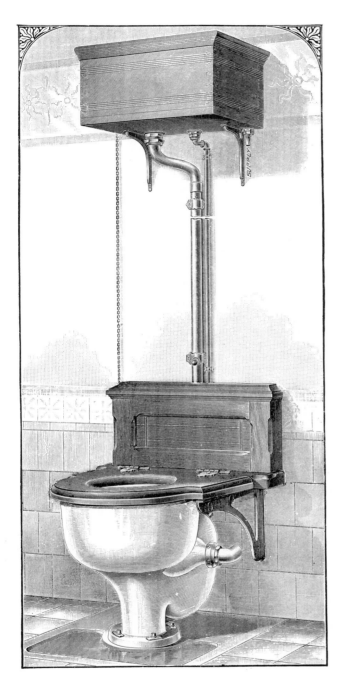

PLATE 804-G.

THE "MONARCH" NO 1, IVORY TINTED OR WHITE PORCELAIN,

With Copper-lined Stained Wood Cistern, Cherry or Black Walnut
Automatic Seat and Back, Bronzed Iron Seat
and Cistern Brackets, and Chain.

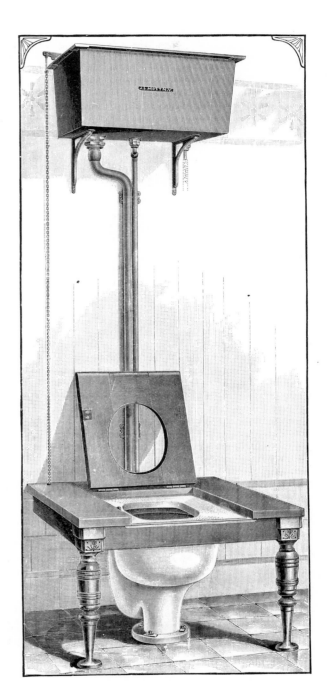

PLATE 805-G.

THE "MONARCH" NO. 1, IVORY TINTED OR WHITE PORCELAIN,

With Iron Cistern, Cherry, Black Walnut or Ash Seat with
Bronzed Iron Legs, Enameled Cast Iron Slop
Safe, Brackets and Chain.

Plates 804-G and 805-G are Automatic in action; when the Seat is relieved the Closet is brought into operation as described on page 269.
The No. 1 "Monarch" must not have a Trap below the Floor.   Directions for setting are sent with each Closet and must be observed
to insure its proper working

PATENT SIDE-OUTLET FLUSHING-RIM SYPHON WATER CLOSET, THE "WARWICK."

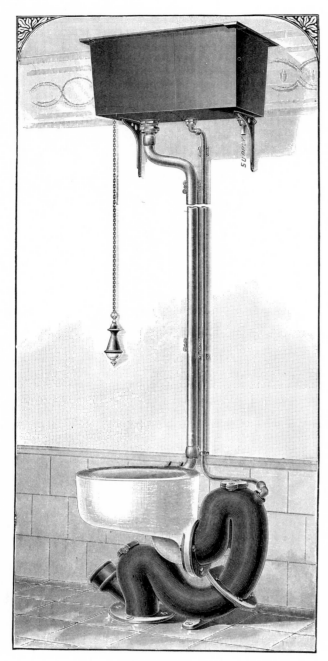

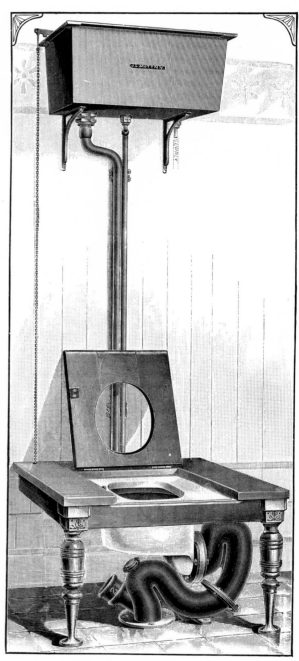

PLATE 806-G.

THE "WARWICK" No. 1,

With Cistern, Brackets, Chain and Pull.

For description, see page 269.

PLATE 807-G.

THE "WARWICK" No. 1,

With Cistern, Cherry, Black Walnut or Ash Seat, Bronzed Iron
Legs, Enameled Cast Iron Slop Safe, Brackets and Chain.

Plate 807-G is Automatic in action; when the Seat is relieved,
the Closet is operated as described on page 269 when Pull is drawn down.

The "Warwick" No. 1, must not have a Trap below the Floor.   Directions for setting are sent with each
Closet and must be observed to insure its proper working.

Demarest's Patent Syphon Water Closets, the "Monarch" and "Warwick."

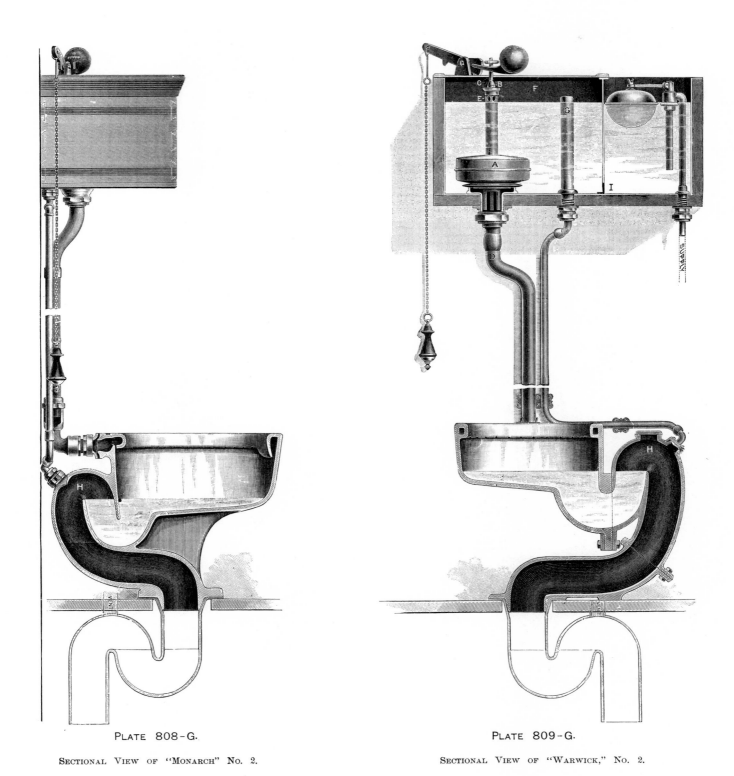

Plate 808-G.

Plate 809-G.

Sectional View of "Monarch" No. 2.

Sectional View of "Warwick," No. 2.

The No. 2 "Monarch" and "Warwick" require a Trap below the Floor, as indicated by the above illustrations. They should only be used when replacing an old Closet having Trap below the Floor which it would be inconvenient to remove.

The "Roman" Patent Embossed Front-outlet Wash-out Ventilating Water Closet.

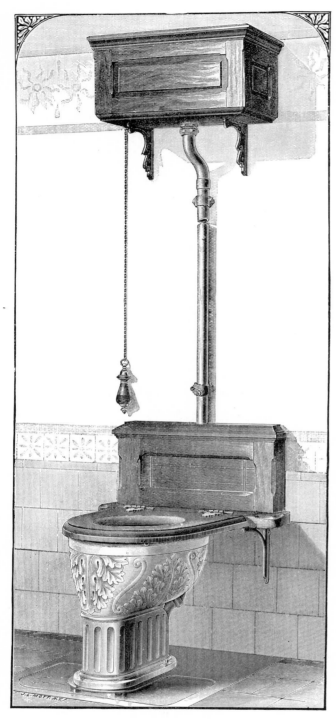

PLATE 810-G.

The "Roman," Ivory-tinted or White Porcelain,

With No. 21½ or No. 4½ Cabinet-finish Copper-lined Cistern, (Design B,)
Open Seat and Back, Nickel-plated or Polished Brass Flush Pipe,
Nickel-plated or Polished Brass Brackets for
Seat and Cistern, Pull and Chain.
Seat and Cistern may be of Cherry, Black Walnut, Ash or Mahogany.

PLATE 811-G.

The "Roman," Ivory tinted or White Porcelain,

With No. 21½ or No. 4½ Stained Wood Copper-lined Cistern, Hardwood
Open Seat and Back, Nickel-plated or Polished Brass Flush Pipe,
Japanned Seat and Cistern Brackets, Pull and Chain.
Also furnished with Iron or Plain Wood Cistern.
Seat may be of Cherry or Black Walnut and Cistern stained to match.

For description of No. 21½ and No. 4½ Cisterns see page 78.

The "Roman" is a Front-outlet Wash-out Ventilating Water Closet, intended to set up open as shown by the illustration. It is ornate and attractive in design, efficient in operation and being of the best English ware, will not craze or discolor.

Our Stained Cisterns are made of seasoned White-wood, stained to represent Cherry or Black Walnut, and unless examined closely it is difficult to distinguish them from the real wood.

For sectional view see Plate 127-G, the "Roman" being practically the same as the "Undine."

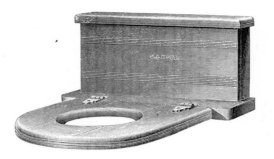

PLATE 812-G.

CHERRY, BLACK WALNUT OR ASH OPEN SEAT AND BACK,

With Plain Brass Hinges and Japanned Brackets.

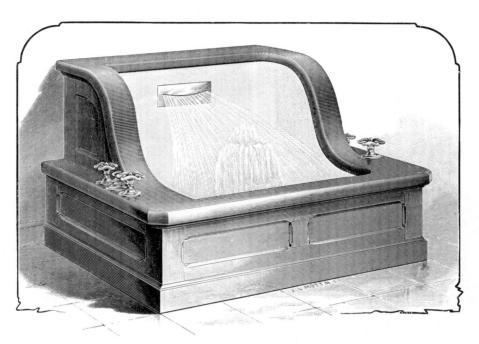

PLATE 813-G.

THE "IMPERIAL" PORCELAIN, PORCELAIN-LINED IRON, OR COPPER SEAT BATH,

With Combination Wave and Douche Spray and Patent "Unique" Waste.

To bring the Wave or Back Spray into operation the two Valves lettered "Cold Wave" and "Hot Wave" are turned. The Bidet or Douche is obtained by turning the two Valves lettered "Cold Spray" and "Hot Spray." The Wave and Spray can be used together or separately. If so desired water may be retained in the Seat Bath by means of the "Unique" Waste.

Plate 813-G is furnished in the following different combinations:

Combination 1, as shown above and described.

Combination 2, as shown above and described, less the "Unique" Waste.

Combination 3, comprising the "Imperial" Porcelain, Porcelain-lined Iron or Copper Seat Bath, with Wave or Back Spray, and Supply Fittings and "Unique" Waste as shown by Plate 72-G.

Combination 4, comprising the "Imperial" Porcelain, Porcelain-lined Iron or Copper Seat Bath with Bidet or Douche Spray, and Supply Fittings and "Unique" Waste as shown by Plate 72-G.

ENGRAVINGS · BY · McCULLOW · & · STURM
·MDCCCLXXXVIII·

◄ INDEX ►